ABOUT THE AUTHOR

Born in Bombay on 10 July, 1949, Sunil Manohar Gavaskar had his schooling at the St. Xavier's High School. His father was a good club cricketer in his days and a keen student of the game. His uncle was also a good cricketer. Sunil's mother helped him to take the first steps in the game. He gave early promise of his batting prowess when he made his debut for his school in the 'Giles' and 'Harris' Shield Tournaments in 1961. He played brilliantly in the All-India Schools' Tournament, scoring prolifically for the West Zone, which won him the 'J.C. Mukherjee Memorial Prize'. Gavaskar joined St. Xavier's College in 1966, and was immediately selected to play for the College XI. He later joined the Dadar Union Sporting Club. In 1967-68, he represented Bombay in the Irani Cup, and in the Ranji Trophy in 1969-70.

Selected to tour the West Indies in 1971, Gavaskar made his Test debut at Port of Spain, Trinidad, in March, 1971; and has since been a regular member of Indian Test teams. He has toured the West Indies (twice), England (twice), and New Zealand. Gavaskar was one of the three Indians who played for the 'Rest of the World' against Australia in Australia in 1971-72. Gavaskar has captained Bombay in the Ranji Trophy and the West Zone in Zonal competitions. He is completely fearless while facing any type of bowling. Carelessness is totally alien to his nature. He is always friendly and quite difficult to ruffle. He is fond of reading, dancing and listening to pop music, and plays an occasional game of badminton to keep himself in good trim.

SUNNY DAYS

In this autobiography, Sunil Manohar Gavaskar tells the story of his cricketing life in a simple and straight forward manner. Few cricketers have attained such heights so early in their career. In spite of all the adulation he has received in his own country and other parts of the world, he remains a modest gentleman and a fine sportsman. The impressions that he has imbibed in the course of a crowded and exciting career make interesting reading. His comments on players, colleagues, umpires and officials are told without malice. Sunil Gavaskar has many more years of cricket ahead of him, and this first essay into the realms of 'autobiography' may well be the beginning of the 'Saga' of a cricketer who will always live in the minds and hearts of those who play and love cricket.

Sunil Gavaskar emerged on the international cricketing scene with meteoric brilliance. His 1971 Caribbean Odyssey dazzled the cricketing world and he was compared with the great cricketing personalities of the past. He scored 774 runs in that series—including a century and a double century (124 and 220) in the fifth Test at Port of Spain—the highest aggregate in a Test Series by an Indian. He has scored over 2000 runs in Test cricket, with an average of 51 runs an innings, which is, by far, the fastest by an Indian cricketer. He is an opening bat with the requisite qualities of stamina and sprightliness to face top-class bowlers even under pressure. Indeed, Sunil Gavaskar has proved to be the best opening batsman that India has produced so far.

Sunny Days

an autobiography

SUNIL GAVASKAR

Foreword by
M. L. Jaisimha

Rupa & Co

CALCUTTA * ALLAHABAD * BOMBAY * DELHI

© SUNIL GAVASKAR

First Published : 1976
Printed in Paperback: 1977
Reprinted 1978, 1979 (thrice), 1980

Cover Design :
Susanta Karmakar

Published By :

Rupa & Co

15 Bankim Chatterjee Street, Calcutta 700 073
94 South Malaka, Allahabad 211 001
102 Prasad Chambers, Opera House, Bombay 400 004
3831 Pataudi House Road, Daryaganj, New Delhi 110 002

Printed By :
Jay Print Pack (P) Ltd.
8/39 Kirti Nagar Industrial Area
New Delhi-110 015

Price : Rs. 15.00

To
Aai—Baba
My Parents

Contents

Contents

List of Illustrations

(b) When the world was young. The author with his two closest friends, Ramnath Parkar and G.R. Vishwanath (left).

8. (a) Cooling off after a strenuous game.

(b) Sunil with Zaheer Abbas, Rohan, Kanhai and Bishen Bedi in Australia where he went to play for the Rest of the World XI against Australia.

Beetween Pages 128 and 129

9. Author cooling off on the balcony of Lord's The Treasurer of the 1971 team, Mr. Ram Prakash Mehra is in the back-ground.

10. Ajit Wadekar leading the West Zone out to field in a Duleep Trophy match. Sunil Gavaskar (extreme left) running in to join the team.

11. The Indian team being presented to Maharashtra Governor, Mr. Ali Yavar Jung. The Governor shaking hands with the author.

12. (a) A warm welcome at home after the 1971 Windies tour.

(b) The Gavaskar 'Family Score-board' to record the fabulous performance of Sunil in the West Indies (1971).

Beetween Pages 176 and 177

13. The Indian team to the West Indies, 1971.

14. Gavaskar completes a double-century in the second innings ot the 5th Test against West Indies at Port of Spain (1971) after having scored a century in the first innings. M.L. Jaisimha walks down to congratulate him.

15. The Indian team leaving the field at lunch on the 3rd day of the match against Trinidad, 1971.

16. Batting in the Old Trafford Test (1974) against Derek Underwood. Tony Greig and John Edrich (back to camera) are the close-in fielders.

Between Pages 214 and 215

17. England Captain, Mike Denness, protects Gavaskar from the frenzied Indian admirers who invaded the field after Sunil's century in the Old Trafford Test (1974).

18. Sunil Gavaskar with Tony Greig, towering over him, returning to the pavilion after batting for the Rest of the World against Australia (1971-72). With him are the Chappel brothers, Ian and Gregg.

19. Playing for the Rest of the World against Victoria (1971), Gavaskar hooking A.F. Thomson.

20. Gavaskar mobbed by spectators after he completed 1,000 runs in Test in single calender yea, Delhi, 1976.

Between Pages 248 and 249

21. (a) Holding up the Irani Cup after leading Bombay to victory against the Rest of India, Delhi, 1976

    (b) A typical sweep shot by Gavaskar.

    (c) A drive in cover.

    (d) Hooking Derek Underwood to the fence in the Test against England, Old Trafford, 1974. Looking on is Alan Knott.

    (e) Playing an elegant cover-drive.

PHOTO CREDITS
Sportsweek, Bombay, Hidustan Times, New Delhi.

Foreword

Sunil Gavaskar exploded on to the International cricket scene on India's tour of the West Indies in 1971. To those of us on the tour with him, his fantastic success could not have come at a better time and his phenomenal scores could not have been better deserved.

I saw Sunil for the first time when the Indian team touring the West Indies met for a two-week practice camp at Bombay. One had heard a great deal about this young player and of his success in School, University and, finally, in State Cricket. I was most interested in seeing him, as he was so obviously a player of distinction. During these two weeks we got to see this young slip of a boy demonstrate the keenness of eye and perfect balance, which are the hall-mark of a good cricketer.

Already acknowledged as one of our greatest players he does not need any introduction. During the trip to the West Indies, I had the rare pleasure of seeing this boy mature into the scoring phenomenon he became later on the tour. A whitlow on his little finger that needed the surgeon's scalpel kept Sunil out of the first few games of the tour and the first Test. This was a very unfortunate begining to his Test career. As the tour was limited to only four games against the Islands and five Tests, the visiting side got to play only one or two games before the first Test. Sunil made his debut in the second Test match at Port of Spain, Trinidad, after missing the first. His performance on his debut and the heights to which he rose later in the series are already on record and need not be enumerated here.

Cricket is a never-ending subject. Even though one feels one knows a great deal about the game, there is always much more to learn. Sunil embodies this quest for knowledge in his approach to the game and it has been rewarding for me to sit and discuss cricket with Sunil whenever the opportunity arose, as it is with most cricketers. I found on these occasions that he has discovered a new dimension to some aspect or other of cricket. His insight into the finer points of the game, his demeanour on and off the field, his application to the game, his evaluation of fields, have proved that success had given him a sense of modesty. His approach to the game has always been objective and this has given him the broad outlook which enables him to view his successes and failures pragamatically. With his keen analytical mind and his desire to always improve and learn more of the intricacies of this great game, he will always be reaching new horizons.

This book, I am confident, will be of great value to all cricketers, particularly to youngsters learning the rudiments of this delightful game. To Test and first-class cricketers, his technical analysis will be of great interest.

Hyderabad
October 19, 1976

M.L. Jaisimha

Preface

It is always hazardous for an active cricketer to venture into the realm of authorship, especially for one who has won his spurs in Test cricket barely five years ago. Critics will, perhaps, dismiss my haste in getting into print as presumptuous. Even those more charitably disposed towards me may characterise this essay into authorship as a juvenile escapade. I am aware of these dangers and it is only after considerable hesitation that I have decided to publish this personal account of my cricketing experience. I do so with the utmost humility and in the hope that what I have seen and observed will make playing conditions easier for players.

It is inevitable that, in setting down my thoughts and feelings about certain aspects of the game and the conduct of individuals, I have been critical. I do not claim infallibility for these views, nor do I wish to impute motives to people and organisations. It is not my purpose to indulge in gimmicks or mere sensationalism. My sole object is to set the record straight, and to present a faithful picture of the environment in which I have grown to be what I am.

The impetus for writing this book has come mainly from my parents. For as long as I can remember, they have given me every encouargement to play the game, and they have sacrificed so much to help me on the road to cricketing fame. I have looked to them for comfort when things have not gone off well, and we have rejoiced together when my efforts to prove myself have been crowned with success.

My reason for selecting the title of the book is that, to my friends all over the world, I am known as 'Sunny', a nickname which has stuck to me over the years. In a way, the title also reflects the many happy days I have spent playing the game in different parts of the world, and the sunshine it has brought into my life.

I have been singularly fortunate in so far as I have received the love and affection of cricketers and cricket lovers in abundant measure. On the cricket field and off it, I have made so many friends that I feel truly 'rich'. When I think of this, I am reminded of the famous lines of the Poet Rabindra Nath Tagore :

"Thou hast made me known to friends whom I knew not
Thou hast given me seats in homes not my own
Thou hast brought the distant near
And made a brother of the stranger."

I do not know what the future holds out for me. But, of one thing I am certain. I shall always love the game of Cricket and shall ever strive to do my best to prove worthy of the past in the future.

This book is not the result of a conscious or deliberate effort, but an attempt to put down my stray and random thoughts in some order. It does not claim to be the sum total of my experience, but some of the highlights of my career. I owe a special word of thanks to the Publishers for undertaking the publication of the book in record time, to the 'hero' of my school days, M.L. Jaisimha, for writing the Foreword to my book, and to Mr Anandji Dossa for compiling the statistical data.

Bombay,
November 8, 1976   Sunil Gavaskar

1

The First Steps

I may never have become a cricketer and this book would certainly not have been written, if an eagle-eyed relation, Mr Narayan Masurekar, had not come into my life the day I was born (July 10, 1949). It seems that *Nan-kaka* (as I call him), who had come to see me in hospital on my first day in this world, noticed a little hole near the top of my left ear lobe. The next day he came again and picked up the baby lying on the crib next to my mother. To his utter horror, he discovered that the baby did not have the hole on the left ear lobe. A frantic search of all the cribs in the hospital followed, and I was eventually located sleeping blissfully beside a fisherwoman, totally oblivious of the commotion I had caused! The mix-up, it appears, followed after the babies had been given their bath.

Providence had helped me to retain my true identity, and, in the process, charted the course of my life. I have often wondered what would have happened if nature had not 'marked' me out, and given me my 'guard' by giving me that small hole on my left ear lobe; and if *Nan-kaka* had not noticed this abnormality. Perhaps, I would have grown up to be an obscure fisherman, toiling somewhere along the west coast. And, what about the baby who, for a spell, took my place? I do not know if he is interested in cricket, or whether he will ever read this book. I can only hope that, if he does, he will start taking a little more interest in Sunil Gavaskar.

My most vivid recollection of my childhood cricket-playing days is the time I almost broke my mother's nose. She used to bowl to me in the small gallery of our house where we played our 'daily match' with a tennis ball. Since the area was small she would kneel to bowl, or rather lob the ball to me. I hit one straight back and caught her bang on the nose, which started bleeding. Although it was a tennis ball, the distance between the two of us was very short, which accounts for the force with which the ball hit her. I was frightened but she shrugged it off, washed her face and, as the bleeding stopped, we continued the game. But, for the rest of the day it was only forward defence for me. I restrained myself and played no attacking shot.

Cricket, to use a cliche, is 'in my blood'. My father was a good club cricketer in his days and a keen student of the game. Even now we have interesting discussions on various aspects of the game and I have found his advice invaluable in the development of my career. And, as I have already said, I have had the privilege of having a cricketing mother, who helped me to take the first steps in the game I have come to love. My uncle, Madhav Mantri, who played for India in four 'official' Tests, though not very successfully, was a force to reckon with in first-class games. Whenever I went to my uncle's house my favourite pastime used to be to take out his pullovers and caress them with a sense of longing. I was so attracted by the India Test pullovers that once I even dared to ask him if I could take one, since he had so many. My uncle told me that one has to sweat and *'earn'* the India 'colours' and I too should work hard to earn the distinction. That is a lesson I have never forgotten. Looking back, I am glad that my uncle did not succumb to my childish fancy and, instead, taught me that there was no short-cut to the top. I was also fascinated by the many souvenirs he had and the large number of trophies he had won. What I liked most was the stump bearing the autographs of the 1952 India and

England teams, and I loved to linger over the autograph of every player.

Right from the beginning I wanted to become a batsman and I hated losing my wicket. This became such an obsession with me that, if the rest of the boys ever got me out, I would fight and eventually walk home with the bat and the ball. This would bring the game to an abrupt end since nobody else had a ball or bat. The boys cursed and called me names, but the tension did not last long and we generally got on very well. Among these early comrades with whom I played were the Ambaye brothers, the Mandrekar brothers and several others who made up our team. Whenever I batted they would decide beforehand that they would appeal at a particular ball and, whether I was out or not, I had to go by the majority verdict! We often played matches against teams made up of boys living in the neighbouring building and there was tremendous interest in the 'trophies', as we called them. These trophies were small white-metal cups for which we all contributed and bought for as little as Rs. 1.50.

In our neighbourhood were Sudhir Naik, Sharad Hajare and, of course, Milind Rege, who lived in the same building in which we had a flat. We often played against each other in those days. Years later, when all of us were in the Bombay Ranji Trophy team, it seemed as if Chickalwadi and Shivaji Park were representing Bombay!

I joined St. Xavier's High School, which had a fairly good cricket team at that time. While we were just juniors we would run during the lunch recess to watch the senior boys play. Feroze Patka was then the idol of almost every Xavierite and Vinay Chaudhari, the skipper, was equally popular. When St. Xavier's won the Harris Shield under Chaudhari's captaincy, every Xavierite went delirious with joy. We had inter-class matches which were very important, because the School junior team was selected on the basis of performances in these encounters. Even on holidays we went to play the school matches, very often with just one leg-guard and no batting gloves. I used to bowl, also, at that time and managed to bag quite a few wickets.

One day, as I was leaving home to play a match, my father stopped me to introduce me to Mr Kamal Bhandarkar, the former Maharashtra player, who is always prepared to coach anybody who shows a keenness to learn. He had come to invite us for a wedding and, seeing that I was going for a game, he asked me to show him my stance. After I showed him my batting stance, he asked me to show him my forward defence. When I did so Mr Bhandarkar pointed out that my bat was at an angle and there was the danger of the ball being deflected towards the slips. Then he showed me the proper grip and, even now, when I find myself in difficulties I remember those words and check if my grip is correct. Anyway, the ball still goes to the slips! Mr Bhandarkar is, I think, one of the best cricket coaches in India and he is prepared to sit up all night to discuss any cricketing problem one might have. Years later I was thrilled when he invited me, along with Dilip Sardesai, to his Coaching Camp at the P.Y.C. Gymkhana to talk to the young boys under his charge.

My first chance of playing in the Harris Shield came when Milind Rege went down with chicken pox. I went in to bat at no. 10, and remained unbeaten with 30 runs. Next morning I got up early to look at the newspaper, all excited in the expectation of reading my name in print for the first time. I was, however, disappointed because the name had been printed as "G. Sunil 30 not out". Thus began my career in school cricket. The next thing I had set my heart on was to earn the Bombay Schools 'cap'.

My first season for the Bombay Schools began disastrously. I fielded badly and was dropped from the side after I had scored only eight runs. It was then that I realised that I had to improve my fielding. I worked hard to become a good fielder and soon my efforts bore fruit. I became a close in fielder, specialising in the slips. Concentration, I feel, is my strongest point and this keeps me going in the slips even when the batsmen are batting so well that there is no chance of their edging or snicking the ball in my direction.

My second year for the Bombay Schools was better and the third and final year (1965-66) was the best. In the quarter-finals of the Cooch-Behar Trophy I scored 246 not out and put on 421 runs for the first wicket with Anwar Qureshi, who also got a double hundred. In the semi-finals I got 222 and in the final my score was 85. This led to my selection for the All-India Schools' Team against the London Schoolboys, who were touring India. I was also the proud recipient of the J.C. Mukherjee Trophy for the 'Best Schoolboy Cricketer of the Year'—my first prize in a national competition.

In the first 'Test' against the London Schools I scored 116. I did not wear a thigh-guard till then and, during the early part of the innings, I was hit by a ball on the thigh. It hurt me terribly, and the skipper of the team, realising my dis-comfiture, asked the bowlers "to do it again". This only made me more determined and I batted on without flinching. I have found that any physical pain now puts my back up and I invariably play better.

I played in the first four 'Tests' and scored an aggregate of 309 runs. I had to stand down from the last 'Test' because I had the annual examination coming. The Indian Schools, however, won the match and, with it, the series. This was my final year at school, but before going on to the university, I attended a Coaching Camp organised by the Board of Control at Hyderabad. There were 30 schoolboy cricketers in the camp, and Mr T.S. Worthington, the former England player, was our coach. Mr Worthington changed my Indian technique to the English one and gave me many invaluable tips. The month I spent in Hyderabad meant that I missed my first ten days of college life.

2

Lotuses in the Slush

St. Xavier's College at that time boasted of a cricket team that had several first class players. Ashok Mankad was the captain and later on Kailash Gattani led the side. We, however, invariably lost to Siddharth College, except in my final year when we beat our traditional rivals by a convincing margin.

My parents gave me every encouragement and, as an inducement, they promised to give me Rs. 10/- for every hundred I scored. Even in those days the value of money was not lost on me, and I remember one year when I almost put the household budget in disarray with my centuries. My father, however, was delighted and paid up cheerfully. Often, when he returned home in the evening, he would take out his wallet and ask me if I had scored a century and would be most disappointed if I said 'no'.

While I was encouraged to develop my talents as a cricketer, my parents never failed to emphasise the importance of doing equally well in my studies. In fact, cricket was never allowed to interfere with my studies. Once, when I got a really bad report from school, my father was so upset that he refused to let me play in the Inter-School Tournament. My Principal, the late Reverend L. Serkis, however, met my father and assured him that he would personally look after my studies. It was then that my father relented and I was allowed to play in the tournament.

I'll never forget my first match against Siddharth College. We scored about 311 runs, of which Ashok Mankad alone contributed 140-odd. When Ashok reached his century, some Xavierites drove a car, almost up to the wicket, and garlanded their hero. When Siddharth College batted, Kiran Adhikari scored a century and when he completed his ton, some of the Siddharth boys came up in a motor-bike and garlanded him. This must have upset Adhikari's concentration because he was soon out lbw, leaving Siddharth's last pair to score 20 runs for victory. They did so, but even now I feel they should never have won. I was keeping wickets then and the first ball that the no. 11 batsman faced caught him on the backfoot plumb in front of the stumps. It was a plain straight delivery, and it could not possibly have missed the middle stump. However, the more aggressive among the Siddharth College boys, wielding knives and sticks, looked very menacing and the umpire dared not give the batsman out. Frankly I don't blame the umpire at all for adhering to the old adage, "discretion is the better part of valour."

Immediately after this incident, there was the tea interval. Our Cricket Secretary, however, told us not to bother to come to the pavilion, but run straight to the cars they had lined up and make a quick get-away. Being the wicket-keeper I was stranded, and soon found myself encircled by the mob. Luckily one of the 'dadas' (senior boys) of Siddharth College escorted me, all the time assuring me that there was no cause for worry. I was safe, but I wondered what would have happened if St. Xavier's had won. My team-mates, who were able to reach the cars and were rushing away from the ground, were not, however, lucky. The waiting crowd smashed the windscreen and caused considerable damage to the cars.

Soon afterwards I was selected to play for the Bombay

University Team. The West Zone tournament that year was held in Poona and in the first two fixtures I hit centuries. The second century was a better effort as we played against bowlers like Uday, Ashok Joshi and Pankaj Zaveri, all established Ranji Trophy players from Gujarat. I used to bat one wicket down at that time, because Sudhir Naik and Ramesh Nagdev were the regular openers.

We lost in the final to Osmania University, who won the Rohinton-Baria Trophy for the first time. Osmania, with their balanced attack, used to bundle the other sides out on the matting track. Their left-arm spinner Mumtaz Hussain, the hero of the tournament, proved deadly with his disguised 'chinaman' and regular orthodox spin. In the second innings Ramesh Nagdev and I were going strong after Naik's cheap dismissal. But, Nagdev was not able to fathom Mumtaz Hussain's spin when he bowled the 'chinaman'. I thought I knew, so in a purely psychological move I called out loud to Nagdev at the non-striker's end: "Don't worry, Ramesh, I know when he bowls that one." When Mumtaz heard this, he smiled mysteriously and tossed the ball up to me for the next few deliveries. I came down the wicket, but managed to hit only one four while the others went straight to the fielders. Mumtaz tossed up the last ball of the over slightly outside the off-stump. Too late I realised that he had bowled a googly and was stranded yards down the track, to be easily stumped. We had learnt our lesson and when South Zone met West Zone for the first-ever Vizzy Trophy Inter-Zone final, Mumtaz got only three wickets in two innings. Unfortunately, the next time I saw him bowl at Hyderabad he seemed to have changed his style, and from a lovely high action he seemed to be bowling almost halfway down. He still does a good job for Hyderabad, but the magic seems to have disappeared.

Conard Hunte, the West Indies stalwart, who was the Chief Guest at the Vizzy Trophy final, came in the afternoon when I was batting. He seemed quite impressed with my performance and was kind enough to make a reference to me in his speech. Jayantilal also came in for some praise from Hunte.

Earlier in the season Hunte's batting technique had been evident during his century against India in the Bombay Test. His backlift, so straight and high, was the thing I had my eyes glued on, and also the way his front-foot was always where the ball was pitched. It was an unforgettable and rewarding experience. I must confess that I have tried to model my batting on Hunte's style.

While returning from the Inter-University Tournament, we read that four University players were in the Bombay Ranji Trophy team, announced the previous day. Rege and I were the two newcomers, while Naik and Varde had already played in the Ranji Trophy. Both of us, of course, never made the XI, but I was made twelfth man. It was here that I really got to know Ajit Wadekar. I had met him earlier, but it was as Madhav Mantri's nephew. Now, I was in the same team, we shared a lunch table, and I could talk to him freely. Ajit completed a magnificent century and then his bat broke. I rushed out with some bats after searching his kit-bag, in vain, for a spare bat. I carried my own bat also, and I don't know why, but somehow of all those bats, Ajit chose mine. He banged the next three balls for boundaries, and going for a fourth, was caught behind.

As he sat in his corner in the dressing room, he handed back the bat to me with a "thanks". I ventured to say, "It brought you bad luck". To which Ajit replied, "May be, but those three shots were the best of the innings." Ajit Wadekar always had a word for me then and though he and Ramakant Desai often pulled my leg it was in good spirit and I liked it. Baloo Gupte was another player who helped me along and made me feel at ease in the company of the other stalwarts I had only read about, but had never come in contact with. Somehow 'Baloo Kaka', as I call him now, got wind of the fact that I could do a fair mime of film star, Dev Anand, and even now he never forgets to ask me to mimic Dev Anand, whenever we meet.

Soon after the first Ranji Trophy match I was dropped from the 14, and it not only disappointed me but I felt rather confused. After all, I had nothing to do but field and, when there, I had taken a good running catch. This is one thing which has always foxed me. How the 'reserves' get dropped remains a mystery. Do they suddenly become so bad after one game that they do not merit a place, even as a 'reserve'? How can one merit such treatment, even without playing ?

At this time I had become a member of the Dadar Union Sporting Club, which has a tradition for excellent fielding, discipline, tenacity and ability to fight back. Dadar Union was then a 'dream side'. Madhav Mantri had built up the team, and under his captaincy it had earned a great name for itself. When I joined Dadar Union, Madhav Mantri had retired and had taken under his wings a weaker neighbouring side full of youngsters. Vasu Paranjpe was captain of the Dadar Union. His outlook on the game was a blend of the care-free approach of the West Indians and the bulldog tenacity of the Australians. He was positively in love with Australian cricket and his dream of a tour to Australia was realised when he went there with the Cricket Club of India team in 1971-72 when I was also in Australia. Throughout his stay in Australia, Vasu wore a broad smile, even when he was dumped into the swimming pool at a party. Incidentally Vasu cannot swim, and he had to be fished out of the pool! As a fielder he was magnificent and his aggressive batting won many a hopeless match for Dadar Union. His captaincy was as dynamic as his batting, and he loved a challenge. It was Vasu who gave me my nick-name 'Sunny', which has stuck to me ever since.

But, more than Vasu, one man who has literally carried

Dadar Union on his shoulders was Vithal 'Marshall' Patil. 'Marshall', with his swing bowling, was almost unplayable in the first few overs and in the limited overs matches he seldom proved expensive. Besides, he also 'doubled' as Secretary of the Club and has done a good job. 'Marshall' literally lives for cricket. Morning and evening he would bowl to aspiring young cricketers, find the chinks in their armour and guide them accordingly. In later years, his bowling lost its sting because the nip off the wicket was gone and the batsmen had enough time to change their strokes. However, his length never wavered. If there is one man who has taken a great deal of interest in my cricket and encouraged me at every step it is 'Marshall'. Often he would drop in at our house late after dinner and say "Sunny, century tomorrow". I think he had more confidence in my cricketing ability than I had myself.

P.K. 'Joe' Kamat is more famous as the guiding spirit behind Ajit Wadekar. I, however, remember him more for his 158 against Maharashtra at the Bombay Gymkhana ground. He just about hit the ball everywhere and almost every blade of grass must have felt the sting of his power-packed shots. A fearless hooker, he believed in going for the bowling right from the first ball. I think this adventurous spirit cost him a lot because he did not stay in the Bombay team for long. An absolutely brilliant fielder anywhere, he took amazing catches at gully and, I remember the time when, after splitting his palm catching a full-blooded Budhi Kunderan hit, he just ran to the doctor round the corner, had his palm stitched and was back again at gully. 'Joe' can discuss cricket at length and his views are clear and arguments convincing. He is always ready to discuss any cricketing problem with you and will try to sort it out. 'Joe' and 'Marshall' are so deeply dedicated to cricket that they are still bachelors!

The next year I was back in the Bombay 14 though I did not play in the first two Ranji Trophy matches. However,

I found a place in the XI against the Rest of India in the annual Irani Trophy match. At the end of the match the team to tour Australia and New Zealand was to be selected. So, while everybody else was trying to get a place in the Indian team, I was the only player trying to earn a place in the Bombay side. However, I was a complete failure in my first outing for Bombay.

The wicket had the typical first morning 'life' when we batted. Dilip Sardesai, who opened with me, was caught off the splice when a ball cocked up. My pleasure at seeing Ajit Wadekar at the other end and the dream of having a big partnership with him vanished when I was also caught at leg-slip, off Chakravarty, who had earlier claimed Dilip's wicket. Ashok Mankad and Hardikar, however, took Bombay to a safe position. The wicket still had a bit of life when the Rest started batting. Ramakant Desai, who had not been selected for the earlier England tour and who was not even in the 30 called for a Camp prior to the Australia-New Zealand tour, bowled with fire. With Umesh Kulkarni giving him valuable support, they bowled themselves into the team for Australia and New Zealand. In the second innings I offered no stroke to a ball and was out plumb leg-before, again to Chakravarty, for a 'duck'. Six Bombay players were selected for the Australia-New Zealand tour and since they were to leave within ten days, the Bombay Selectors recalled Madhav Apte, among others, for the next Ranji Trophy match. Although Madhav Apte had been playing club cricket regularly he had not played first-class cricket for a number of years. Sudhir Naik was also recalled and I found myself left out of the eleven. I was quite bitter about this because I thought that I should have been given another chance, instead of recalling Madhav Apte. This feeling was strengthened when Apte was bowled first ball by Urmikant Mody, my Dadar Union colleague, who played for Saurashtra. However, I was thankful to the Selectors because I realised I was very immature then and another failure would have demoralised me completely. Madhav Apte himself was very sympathetic and comforted me. It was, however, quite sad to see him struggling to make runs, and such is the Bombay spirit that towards the end of the Tournament, especially in the knock-out stage, I wanted him to succeed in giving Bombay a good start. Madharao, as he is popularly known, had a very good series against the West Indies in 1953, but he played only a few Tests thereafter. His fielding even in 1968 was good enough for the batsmen to think twice before taking a run. He retired immediately after the end of the 1967-68 season, along with Hardikar and Baloo Gupte.

When Bapu Nadkarni also retired from first-class cricket at the end of the Australian tour, the Bombay team for 1968-69 suddenly had a lot of vacancies. Luckily, Bombay has always had reserves who are only waiting for their chance. Solkar was already an established Ranji Trophy player and Sudhir Naik, with a good season behind him, had also established himself in the team.

In the 1967-68 season I had not gone on tour with the University team because I wanted to concentrate on my studies. The next season I became Captain of the Bombay University team, but I was not included among the 14 players for the Ranji Trophy. Ramnath Parkar had replaced me in the Bombay 14, but for the next three seasons he had to be content with being the 12th man. I had a wonderful season otherwise, but I was still unable to find a place in the Bombay team.

Bombay University lost in the semi-final of the West Zone matches of the Inter-University Tournament to Indore in a thriller. Bombay took a first innings lead of 52 runs, and, on the third and final day, were required to score 202 runs to win. Meanwhile, in the other semi-final Baroda, the hosts, had won and were awaiting the result of our match. Ours was the best side in the West Zone and, to ensure a smooth final for Baroda, the local umpires started raising their fingers for practically every appeal by an Indore player. As a result, Bombay at the time were 110 for 8 and with 90 runs to make we had given up all hope. But Dilip Galvankar (a medical student) had other ideas. He played a cavalier innings of 52 and carried the side to within ten runs of victory, with about 15 minutes left for draw of stumps. The entire crowd, which by then was pronouncedly anti-Bombay, suddenly became pro-Bombay and, as our last man walked in, there was tremendous excitement in the air. Having taken a first innings lead we had only to draw the match to qualify for the final. Navin Ambulkar, a great character to have around, was playing a dogged innings and, with only two runs and seven minutes to go, glanced the ball to deep fine-leg. Surprisingly, he was half-way down the wicket when he was declared out leg-before. Ambulkar was so shocked by the decision that, for almost ten minutes after that, he could not speak even though he tried to. In the meanwhile both the umpires had run off and had not bothered to sign the score book, as is the rule. The Indore boys also were sympathetic and our players were clearly agitated. But we wended our way back slowly to our hostel, being comforted by the fact that from a near hopeless position we had almost won, and we would have done that, but for those two gentlemen in white coats.

The Vizzy Trophy final against North Zone that year was played at New Delhi. I had an innings of 247 not out against South Zone, followed by an innings of 113 not out in the final against North Zone at New Delhi. Though the North Zone was strongly fancied to lift the trophy, the West finished victors for the third time in a row. Even this performance did not impress the Bombay Selectors and I was not included in the team for the Ranji Trophy. This served only to make me more determined to assert my claim. In the Purshottam Shield final at Bombay, just before the team for the Ranji Trophy final was selected, I scored 301 not out. Well, it was still 'no go' as far as the Selectors were concerned. They probably did not want to change a winning combination. I was, however, satisfied that the season had been a marvellous one for me.

It is really an amazing part of cricket that after a good season, the next one turns out to be a barren one. And so it happened with me. Right from the club games to the University matches, I found run-getting extremely difficult.

This time the Inter-University matches were played at Jabalpur. We got past the first round easily and, in the second round, clashed with Gujarat. After being dismissed cheaply, we conceded a first innings lead to Gujarat. Then we fought back and scored 200 runs, leaving Gujarat to score 162 runs for victory. We dismissed Gujarat for 150, with just about 10 minutes to spare. Dilip Mulherkar, who was so short that he had to shout before anyone looked down on him, bowled his off and leg-spinners so effectively that the Gujarat batsmen had no clue as to what was happening. Our victory was achieved when Jayprakash Patel, Gujarat's captain, tried to swing Mulherkar out of the ground and the ball rose up at mid-off. Hemant Waingankar, not the best fielder in the side, got himself underneath and waited. I turned my face away and kept on looking at the wicket-keeper. Only when he let out a smile and a 'well done skip' did I turn around and congratulate Mulherkar on his excellent bowling.

Somehow after his sensational start Mulherkar just went into oblivion. Perhaps his small frame was not up to the task of toiling and spinning away for hours. But he did a great job that year for Bombay University, and it was he who was mainly responsible for our winning the coveted Rohinton-Baria Trophy. We had a good team that year and all of us were keen to avenge our previous year's defeat by Indore. Indore, however, did not have its stalwarts of the previous year and our victory was an easy one.

In the All-India final we played Bangalore. It was a good

match and we won mainly because everybody contributed
his bit to the victory. It was a proud moment for me when I
received the Rohinton-Baria Trophy and we had a real
celebration that night.

West Zone, however, lost their hold on the Vizzy Trophy
that year, convincingly beaten by East in the semi-finals. It
was a great disappointment, but also a relief to be able to get
back home and to one's books.

A word about the Inter-University Tournament. These are
the very matches which are the stepping stones to first-class
cricket. Every University in each Zone gets to host the matches
by rotation and the All-India final and the Vizzy Trophy
matches are played at the same centre. The tournament, which
is played during December-January in cold weather, can take
quite a toll of one's resources. The teams are asked to stay in
rooms where eight to ten boys are crammed. There is hardly
any hot water to bathe and shave and the boys have to sleep
on the floor in freezing weather. It's all very unhygienic, apart
from being terribly uncomfortable. The boys get a very nomi-
nal allowance from the University for their meals and one
has to spend from one's own pocket to make up the deficiency.
The University also does not provide sweaters and blazers.
Actually, Bombay University gives blazers only to the teams
that win, and that too after the tournament is over. Because
of their tremendous enthusiasm, the boys overcome these
handicaps and appreciate the difficulties of the host University.
I feel that the participants in this prestigious tournament
deserve a better deal and the basic necessities must be looked
after. Many schoolboy prodigies fade out when up against
tougher competition, and it is seldom that they succeed in
first-class cricket. It is the University lads who eventually hit
the top and if they are treated better it will be an investment
for the future, and also help to create the climate for the
proper development of latent talent.

3

Bombay Blues

By early 1970, Bombay had made their way to the knockout stage of the Ranji Trophy Tournament and I was surprised to find my name in the team. Obviously my selection was not prompted by my performance. In the University matches it had been awful, and my only big score was a double century in the Inter-Collegiate final against a none-too-impressive attack. I had replaced Sudhir Naik, who also had a poor Ranji season. Ashok Mankad, having earlier been asked to open for India in the Tests against Australia, was the other opener for Bombay.

Bombay lost the toss. We, however, dismissed Mysore (as Karnataka was then called) for 220 runs. When our turn to bat came I requested Ashok to let me take the first strike. After playing four balls I missed the fifth one and was plumb lbw and was out for a 'duck'. I will never forget the booing of the crowd that day, accusing me of coming into the side because my uncle was a member of the Selection Committee. Actually, I learnt much later from the other Selectors that whenever my name was proposed or discussed, Mr Mantri would not take part in the discussions and would seldom venture an opinion. Yet, the average man never believed it and I was the target of the crowd's displeasure every time. When I entered the dressing room there was a deathly silence and the players completely ignored me. As I was removing my leg-guards I realised what a great opportunity I had missed and what a mess I had made of that shot and I started laughing. Some of the players were worried and began to wonder whether I had lost my mind. But when I explained how I had missed a half-volley, which was the reason I was laughing, they relaxed. We then sat out and watched Mankad, Wadekar and Sardesai score runs almost at will against Prasanna and Chandrasekhar. In the second innings, Vishwanath, making his first appearance in Bombay after his triumphant series against Australia, scored 95 runs. He missed his hundred when he tried to cut a ball from Abdulla Ismail and was caught behind. He played a variety of strokes all round the wicket, but there was one cover-drive which stands out in my memory. He stepped out to a flighted one from Rege and, at the last minute, with a flick of the wrist, guided the ball between short third-man and cover-point. From my position at first slip, I had seen exactly how he had changed his shot at the last minute. Vishwanath too remembers that shot.

Brijesh Patel scored a century on that occasion and Budhi Kunderan, the Mysore captain who was retiring from first-class cricket at the end of the match and migrating to England, declared his innings, to give us the last 90 minutes of batting. Of the fifth ball, again of the first over, I was dropped at leg-slip and thus avoided a 'pair'. Both Ashok and I played out the 90 minutes, and I scored 27 not out, while Mankad was beaten when he was 28. When the team for the next match against Rajasthan was announced I was expecting the axe. But the Selectors had decided to give me another chance. Probably my three catches in the slips in the earlier match had influenced them. Whatever it was, I was glad to have another go, which I knew would truly be my last chance.

Rajasthan won the toss and batted first. However, Ismail and Saeed Hattea skittled them out for 217, just before close of play. In the few minutes left, I got off the mark and the next day I was lucky to see a simple snick being dropped by the wicket-keeper. After that I gave only one more chance before reaching a century. That was at 95 when a cut went through Parthasarthy Sharma's hands in the slips, to take my score to one run short of my first century in the Ranji Trophy. All this while Ashok Mankad had already notched up his century, carting Kailash Gattani repeatedly over square-leg. We struck up a good understanding and took some cheeky singles. It was with one such run of the last ball of the over before tea that I got the century. As we were returning to the pavilion, Raj Singh and Hanumant Singh came and offered their congratulations. Raj Singh said he hoped this would be first of many I would get in the Ranji Trophy. Both Ashok and I had overhauled Rajasthan's score without being separated and we broke the previous record for the opening stand for Bombay when we passed 273 runs. We were eventually separated at 279 when I was caught behind, off Salim Durrani, for 114. Ashok went on to score 171 runs. It was a great knock. We got Rajasthan out cheaply again in the second innings and, once again, I held three catches. Thus another win was registered for Bombay and I ended up with renewed confidence and hope that I could make it big.

Earlier in the season the Combined Universities had played the touring New Zealanders and I had been selected to play against the visitors. Collinge and Dayle Hadlee, their bowlers, were fast and it was the first time I had faced bowling above medium-pace. I stuck around for almost two hours and scraped 25 runs before a great piece of cricket got me out. Bryan Yuile, the left-hand bowler, induced me to go for a cut. I bottom-edged the ball on to the wicket-keeper's pads. From there it flew to Hastings at gully, who knocked it up behind him Glenn Turner from first slip ran and dived behind Hastings to take a left-handed catch, inches from the ground. This was incredible, but I was out. I was satisfied with my first encounter with pace and thought I had done a good job to see the new ball bowlers off in both the innings.

The Selectors, who were watching, also must have been

impressed, because they called Ramesh Nagdev and me for trials on the 4th day of the first Test against Australia at Bombay. Ramesh was then selected as 12th man for the second Test at Kanpur. After these trials were over I had a problem because I had no pass to sit in the pavilion. Mr Chinnaswamy, probably the nicest of all the Board officials, immediately gave me one.

I watched the Bombay Test being slowly grabbed by Australia. They knocked out all the Indian batsmen, and only Wadekar and Venkataraghavan were able to withstand their attack somewhat. Then Venkat was declared out, caught behind and as he didn't seem happy with the decision the crowd also showed its displeasure. Suddenly, a section of the spectators became violent, and the rest is now history. The next day, when I came to the game, my gloves had been smattered with blood and the whole dressing room was in a mess.

4

Going Places

The 1970 season began with the Indian Universities' Team going to Sri Lanka. Ashok Gandotra was the captain and I was his deputy. We had a Camp in Madras and then flew to neighbouring Sri Lanka. Our trip was a successful one and we won all our matches. Unlike in India, Sri Lanka's University boys are not half as good as the Sri Lanka schoolboys. In the Island school cricket is very competitive and people throng to watch these games.

We had an interesting match against the Sri Lanka Cricket Board XI, led by Anura Tennekoon, and including many other Sri Lanka players. After we won the toss Vinay Lamba and I put on 60 runs, before both of us were dismissed in succession. The others followed. The Sri Lanka team took a lead of about 70 runs. While fielding at silly mid-off my thumb was injured when I tried to stop a fierce drive. This prevented me from opening in the second innings. There was a bit of rain and the wicket had just that little bit of life to encourage the Sri Lanka bowlers. They had us on the hop. I went in at no. 7, and, first with Kailash Gattani and then with Dilip Doshi, managed to avert a collapse. We declared, leaving the Sri Lanka team to score 130 runs in 90 minutes. They almost made it but eventually fell short by just 11 runs.

The next match was against the Sri Lanka University.

Jayantilal and I put on 174 runs before Jayanti was out. I went on to score 203 not out. In the last match, on a matting track, Vinay Lamba scored 150 and thus we ended the tour on a satisfactory note. Ashok Gandotra, however, did not have a successful tour and disappointed many people who had come specially to watch him.

In the meanwhile I had a cable from home informing me of my selection for the Bombay team for the first Ranji Trophy match of the season. Of course, I could not leave the tour midway and so I missed the first match. Sudhir Naik replaced me and scored 74 runs. Thus I found myself left out of the XI for the next game against Gujarat.

Since I was not going to play in the team I did not carry my leg-guards to the nets on the days preceding the match. Seldom does a reserve player get batting at the nets because all the eleven want to have a go. So the reserve's main job is to bowl and field at the nets.

So, imagine my embarrassment when, on the morning of the match, skipper Ajit Wadekar declared himself unfit and Dilip Sardesai, deputising for him, told me that I was playing. I phoned home frantically for my leg-guards. My mother, poor thing, rushed in a taxi with the leg-guards and returned home in the same taxi after leaving the leg-guards with the doorman. One would wonder why she did not stay to see me play; and thereby hangs a tale. Ever since I was out for a 'duck' in my first Ranji Trophy match against Mysore, my mother had not watched me batting. She would refuse to come on the first day, not knowing whether we would bat or not. Then if I had finished batting, she would come the next day. If we had to field first, she would not come at all.

Meanwhile, seeing my predicament, Wadekar offered me his leg-guards, since he was not playing. When I came at lunch unbeaten with 71 runs, he advised me to continue with

his leg-guards, instead of changing over to mine. I went on to
score a century and was out soon after. My innings had lasted
160 minutes.

Saeed Hattea could not produce the same speed as in the
previous year and broke down with back trouble. This, together
with some fielding lapses, enabled Gujarat to force a draw.
Incidentally, in Gujarat's second innings, I got my first wicket
in the Ranji Trophy when I clean bowled Saldhana, their opening batsman. Sudhir Naik who had opened in the first match
had to bat lower down   the order in this match, in spite of his
big score in the first game.

With Wadekar being fit for the next game it was a problem
as to whom to drop. This was solved when Sardesai found he
had cracked a rib and could not play. This was the match
which was to prove a crucial one for me. It was always the
Maharashtra-Bombay tie that decided the West Zone championship. The Poona wicket was a featherbed and there would be
no alarms for the batsmen. Bombay, batting first, were 322 for
two at the end of the first day. Sudhir Naik, batting no. 3,
and I added 227 runs for the second wicket. Earlier, Ashok and
I had a partnership of 52 runs. Sudhir scored 110 and I was
unbeaten with 144 at the end of the day.

The next day we went for the bowling and lost wickets in
the process. I was out for 176, giving me my third century in
three Ranji Trophy matches after my disastrous debut against
Mysore. The match ended in a dull draw, as Maharashtra
were just content to plod along. They achieved their aim of
not giving us even the first innings lead. So we shared points.

Sardesai reported fit for the next game, and this time I was
down with influenza. So, once again the ticklish problem of
dropping a good player was avoided.

After this, the West Zone team against the South Zone was

announced and I was surprised to find myself excluded. People
sympathised with me and consoled me by predicting that I was
a certainty for the forthcoming West Indies tour. Because of
this, they said, the Selectors had decided to watch the others.
I did not derive any comfort from this, because, until then, I
had played only four first-class matches and I feared that my
inexperience could have gone against me.

I consulted Madhav Mantri and he advised me to go ahead
and lead Bombay University in the Inter-University matches
to be played at Poona. He said that I should not worry unduly
about the selection of the team and play my natural game. I
then asked him a question that was uppermost in my mind.
Supposing I was selected to play in the final of the Duleep
Trophy what should I do? Should I return from the Inter-
University matches? His reply was typical of him: "You are
the captain of the Bombay University. Just go and forget
everything else. We'll cross that bridge when we come to it."

Poona is just a four-hour drive from Bombay, and I completely forgot about the impending selection as the boys
started their usual bantering and joking in the train. As soon
as we arrived in Poona, we had a net practice session, because
we were playing the next day. In the four innings I played, my
scores were 226, 99, 327 and 124. Only the last innings was
really worth something because the attack was better than the
rest. Incidentally, the 327 bettered Ajit Wadekar's record of
324 runs set up 12 years ago. And it came just before Ajit was
selected as the captain of the Indian team to the West Indies.
The University boys were happy and we went on to beat
Poona University in the final to reach the All-India semi-
finals.

My mother had telephoned me the previous evening and
said that she wanted me to do her a favour. When I asked
her what it was, she replied that she wanted me to break the

individual batting record of 324. I promised to try my best, but 325 was a tall order in Inter-University Cricket.

How the record came about is rather interesting. Avi Karnik said to me after I was out for 226 in the first match that I should have gone on to better the record. I told him that I had not thought of it and, besides, there was hardly any time. During the innings of 327, when I was not out with 269 at tea, he came and said, "Now there is plenty of time and so don't throw it away." I did not but, after the boundary that gave me the record, the next ball sent my off-stump cartwheeling to the wicket-keeper, as I tried to steer it past third-man. Imagine being out like that after scoring 327. All my elation vanished with this ignominious dismissal.

The team came back to Bombay before travelling to Waltair down south, for the All-India Championship. The day the team was to leave for Waltair, the Indian team for the West Indies was to be announced, so I stayed back in Bombay promising the boys that I would fly to Waltair and join them.

I remember how I spent that afternoon with Saeed Ahmed Hattea. He was also strongly tipped to make the team, and both of us went to a cinema show to while away the time. However, we did not feel interested in the show and walked out after sitting for a short while. When we went to the Bombay Cricket Association office to inquire if the team had been announced we were told that the Selection Committee meeting was still on. We spent another half-an-hour and I suggested to Saeed that we should better go home. The suburban train was crowded with office workers returning home. Saeed, with his long hair (quite a new fad those days), was easily recognised and many commuters 'selected' him in the team. When Saeed very politely pointed to me and asked, "What about Mr Gavaskar?", they said, "O.K. he will also be there", but they did not sound very convincing. We parted company wishing each other luck and promising to phone on hearing the news. When I reached home everybody was relaxed, except my mother, who looked tense and asked me anxiously whether there was any news. My father and sister were, however, confident that I was 'in' and showed no signs of anxiety.

I played around a bit with my cousin and, just before dinner, decided to drop the little kid home. I was hardly out of the door when the telephone rang. I waited outside the door and did not ring the bell, waiting to see if it was for me. It was! Ashok Mankad was on the line telling me that I was in the squad to tour the West Indies. I felt a tremendous surge of happiness and hugged my parents, who were shedding tears of joy. I immediately went to the room in which the daily *pooja* is performed and prayed for the Almighty's blessings.

I was on my way to Madhav Mantri's house when the telephone call had come. I told him the good news and he embraced me and we sat down while he told me a few things. But, my mind was in a whirl. I came home soon afterwards and had dinner. There was tremendous excitement in the house. The telephone did not ring again, because the team had not been officially announced. But, through it all, I could not help thinking of Saeed, who was not 'in'. I felt sorry for him and didn't have the heart to telephone him as I had promised.

About the same time I was asked by the Board Secretary that I should go and play in two fixtures against the visiting Sri Lanka team. Earlier, I had asked for permission to continue with my Inter-University matches, which had reached the All-India stage and Bombay University were in the final. However, I was refused permission on the ground that I might get injured. At the same time, I was surprised at being asked to play against the Sri Lanka team, apparently because "it was always nice to be in the good books of the south". This stunned me, but I had no choice, so I went. Ashok and I decided that we would just throw our bats around. We did just that, though in both the matches my throwing the bat around fetched me quick runs and the crowd's approval. Meanwhile, Bombay University played and lost in the final to Madras. I am sure all the boys must still be thinking that I had let them down. I hope, after reading this, they will change their minds. If I hadn't played any game at all, it would have been all right, but the reasons given as to why I should play against the Sri Lanka team were stupid, because I had to play against better and quicker bowlers on matting. As it is, Jayantilal fractured his thumb, but as he was having only slight pain, he went to the West Indies. This fracture was finally diagnosed when he had his hand x-rayed after an injury to another finger just before the last Test in the West Indies.

5

Caribbean Journey

We had about ten days' practice before we left for the West Indies. There were the usual tour formalities, which were all new to me, to be completed. I was all at sea, but 'Mama' Karmarkar, the genial but live-wire Assistant Secretary of the Cricket Control Board did everything and asked me not to worry. I am sure, the Board officials, especially the players, would feel completely lost if 'Mama' wasn't there. Everybody loved him, though he would chide the players occasionally, because he is warm-hearted and genuinely anxious to help people.

Three days before we left I began to get a funny kind of pain in the middle finger of my left hand. It was as if some external article had gone in. The doctor diagnosed it as a whitlow and asked me not to do any net practice. Ajit kindly excused me from practice sessions. Instead, I sat and watched the others practise on the last two days. Govindraj told me that he had the same trouble a few days earlier and how he had got rid of it. I didn't pay any attention to him then and did only what the doctor had told me.

The Chairman of the Selection Committee, Mr Vijay Merchant, met the members of the Indian team before we left for the Caribbeans. He conveyed his good wishes to us and expressed the hope that we would acquit ourselves creditably. During his talk, Mr Merchant said that the batsmen should give our bowlers enough runs to bowl with. A hundred should only be the stepping-stone to another hundred. He said that the only player who followed this precept was Sunil Gavaskar. "Though he is the youngest player in the team, the senior players would do well to follow his example," he added. This was very flattering indeed. It also made me aware of the high expectations, not only of the Selection Committee, but those who followed Indian cricket. I am glad I didn't disappoint them.

We left for London on our way to the West Indies on February 1, 1971. I had bandaged my finger to protect it from hurting myself as a result of the jostling we might get from the enthusiastic crowd that had turned up to see us off. During the flight I decided to follow Govindraj's method to reduce the pain. I asked the air hostess for some sweet lime, sliced into two. When I got this I shoved my finger into one half and kept it there for an hour or so. According to Govindraj, this would draw out the puss and the finger would be healed quickly. Since the flight to London takes about 9 hours, I disturbed the hostess a few more times and continued the treatment until we reached our destination. We had a night's halt in London and we used it to do a bit of sight-seeing. Ashok Mankad, who had spent the previous English cricket season in Manchester, was my guide and we went around in our tropical suits, cheerfully ignoring the startled Londoners in their overcoats. The finger had not started its tricks till then and I had my hand in my trouser-pocket all the time, while going around Piccadilly Circus.

The next morning we left for New York. By this time the finger was painfully throbbing, probably because the condition was aggravated by the cold of London. Hardly had the plane taken off when the pain started increasing in intensity until I couldn't even move it one way or the other. I was feeling miserable. I endured the pain for a couple of hours, by which time the air hostesses had finished their work. When I couldn't bear the pain any longer, I talked to our Manager, Mr Tarapore. He looked worried and he had an emergency announcement made over the aircraft's public address system, to enquire if a doctor was on board. Luckily for me, there was; and he gave me some capsules that reduced the intensity of the pain and kept me from howling in agony.

As soon as we checked into our hotel near the Kennedy airport in New York, Mr Tarapore took me to a hospital. I was asked what my problem was. When the nurse on duty saw my finger, she turned her face away, because it was badly swollen and was full of puss. The doctor examined me and said he would have to operate immediately. He assured me that it would take less than ten minutes, but I would be out of action for two weeks. He said, "Thank God, you've come now. If you had delayed even by twenty-four hours, gangrene would have set in, and the finger would have had to be chopped off." The operation, which was a minor one, did not take long, and I felt very much relieved. The pain was gone. I am deeply grateful to Mr Keki Tarapore for the prompt action he took, and for taking me to the hospital. Keki came to the hospital and stayed with me all the time. He comforted me, saying I would be well soon. And, when we returned to the hotel, he packed me off straight to bed, as I had lost a bit of blood and a night's rest would do a lot of good to me. He was right and I woke up feeling very much refreshed, with the finger looking tender, but certainly better. While I was at the hospital, the other members of team went on a lightning tour of New York, making the most of the night halt in the fabulous city.

Our flight to Jamaica from New York was short, compared to the long flight from Bombay to London and New York—16 hours in all. We landed at Pallisadoes airport in Kingston, where the West Indies cricket officials received us. The people were nice and friendly and began to talk to our players. Jaisimha, Sardesai, Prasanna and Durrani, who had been in the West Indies with the 1962 team, were especially sought after, but nobody paid much attention to the others. While we waited for our luggage, a round of rum-punch was served. When I said I did not drink, the person serving the drink looked at me flabbergasted and said, "What maan, you, a batsman! You can't score runs here unless you drink rum." Still I declined, and so did a few others. The welcome was friendly though naturally not overenthusiastic after the 5-0 drubbing we received in 1962. It was frustrating for some to find their kit-bags misplaced, as they had not arrived from New York. We had just one day before our first match against Jamaica. I, of course, was out of it all, though I earnestly wanted to get into the thick of things. I did quite a bit of running and bowled a lot to our batsmen, just to keep myself fit, especially my legs.

Just before the match against Jamaica, Vishwanath had to drop out. He had twisted his knee very badly in the South Zone vs. Central Zone final at Bombay and now it had started to trouble him. So, Dilip Sardesai, who was not in the XI for the match, and was, in fact, a last-minute choice for the tour, got in. And, how he made full use of his opportunity! Even before he was selected for the tour, Dilip used to say that he would score two or three centuries in the West Indies, and then retire from first-class cricket. This self-confidence was justified when he slammed three centuries in the Tests, all of them under the most difficult circumstances.

In the match against Jamaica, Dilip scored 97 runs before being run out in a mix-up with Ajit Wadekar. Both Ajit and Dilip, in spite of their innumerable long partnerships for Bombay and West Zone, were terrible runners between wickets, and, more often than not, the only way to get them out was through a run out. Dilip thus missed the distinction of being the first to hit a century on the tour. In a way it was good, because generally those who start with a century always find runs hard to come by later on. This proved true in the case of Salim Durrani, who hit a century (131) in the second

innings, but failed to make any substantial contribution with
the bat thereafter. Ajit had a long look at the bowling and the
wicket and scored 70 runs in 240 minutes. It was Sardesai,
however, who stole the show. Equally comfortable against pace
and spin, his innings was an object-lesson to players like me.

In the second innings Durrani played as only he can. With
the minimum movement of his feet he still got the maximum
power behind his shots, which fairly sizzled over the grass. He
hooked Dowe out of the small Sabina Park ground and then
cover-drove him to the boundary. This caused excitement
among the tree-top spectators, who began to jump and clap
with such gusto that a branch of the tree crashed down with
its human load. While some people who had fallen were dust-
ing themselves and looking for broken bones, the others quickly
scrambled back to their high perch. It was a great sight, and
it shows how keen the West Indians are where cricket is concerned. The spectators in the Caribbean want to see bumpers
bowled and love to see the batsmen wilt. They are annoyed
if a batsman (especially Indian) hooks the bumpers for
boundaries.

During this match we had our first look at Lawrence Rowe.
According to one player, Rowe is in the habit of whistling
while playing a shot. He clipped a few shots but was out
quickly in the first innings for 19 and scored 19 not out in
the second knock. We played our second match at Montego
Bay against the West Indies Board President's XI. Alvin Kallicharran played in the match and got a few runs (57 not out)
in the second innings. At that time he looked like a batsman
ever ready to hit every ball out of sight. But, by the time he
came to India in 1974-75, he had become a complete batsman,
willing to wait for the loose ball, yet elegant at all times. I
remember how Kallicharran was despondent when we met him
at a beach party in the evening after he was out for only six
runs in the first innings. He was apparently haunted by the
fear that he would never be selected to play for the West Indies

The Gavaskar family.
L—R: sister Nutan, dad Manohar the author, wife Marshniel, sister Kabita and mother Meenal.

Gavaskar 'the baby' cricketer, in leg-guards stitched by his mother and sweater knitted by his grandmother

Wedding bells for the maestro.

With his first born after he returned from the dual tour of New-Zealand and West Indies, 1976.

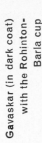

Returning to the pavillion
after playing a Captain's
innings for Bombay.

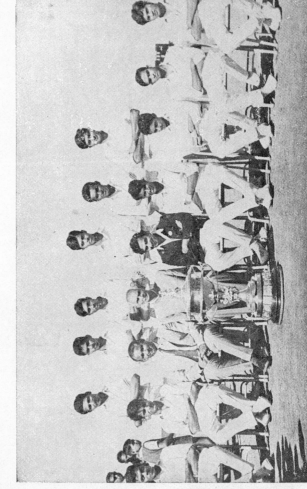

Gavaskar (in dark coat)
with the Rohinton-
Barla cup

Gavaskar receiving the Deodhar Trophy.

and was on the verge of tears. Vishwanath and I did our
best to console him and we have been good friends ever since.

Vishwanath and I, in the meanwhile, were regular visitors
to the hospital, where the doctor who was treating us talked
endlessly about cricket. The doctors were undecided about
the condition of Vishwanath's knee. My finger now needed
only cleaning and dressing, and it was getting better.
Vishwanath and I would be at the hospital when the others
were on the field and, listening to the radio commentary on
the match, we would suddenly look at each other and laugh,
while we really felt miserable. Imagine, two 21-year-olds in
hospital! Vishwanath's leg had been shaved and it was a funny
sight. I never stopped ribbing him about it, and, even in the
hospital, we tried to pull each other's leg.

With both of us unfit for the first two games of the tour,
the rest of the team members had more opportunity of estab-
lishing themselves. Ashok Mankad, finding it difficult to cope
with livelier wickets, was struggling to get into runs and was
not played in the first Test. The tour selectors decided to
experiment with Abid Ali, who had earlier opened for India in
Tests against Australia and New Zealand, both at home (1969)
and in the two countries (1967).

I played my first match against the University of the West
Indies, which was a one-day game played over 45 overs a side.
We scored freely and I got 71 runs. The finger wound
looked to have opened a bit and I was worried. But it was
a minor thing and the rest I got while we played the first
Test was enough for it to heal. Vishwanath also played in the
match, his first on the tour, and got 50 runs. Dilip was his
usual self but was run out again, when he was on 55.
After his third run out in three matches, Dilip swore that
if he was ever run out again he would pack up and go home.
In this game he got into a muddle with Salim Durrani and
Salim saw to it that Dilip didn't get 'home'. Salim and Dilip

were roommates and they got on famously, and it was this
that probably also prompted Durrani to throw away his wicket.
We won the match, fairly easily, by 101 runs.

The first Test at Kingston started late, as there was a bit of
rain and the first day's play was washed out. On the second
day, Sobers won the toss and asked India to bat. The wicket,
freshened by rain, had a lot of life which the Caribbean pace
bowlers fully exploited. Shillingford sent back Jayantilal with
only 10 runs on the board. Jayantilal withdrew his bat at the
last moment, but the ball came back sharply, got an edge and
travelled like lightning between second and third slip. There
was a flash of movement, and Sobers came up laughing with
the ball clutched to his chest. "What a catch!" I told somebody. "Now all I want to see is Rohan Kanhai's falling sweep
shot, and my tour is made." Abid followed soon after, sparring
at one outside the off-stump for Camacho to take an easy
catch. Ajit held on grimly till he gloved an attempted hook off
Holder, for another easy catch. Dilip and Salim of Room No.
53, Flamingo Hotel, got together and added runs slowly. The
spinners came on and Test debutante Barrett struck, claiming
the wicket of Durrani, who missed a pull and was bowled by a
ball that kept low. Jaisimha, my boyhood idol, came and
played on to Holder and was bowled. India were 75-5 and
already the radio commentators and critics were sharpening
their knives. One commentator called us a 'club side'. I don't
know whether Eknath Solkar heard it. But, when he went out,
Dilip met him halfway and had a word with him. With Dilip's
constant encouragement, Eknath, who was playing his first
Test abroad, put his head down, and the pair slowly wore out
the Windies attack. They added 137 runs, a new record for
the sixth wicket, and batted up to the third day, before Solkar
was bowled by Sobers for 61. India were 8 for 260 when
Prasanna joined Dilip. Those who complain that Prasanna
is chicken-hearted and is afraid of a contest should have been
there to see how well he stood his ground against pace and
spin. In between, he played a delightful square-cut when Hol-

der took the third new ball. The Dilip-Prasanna partnership flourished and 122 runs were added before Prasanna (25) was bowled by Holder. This was yet another wicket record in Tests against the Windies. And then, Dilip (212) was caught behind off Holder. India were all out for 387, which was a remarkable improvement on 75 for 5. We were on top right through after that initial debacle. When the Windies batted, their stroke players found it difficult to score against our spinners. Only Kanhai and, to some extent, Sobers batted comfortably. Once they were gone, the others just collapsed and the West Indies were all out for 217.

The first day's play having been washed out, we could enforce the follow-on, which we did. Incidentally this was the first time in 23 years that the West Indies had to do so against India. Ajit told us how the Windies were looking downcast when he went to their dressing-room to ask them to bat again. This time they played sensible cricket and Kanhai remained unbeaten with 158, while Sobers scored a dazzling 93, and Clive Lloyd was run out for 57. Kanhai played his falling sweep shot in this innings, and it made my day. Earlier, Dilip, nursing a strained thigh muscle, came in to rest. While watching the match with Grayson Shillingford, Dilip suddenly turned round and told the West Indian bowler, as he pointed to me, "Watch him, he'll also score two hundred against your bowling." For a moment I was stunned and could only manage a weak smile. I had not, until then, played a first-class match in the Windies, and a statement like that from somebody, who was the first to score a double-century against the West Indies, was a bolt from the blue, so to speak. Dilip's thunderbolt was even faster than what Shillingford was to bowl in the two Tests I played against him!

The Test ended in a draw, and our performance had put us back in the game and salvaged a lot of our prestige. The critics turned their comments against the West Indies and their players came in for a bit of lashing.

We went to St. Kitts for a three-day game against the Leeward Islands which we won by nine wickets. This was my first first-class game in the West Indies and I was happy to be able to get off the mark with a score of 82, before hitting a full-toss back to Willett, in the first innings. Ajit was unbeaten with a brilliant 128 and Abid was 64 not out. Left to get 57 runs in 12 mandatory overs to win, we got 60, with an over to spare. Andy Roberts played in this game and bowled with a lot of pace, but he lacked direction. When we next met him in 1974-75, he had matured a lot and we found him very accurate, and he had increased his pace by a couple of yards.

6

Glorious Victory

After an overnight flight, due to some mix-up, we landed at
Trinidad airport pretty late. The drive to Guaracara Park,
about 60 miles away, was tedious and the match against
Trinidad started late. Ajit won the toss and we batted, while
everybody from no. 5 downwards went to sleep to make up
for the previous night. They must have slept soundly because
Ashok and I were not separated until just before tea. We had
scored 155 runs, Ashok contributing a strokeful 79. Durrani
then clouted two mighty sixes out of the ground, before he
was run out for 43. I got my century (119), with Dilip as my
partner. Next morning I was run out for 125, while Dilip
went on to score 94 before he was out. The disappointment
was Vishwanath, who hooked a bumper straight to Gabriel
at mid-wicket. For Trinidad, Charlie Davis scored 100, while
his brother Bryan Davis contributed 61 runs. Almost all the
Trinidad batsmen made runs and they totalled 338 runs.
Before Ajit declared our innings at 5 for 162, I got 63 runs in
90 minutes when I played a lazy shot and was caught at
extra-cover. The match ended in a drab draw. After the
match, the Trinidad Cricket Council presented me with a
magnificent Trophy, which holds a very prominent position
in my house. It was terrific getting a trophy, even before
I had played a Test and did wonders to my confidence.

In the second Test at Port of Spain, Ashok Mankad and I
came into the team. Ashok was staging a comeback after

being dropped for the first Test, while I was making my debut. At dinner that night my team-mates wished me luck and I went to sleep with the thought that the next day I was going to play my first Test for my country. I don't think I slept well, and as I lay tossing in bed, I could see Vishwanath fast asleep, without a care in the world. He wasn't playing in the game!

Sobers again won the toss and elected to bat. Opener Fredericks was bowled off his pads off the very first delivery by Abid Ali. After that, the West Indies lost wickets at regular intervals and were all out for 214. Only Charlie Davis batted well to remain unbeaten with 74. We had about 30 minutes' batting before close of play. As I took strike, after Ashok had got three runs, I was a little afraid that I might not be up to the mark. Holder thundered down and bowled on the leg-stump. The ball struck my leg-guards and went down to fine-leg for two leg-byes. But I was surprised to see that the umpire did not make any signal, so I was off the mark with two runs, when actually I shouldn't have had any. This helped me to get rid of the fear of failure, and I was soon middling the ball and clipped Holder to the square-leg fence for my first boundary in Tests. We ended the day with 22 without being separated. Ashok was on 14 and I on 8.

The next morning I was glad to see Sobers grass a low, fast edge off Holder as I tried to drive him off the back-foot. Sobers tumbled in the attempt but spilled the ball. This was a lucky break and I went on with greater confidence and got my 50 after lunch. It was a slow innings, but I was encouraged when Kanhai, fielding in the slips, said, "Well played, son". That gave me a terrific boost and after that I seemed to play much better. I got to 65 before I pulled a short ball from Noreiga, for Clive Lloyd, half-way to the square-leg boundary, to take a simple catch. My baptism in Test cricket was over and I hadn't done too badly. Ajit was out next ball before he had scored, but Solkar prevented the hat-trick. Dilip, in the meantime, had settled down and, with dazzling footwork, was neutralising any spin that Noreiga and Sobers were getting from the wicket. It was an object-lesson on how to play spin, and Dilip made 112, before he fell to a catch off Noreiga. India were all out for 352, which gave us a lead of 138 runs. In the second innings the West Indians lost Kanhai cheaply, but Fredericks and Charlie Davis settled down and at the end of the day's play they had just about wiped out the arrears.

It was one of those freak accidents which gave us an opening. Fredericks and Davis were batting at the nets when a shot by Fredericks went through and hit Davis on the right eyebrow, splitting it. He had to be carried to hospital and Lloyd came out with Fredericks to resume the innings. Fredericks was, however, run out without any addition to his overnight score. Lloyd, after hitting an uppish shot past mid-wicket, was caught brilliantly by Ajit, who had stationed himself at short mid-wicket just before the previous ball was delivered. Then Durrani bowled a prodigious break-back that went through Sobers' bat and pad and lifted the leg-bail. The way 'Uncle' Salim jumped up after this and kept on jumping was a sight worth seeing. After this, the West Indies batting collapsed, though Davis came back and was unbeaten with 74. India had to get 124 runs to win, with half of the fourth day's play still left. However, we finished the match that day itself and celebrated our victory on the last day. I was 67 not out without even being aware that I had passed the 50-run mark. We had lost three wickets for 84 runs, but Abid Ali, promoted by Ajit, which proved to be an intelligent move, joined me. We then required 40 runs to win, and went on serenely towards the target. During our unbroken stand we were just tapping and running and, in the bargain, got some bonus runs from overthrows. Though we thoroughly enjoyed ourselves, I was sure that we must have given a real fright to our colleagues in the pavilion. Victory, the first against the West Indies in 23 years, came 15 minutes before the end of the fourth day's play.

As I returned to the pavilion after our historic win, Keki Tarapore came out and embraced me, followed by Ajit and the others. It was a sweet moment. Our first-ever victory over the West Indies! The Windies players also trooped into our dressing room and joined in the handshaking and back-slapping. The Indians in Trinidad were thrilled and we had quite a celebration that night and a wealthy Indian gave us a champagne party at his fabulous estate. But we were well aware that the West Indies were smarting under defeat, and we were determined to see that our success did not make us complacent. It didn't.

I have often been asked about my feelings after my Test debut in an encounter which is a landmark in the annals of Indian cricket. Frankly, I felt satisfied with my performance, even though I did not do anything outstanding. However, I had taken the first step, and I had the satisfaction of having scored 132 runs in two innings, and had remained unbeaten once, to give me the very high average of 132. But to me it has always been a matter of great pride that I was able, in my very first Test, to be associated in India's maiden Test victory against the West Indies and that too in the lion's den.

7

Sardee Maan Tops

Our victory had raised our stock and Dilip with a double-century and century in two Tests was the hero of all the West Indies. Everywhere we went, people wanted to see 'Sardee maan', as Dilip was affectionately called. Dilip was prepared to talk cricket with anybody, which made him a big hit. The department stores threw open their doors to him, and people were falling over each other to invite him to their homes for a meal.

I remember, once Dilip had charged out leaving his food, which he loves, to take up cudgels against a young Indian who had said to me in Jamaica, "Sobers will get you out, first ball, bowled behind the legs." One of the other boys reported this to Dilip, who was about to bite into his chicken, left and caught hold of the Indian, and nearly started a row. We stopped him, but Dilip was fuming. He was touchy about what was said about the team, especially any of the younger players.

Just before the third Test. we played Guyana at Georgetown, and though I was included in the team I had to drop out due to shin trouble, after the toss was over. The Guyanese captain, Rohan Kanhai, very sportingly agreed to allow the change. For India, Jaisimha (108) and Jayantilal (122 not out) batted well. The match was drawn.

The third Test was also played at Georgetown. The only

change in our team was Vishwanath in place of Jaisimha.
Poor Vishwanath was struggling to shrug off his knee trouble
but he was so conscious of it that it hampered his game.
Normally a very mobile fielder he took a longer time to turn
and run for the ball. But there was never any doubt in the
minds of the West Indian cricket lovers about his class. It
was writ large from the moment he took strike. We shared a
room after the Jamaican leg of the tour. He did not, however, come to St. Kitts, but went directly to Trinidad for
treatment of his knee. I came to know him closely then and
realised what a tremendous sense of humour he has. He was
miserable about his knee but in his inimitable way of speaking, he made light of it. Being about the same height as myself, he could use all my clothes, and he did so nonchalantly.
But, I was then heavier than him and so couldn't return the
compliment by using his clothes. The position was reversed,
however, within a couple of years when Vishwanath put on a bit
of weight. He loved his beer and when he got going he could
go on and on. But he hardly drank a drop before and during
Test matches.

Ajit lost the toss for the third time in the series and we
went in to field on a hot and humid day. Things didn't go
too well for us, as the openers Carew and Fredericks settled
down. Carew swept a no-ball from Durrani to Ashok Mankad
at square-leg. Not learning from experience he again
swept the next ball to Ashok and was caught. Kanhai
played some nice shots and then, jumping out to drive Bedi,
missed and was easily stumped. Charlie Davis and Clive
Lloyd then got together and pushed the score along briskly
before Davis, trying to sweep Solkar, was out leg-before. Lloyd,
in the meanwhile, was getting into top gear. A freak collision,
however, got rid of him. He swept a ball to deep square-leg,
took one run and, with his eye on the ball, turned for a
second and collided with Sobers. The impact was terrific.
Meanwhile Bedi's throw had come to wicket-keeper
Krishnamurthy, and Lloyd was run out once again, just as he

was beginning to look dangerous. Sobers was so stunned by the impact that he made a feeble attempt to cut Bedi and was caught by Venkataraghavan at slip off Krishnamurthy's pads. This was a lucky break for us and we surrounded Desmond Lewis, who was making his Test debut. Lewis slashed at Bedi and was dropped by Sardesai at slip when he was only three. Dilip, who had pulled a thigh muscle, had come to stand in the slips so that he did not have to run. That was a bit of bad luck for us, because Lewis went on to score 81 not out and helped West Indies recover to a respectable total of 363. Lewis and the local hero Lance Gibbs, who invariably raised a laugh with his antics but batted with purpose, added 84 runs for the ninth wicket.

India batted soon after tea on the second day. Ashok and I started cautiously against Shillingford and Boyce. When I was six I cut at a short rising ball from Shillingford and the ball flew like a bullet straight at Sobers' neck. He got his hands to it but dropped it. Later he told me that he didn't see the ball at all and it was only when it was almost on him did he realise it was coming at his face. I celebrated my luck by hooking the next ball, a predictable bouncer, for four. Ashok then opened out and we had added 78 runs when, in trying to cut Noreiga, Ashok played on to his stumps. Ajit and I played out time and when stumps were drawn I was batting with 84 and Ajit with 16.

The next day was another glorious morning and we went out to resume the innings. Ajit muttered something like "We must |stick| around and score." But he got out to a ball from Sobers that kept low, without adding to his overnight score. Vishwanath joined me for his first Test innings in the West Indies, to a lot of humming among the expectant spectators. When he passed Clive Lloyd at cover there was a big laugh from the crowd because of the difference in their heights. From the beginning Vishwanath was middling the ball. With him there is no edging. He either middles it or misses and more often than not it is the sweet sound of the bat meeting the ball. We went on to add 112 runs for the third wicket. As I was nearing my first Test century, dark clouds began gathering over the ground and it started to drizzle. Play continued, however, and on 94 I survived what was probably the simplest of catches. I played forward to a flighted delivery from Noreiga. The ball spun and jumped hitting me on my glove and went to Sobers, who would have taken a dolly catch if he had been standing where he was before the ball was delivered. But Gary, anticipating my forward defensive stroke, had moved forward to try and get me. Thus he had to jump and stretch for the ball, which eluded him and in the bargain I got a run. At the end of the over, Gary stood in front of me and said : "Maan, why are <u>you</u> after me, can't you find some other fielder?" He had dropped me thrice so far and this last one was the easiest of the lot. We came in because of rain when I was on 98. We resumed after a while and I duly got my first Test century. Many people must be wondering as to what is the feeling when one gets a century in Tests. My own reaction was simply to think of my parents who had given me every encouragement and they would be beaming when the news reached them. Soon we had another stoppage due to rain. When we resumed, Sobers took the new ball himself. I drove him through the covers and in trying to repeat the shot managed only to edge it to Carew at second slip who, after a lot of juggling, clasped it to his stomach. That was the end of my innings, which had lasted 265 minutes and fetched me 116 runs. Keith Boyce then captured his first Test wicket, bowling Vishwanath, and then Durrani was out leg-before to Sobers. Sardesai, who batted at no. 6 because of his leg trouble, played a dour innings and with Abid hitting boldly, we overtook the West Indies total to lead them in the third successive Test.

When the Windies batted again Eknath Solkar ripped through Fredericks' defence and had him leg-before for five. Carew was again harassed by Bishen Bedi, but he struggled gamely to score 45 runs. Lloyd and Kanhai got out early, and Sobers, when he was on seven, survived a bat-pad catch appeal. I was fielding at long-on and I saw the deflection clearly and naturally jumped with joy in anticipation of our having taken the prize wicket of the great Sobers. But Gary waited and the umpire ruled 'not out'. For once Salim Durrani lost his cool and flung down the ball in disgust. I don't blame him. He had started the tour brilliantly and was now on the verge of losing his Test place. Also, there was the England tour in the offing and he was keen to make it as he had missed the 1967 tour. The crowd reacted predictably and booed Salim. Gary then hammered us for a century (108 not out) between lunch and tea and Charlie Davis also scored a century (125 not out). Gary's innings included a six when he hit Solkar out of the ground. At this stage Sobers declared his innings, with the total at 307 for 3.

We had 90 minutes' batting and Ashok (53) and I (64) put on 123 runs without being separated. My personal Test aggregate had gone up to 312 in four innings, twice not out and an average of 156. We ended the Test on a high note and went to Bridgetown for the Colony game against Barbados, followed by the fourth Test at the same venue. I was in good form. So was Ashok. Vishwanath had also played well. We were a little worried about Dilip's pulled muscle, but he was better after the intensive treatment he had received at Barbados. And how Dilip put us back in the game is now a part of India's cricketing history.

8

Deflated in Barbados

Barbados is a beautiful place. It has many lovely beaches, which are invariably crowded with tourists from America, Canada and Europe. It is also the country which has given some great cricketers to the world, including the then West Indies skipper Gary Sobers. When we arrived at Bridgetown (Barbados), the customs officials wanted to see Sardesai. Asked if he had anything to 'declare', Dilip said with a broad smile: "I have come here with runs, and I am going to leave Barbados with more runs." It was a sight to see Dilip being bombarded with questions by the officials and the ready answers he had for them. Dilip was, by far, the most popular man in the Indian team. At the airport he was told that Wesley Hall had been included in the Barbados side. Dilip's reply was typical of his self-confident self. "Ha! By the time I come to bat we will be 200 for 2 wickets so what is your Wes Hall going to do?" The officials loved him. He was a man after their own heart.

We were staying in a hotel on the beach and whenever we were not at the nets the boys spent their time at the beach, swimming and ogling at the bikini-clad beauties. This was, of course, a temporary respite before we got down to the real job, I mean the match against Barbados, later. Now, in Barbados, if you beat the West Indies the crowd will not feel very sorry. But, if Barbados lose, then it is 'a national catastrophe'.

Nothing delights a 'Bajan', as Barbadians are called, as much as a Barbados victory over a touring side.

We won the toss against Barbados, led by Sobers, and elected to bat. I was to take strike and saw Wes Hall go almost up to the screen for his run-up. I thought to myself, "I'll need binoculars to know when he starts running in." As is normally the case with me, I am always a bit apprehensive when I face a bowler for the first time. But only when he delivers the first ball. So, as Wes Hall started running up to bowl, I was expecting something like a rocket. In this event it proved to be a less dangerous delivery, which was down the leg-side and brushed my leg-guards as I let it go. And, wonder of wonders, the strap of the leg-guard was broken. However, instead of changing the leg-guard, I just tied a handkerchief round it. As it proved later it would have been a useless waste of time, because I was out in the next over.

Jayantilal played a ball from Holder down towards square-leg. I thought we could take a quick single and I took off, expecting Jayantilal to respond. When I found he wasn't moving, I tried to stop, slipped and fell heavily. I was so stunned that I couldn't even get up as the fielder rushed past me and knocked off the bails at the bowler's end. This was the first time that I had 'failed' in the West Indies, and I walked dejectedly back to the pavilion with a 'zero' to my name. We then collapsed and were all out for 185. When Barbados batted, Govindraj bowled a good spell which had Seymour Nurse ducking and sparring at outgoing balls. Nurse, however, survived, but before he got off the mark he fell to a catch by wicket-keeper Jeejeebhoy, off Abid. However, Sobers chose this moment to get back into the century habit, with his cousin David Holford (111) to keep him company. Barbados thus ran up a mammoth total of 449.

In the second innings I was determined to score. In Hall's second over, when he bounced one at me, I played the best

hook shot I've ever played. The ball went skimming to the
mid-wicket boundary. I wish I could play shots like that more
often. We had an opening partnership of 149, before I was
bowled by a shooter from Holder for 67. After that, there was
very little resistance and we were all out, leaving Barbados to
score 50 runs for victory. Again Govindraj bowled well, but
was positively unlucky not to get Nurse's wicket. Barbados
won easily by nine wickets.

There was an incident during the Barbados match, which
involved Russi Jeejeebhoy and Seymour Nurse. Nurse, annoyed
by Russi's constant thrusting of his pads to the ball, made a
sarcastic comment that Russi had a bat to play the ball with.
Russi resented the remark and walked down the wicket gesturing that he wanted to have a word with Sobers, who was
then bowling. Sobers told Russi off and Russi was so upset
about it that he refused to talk to anyone in the dressing
room, when he returned after he was out. Dilip ribbed him a
lot about this and even his room-mate Solkar did not spare
him. The sight of the outraged Russi walking down the wicket
to remonstrate with Sobers is one of the memorable events of
the 1971 West Indies tour.

The fourth Test was to start on 1st April, which was Ajit
Wadekar's birthday. As if to give himself a birthday gift, Ajit
won the toss, for the first time in the series, and elected to
field. This decision was prompted by the greenish wicket and
the fact that the West Indian team did not have a spin bowler
to exploit the worn wicket on the last day. Lewis (88) and
Kanhai (85) had a partnership of 166 runs for the second wicket
before both fell. Charlie Davis and Sobers went on to score 178,
in his team's total of 501 for five, before declaring on the second
day. This left us about 40 minutes of batting. The West Indians
had capped Uton Dowe, a fast bowler, for the Test. The 15,000
Barbadians were yelling their throats dry and giving Dowe
just the encouragement he needed as he pounded in to bowl.
He was fast, but nowhere near as frightening as he was

reckoned to be. By this time dark clouds were gathering and
the light was deteriorating fast. Ashok Mankad came up to me
and asked me whether we should appeal against the light. I
suggested that we wait for another over. Ashok appealed against
the light before Dowe bowled his second over. The umpire
C. Jordan, however, turned down our appeal. Off Dowe's fourth
ball I was out to a simple catch by Holder at mid-wicket when
I had scored only one run—my lowest score in Tests. Two balls
later, Krishnamurthy, who went in as night-watchman, also
appealed against the light. This time the appeal was upheld
and play ended 20 minutes before time. It is amazing how the
light could have deteriorated after just two deliveries, which
justified the umpires calling it a day!

The next day we lost quick wickets, and plunged to 70 for
six, when Solkar came in to join Dilip. At this stage Dilip
was batting magnificently. At 96 he played a perfect cover-
drive off Sobers to reach his third century of the series. As if
to prove he could do it again he repeated the shot off the next
ball. This time the grass sizzled as the ball sped to the boundary. Dilip (111) and Solkar (59) resumed the innings on the
morning of the fourth day and carried the total to 256, when
Solkar (65) became Dowe's fourth victim. Their partnership
had realised 186 runs for the seventh wicket—yet another
wicket record for India. The danger of follow-on had not passed
when Bedi joined Dilip for the last wicket. Bishen, though good
enough to go in as night-watchman against the Australians in
1969-70, was not in his best batting form. In between some airy
shots and a simple edge that wicket-keeper Lewis and Kanhai
let by, he played some firm shots. With Sardesai also putting
his weight behind his shots we avoided the follow-on amidst
excitement. India had totalled 347 runs—the last four wickets
putting on 277 runs. The last-wicket partnership between Dilip
and Bedi had realised 62 priceless runs—again a new record for
India.

The West Indians went on a run spree in their second knock,
and Lloyd in particular hammered away as if he was having a

batting practice. We were expecting a declaration leaving us 30 minutes' batting, which is the kind of declaration every opening batsman dreads. But Sobers, who had other ideas, did not declare until he played an over on the last morning. That left us with a little over five hours to save the game. With no off-spinner in the West Indies side this was not going to be a tough task if we kept our wits about. That's exactly what we did, and we easily saved the match. Early in our second innings Ashok Mankad fractured his right wrist in trying to fend off a delivery from Dowe. Ashok, however, did not flinch, but carried on pluckily for almost an hour, playing most of the time with one hand. I had to shield him from the bowling and often I had to forget taking singles off the first few deliveries of the over, and where we could take three runs we ran only two.

Ashok's courage in the face of physical disability was not lost on the rest of the boys and they helped me to save the match. In the process I got a century (117 not out). It was a purely defensive innings since winning was out of question. Yet, I played my shots with confidence and authority, and a hook for six off a Dowe bouncer stands out in my memory. My second century of the series somewhat compensated me for my 'failure' in the first innings. My Test aggregate had mounted to 430, but my average had come down to just over 143.

And, so on to the last Test, secure in the knowledge that we couldn't lose the series, and there was more than an even chance of increasing our margin of victory to 2-0. It was a good augury for us that the venue of this last encounter was the Queen's Park Oval at Port of Spain, capital of Trinidad, where we had won the second Test barely a month ago. For me, the beautiful island of Trinidad has a special fascination, because it was here that I took my first bow in Test cricket. Little did I know when we were journeying back to Port of Spain that I would see my finest hour. there

9

My Finest Hour

> *...It was Gavaskar*
> *The real master*
> *Just like a wall*
> *We couldn't out Gavaskar at all,*
> *not at all*
> *You know the West Indies couldn't*
> *out Gavaskar at all.*
>
> —Lord Relator

It was sunny, hot and humid at Port of Spain. I was tired, sweating and very very thirsty. It was Trinidad, after all, where the climate makes you feel as if you have just stepped out of a steam bath—particularly after a strenuous practice session at the nets. The dressing rooms at the Queen's Park Oval are some distance from the 'nets' and, tired as I was, the prospect of having to trudge back through that seemingly endless stretch before being able to get myself a glass of cold water was not a particularly exciting one. Just then I saw a number of boys, along with Ashok Mankad who was out of the game with a fractured wrist, making their way towards us with the tray of drinks. It was a very welcome sight and all of us automatically started converging on the approaching procession. My throat, by now, was really parched and, instead of

[From A CALYPSO Composed by Lord Relator in Honour of the visiting Indian Cricket Team to the West Indies in 1971]

waiting for the water to be poured into the tumbler, I asked Ashok to pour the delightfully cold water from the jug straight into my mouth for me to gulp it down. I had to pay for this impatience of mine, and how! For, along with the water, a small bit of ice also went down and got stuck in the cavity of one of my teeth. The cavity had been there for a long time, but I let it be as it had not been giving me any trouble. But, after the ice melted in the cavity, the trouble started and from then on it was sheer agonising pain and torture.

Anybody who has been troubled by cavities will bear me out that it can cause excruciating pain. I had hoped that relief would come at night, but I was wrong. I spent the entire night moaning and, in the process, disturbed my room-mate Vishwanath, who loves his sleep. Pain-killing tablets didn't help me much. On the contrary, I became even more acutely aware of the pain, and sleep just wouldn't come.

I spent a sleepless night and was suffering from acute pain when I went in to battle in the fifth Test at the Queen's Park Oval. To make things more difficult for me, Ajit won the toss and elected to bat. And, there I was, with eyes bloodshot owing to lack of sleep, to open the innings, with Abid Ali as my partner.

The Test began on a note of controversy, but this did not come to public notice, and no one was the wiser for it. There was a misunderstanding over the toss. Apparently, both Wadekar and Sobers believed that he had won the toss. Now, in a six-day Test, the toss is vital and Sobers showed wonderful spirit when he conceded the toss to Ajit, who promptly elected to bat.

It was obvious that Gary was a changed man in this Test, for he bowled a great spell in the morning, with sustained pace, moving the ball both ways. He had Abid caught by Charlie Davis, and greeted Wadekar with a bouncer, followed by a yorker. Ajit was having a tough time, but he batted with self-confidence till he fished for a ball outside the off-stump, and Sobers dived to his left to take the catch. In the process the ball jammed between his diaphragm and hands and Sobers was off the field after lunch. When Dilip Sardesai joined me we were 70 for two wickets. Dilip, for some reason, was nervous and he flashed outside the off-stump to Dowe quite often, once escaping being caught by Carew. He, however, put his initial uncertainty behind, and was soon playing with his customary confidence. Dilip overtook me at 70, but was out soon afterwards, when he tried to flick one down the leg-side and Lewis took a good catch. However, we were able to add a substantial 122 runs for the fourth wicket.

Dilip, whenever he batted, was most careless about his appearance. If the pad-straps were loose and were hanging about, he wouldn't be bothered. After a discussion at the end of the over I told him about a strap, which had come loose, and asked him to tie it up. Dilip turned round and saw Clive Lloyd, crossing over to the other side, and asked him in Marathi to tie up the loose pad-strap. Naturally Clive didn't understand what was wanted, and Dilip realised his mistake. He then requested Clive in English to adjust the pad-strap.

In trying to hook a short ball from Sobers I missed and was hit in the midriff, but this didn't cause so much pain, as the tooth. Every run I took caused more pain as the running jarred the tooth. I've had a painful tooth before, but this was something terrible. Surprisingly, however, the pain sharpened my other instincts. My reflexes were quicker and my concentration became more intense as the pain increased. Vishwanath, who had joined me, made 22, while I crawled to the nineties. Vishwanath and Jaisimha, however, got out immediately, and I eventually got my century and at the end of the day's play was 102 not out. Solkar was on three and we were a respectable 250 for five wickets. At the end of the day when we returned to the pavilion I couldn't even laugh at the jokes which Vishwanath and Dilip cracked and, above all, I couldn't even have a cold drink to quench my unquenchable thirst because of the toothache. The Manager, Keki Tarapore, however, refused to let me have the tooth extracted. "Not during the Test, and no pain-killing drugs or injections. It'll only make you drowsy," he said. I groaned, but had no alternative. Imagine bearing the severe pain for another five days, I thought to myself. Sleeping tablets helped a little. Instead of spending a totally sleepless night, I had a fitful sleep for some time around dawn. Eating was also a problem because I could not chew.

As we walked in to bat the next day, Solkar jokingly said to me, "Watch and learn from me." Well, he was out third ball, and I couldn't learn much as he had played and missed the earlier two deliveries. Anyway, Venkataraghavan came in with a determined look on his face. I tried to shield him from the new ball but Venkataraghavan didn't seem to like it, and to prove his point, he smote Dowe's bouncers to mid-wicket. My innings ended when I was caught by Lewis, off Holford, for 124. Venkataraghavan had scored a valuable 51 and India ended up with a fighting score of 360.

Lewis opened the West Indies innings and was lucky to see umpire Gosein negative an appeal for caught behind. He eventually went on to score 72 runs. But the most incredible decision was when Sobers was given 'not out', after Bishen Bedi had taken a low return catch, stumbled and then run on a bit. We didn't appeal, because we thought we didn't have to. But Sobers, who was then 34, stood his ground and the umpire turned down our appeal. After that, Gary went on to score 132, before he was bowled by Prasanna. Davis turned in another good performance, scoring 105 runs—his second Test century in the series.

I was fielding on the third-man fence when Foster was batting on 99. A spectator ran up to me and bet me that Foster wouldn't score a 100. He said he would give me 100 dollars if Foster got that run or else I would have to give him one dollar. Well, Foster was bowled by Abid a few balls later and never got his 100. After tea, I took my dollar and, when I was fielding on the boundary, I gave it to the man. Such is the kind of betting that goes on among the spectators there. In fact, there is virtually 'ball to ball betting' in cricket matches in the Caribbean. The West Indies innings ended on the fourth day with the total at 526, a first innings lead of 166.

When India batted again, I was feeling pretty weak, because I had not eaten well for several days and had spent many sleepless nights. Abid was out early, leg-before to Gary, a decision he didn't appreciate, and quite rightly too. Ajit joined me and we had a fruitful partnership. When I had scored 51 runs I passed 1,000 runs on the tour. It was the latest of the records I was to set. At the end of the day we were 94 for 1, and I was unbeaten with 57.

The next day we carried the score to 159, before Ajit was out for 54, his best score in the series. He had played some classic cover-drives, off Shepherd and Sobers. Dilip came in to join me, and the crowd gave him a great ovation. We still required eight runs to wipe off the West Indies lead. I took two 4's off Noreiga, and moved closer to my second century in the match. Sobers tightened the field, but I eventually got my hundred (twelve 4's), which I had reached in 215 minutes. This was the signal for tremendous cheering by the huge crowd, which invaded the field to congratulate me on becoming the second Indian to score a century in each innings of a Test. With this, I joined the distinguished company of Vijay Hazare, who had accomplished the feat against the Australians led by Don Bradman, just about 24 years ago. I was naturally elated about my success, and thought how proud and happy my parents would be! However, when at the end of the fourth day, I was unbeaten with 57, I had no idea of trying to score a century in each innings. I was just content to try and get some sleep, which I needed so badly. However, I found that runs were more easy to come by than sleep. After I had got my second hundred, Dilip came up to congratulate me and offered a bit of advice. He told me, "I know you are not sleeping well. So, go to sleep at the wicket and don't get out." Anyway, Dilip did not stay with me long, as he fell to a return catch by Foster. In fact Foster was pleasantly surprised that he should have got the prize wicket of Dilip, with an innocuous delivery. But, such are the vagaries of cricket!

Vishwanath and I then added 99 runs when Sobers with the new ball made one scoot through low to bowl him. Jaisimha, in danger of bagging a 'pair', stayed on till the end of the day's play. At the end of the fifth day I was unbeaten with 180, and dead tired. As I returned to the pavilion at draw of stumps the crowd gave me a big hand. The ovation still reverberates in my ears. It was fantastic. But the pain wasn't.

When I woke up on the sixth and last day of the Test it was with a sense of pleasure. It was not because I was expecting a double century, but simply because I knew that, come what may, I was going to be relieved of the pain by evening. But, pain or no pain, I had to resume my innings, with the Indian total at 324. Eventually, I reached the 200-run mark with a cover-drive off Dowe. This brought about a virtual 'explosion' in the stands. The spectators surged on to the ground in their hundreds to congratulate me. One of the Indians even shoved the Indian National flag in my hand. I was hoisted on willing shoulders, as the frenzied spectators danced about with me in joy. It was all very moving, and I shall never forget those few exciting moments on a foreign field far away from home. However, I was scared that, in their enthusiasm, my admirers might pull an arm or a leg apart because, quite honestly, the chaps were not in their senses. And, if anybody by mistake even lightly brushed my jaw I would have been in trouble. Finally, they put me down with such force that not only the bad tooth, but the entire set of teeth rattled!

The pain was somewhat mitigated by the elation I felt at

having scored a century in the first innings and a double century in the second. At that time I did not know that I had crossed yet another landmark when I got my double century. With this I became the second batsman in the history of cricket to score a century and a double-century in the same Test. By a strange coincidence, K.D. Walters of Australia was the first to perform the feat, also against the West Indies, at Sydney in the 1968-69 series.

When things quietened, I got down to the serious business of carrying on from where I had left off. I knew that my task was not yet over. I had to carry on till the lead and time was beyond the reach of the West Indies. I was eager to get a few more runs, but I chopped a ball from Shepherd on to my stumps and was bowled for 220 (twenty-four 4's).

As I walked back to the pavilion, "The Maestro" Gary Sobers smilingly tousled my cap. I was greeted by deafening applause, which is still ringing in my ears. It was extremely touching to see the huge crowd give me a standing ovation.

I had begun to remove my leg-guards mechanically when I suddenly realised that now I could actually have my tooth extracted. Keki Tarapore agreed and immediately took me to the dentist, where we listened to the radio commentary, while the tooth was being extracted. I did not follow Vishwanath's advice that I should keep the tooth as a souvenir, to remind me of those six days of agony and ecstasy I had undergone in Trinidad. By the time I returned to the ground, the West Indies had lost five wickets, Abid getting Kanhai and Sobers off successive balls. The end of the match saw almost all the players breathing down the necks of the ninth-wicket pair of Lewis and Dowe. But they held on. And so, the Test ended in a draw, and the West Indies, who had dominated the match for most part of the game, were struggling to avoid defeat in the end. India had thus won their first series against the West Indies by virtue of the solitary victory in the second

Test at Port of Spain. It had been a wonderful tour and for me, especially, a memorable one.

We spent an enjoyable day in Tobago where we saw some of the greatest sights underwater. On the way back home, we halted in New York, and also went to see the breath-taking Niagra Falls, and returned to a fabulous welcome in Bombay. We had expected a big crowd, but nothing like what we saw at the airport. It was terrific. We were garlanded profusely and officials were swarming around, pumping our hands in real joy.

10

Blight On Blighty

We had functions galore, but soon we had to get down to prepare for the England tour. We had a new manager, the stern but amiable Lt. Col. Hemu Adhikari. He put us through a gruelling spell of training, during which all the icing of the celebrations after our triumph over the West Indies melted away. When we finally took off for London in an Air-India 'Jumbo', we were fighting fit. There were three changes in the side that had returned from West Indies a month earlier. Durrani, Jaisimha and Jeejeebhoy were dropped. Their places were taken by Abbas Ali Baig, Chandrasekhar and Kirmani. Farokh Engineer was to be available only for the Tests, which meant we were carrying two other regular keepers in Kirmani and Krishnamurthy. Just before we left, Prof. Chandgadkar, the Secretary of the Cricket Control Board, promised a red carpet welcome from the airport to the Brabourne Stadium, if the team was as successful in England as it had been in the Caribbean.

As we circled over London, someone in the team remarked, "Look at the greenery around, we are in for green wickets." We practised a few days at The Oval, because the second Test between Pakistan and England was on at Lord's. However, we were to play the first match of the tour at Lord's against Middlesex. Lord's, at first sight, is not impressive. Quite frankly, I don't understand why cricketers are overawed by Lord's. The members are the stuffiest know-alls you can come across, and the ground is most uninspiring. It slopes from one end to the other. I shuddered to think of it as the Head-quarters of Cricket!

We won the Middlesex match with two wickets to spare. It was exciting to start the tour so well. In the second game, however, we were brought down to earth by Essex, for whom the West Indian bowler, Keith Boyce, skittled us out cheaply in the first innings. We fought back in the second innings to make Essex bat again. They had to make 68 runs in 18 overs, which they succeeded in doing only in the last over, winning the match by six wickets.

We then played a series of matches before we clashed with England in the first Test at Lord's. During these matches most of the batsmen scored runs. Vishwanath, Wadekar, Sardesai, Ashok Mankad and I had hit centuries, with Vishwanath leading with three hundreds. With a 109 against Hampshire just before the first Test, Ashok earned a place in the Test side. The other two openers Baig and Jayantilal had not struck form. Seeing Baig bat, we wondered if he was the same person who had scored a maiden Test century against Trueman at his best 12 years ago. Quite clearly, he had lost the appetite to face fast bowling.

For the first Test at Lord's, England fielded a strong side. They had a terrific batting line-up and the bowling was in the hands of Snow, Price and Hutton, with Gifford and Illingworth to provide the spin. Ray Illingworth, leading England for the first time against India, won the toss, which wasn't surprising, as Ajit was not very lucky with the coin even for Bombay. England were, however, in for a shock as Boycott went early fishing outside his off-stump. I very much wanted to see Boycott play a long innings but was disappointed when he fell to a catch by Engineer off Abid Ali for 3. Then our spinners struck and at 71 for 5 England were in a virtu-ally hopeless position. At this stage Illingworth played back to a flipper from Chandrasekhar, which skidded low and benefited from umpire David Constant negativing an appeal for lbw. Incidentally, Umpire Constant was 'constant' in his support for England that year. So, with a spirited partner in Snow, Illingworth slowly built up the innings before he was out. Snow went on to record his highest Test score of 73. England were all out for 304.

Our innings started badly, with both Ashok and I being sent back cheaply. Ajit then played a strokeful innings to score 85. Vishwanath and Solkar chipped in with 68 and 67 respectively and we led England by nine runs. This was the second time that India had left England behind on the 1st innings in a Test in England. The England second innings was a repeat of their first, despite the umpire's support to the batsmen. And we were left to score 183 runs in four hours to win. Ashok and Ajit fell in quick succession and Farokh was promoted in the batting order. We had a partnership of 66, before Farokh stepped out once too often to Gifford and was easily stumped by Knott, his opposite number, for 35. Earlier, during our partnership, just before lunch, an incident, the famous 'Snow charge', took place involving me. Snow bowled to Farokh from the Nursery End, and Farokh trying to turn a ball to leg missed and was hit on the thigh and the ball fell near short square-leg. We set off for a quick run. From the corner of my eye I saw Snow also setting off for the ball. I would have reached 'home' safely as Snow had gone across to the other side on his follow through. However, I found to my surprise that he was level with me and, with the ball nowhere near him, the hefty fast bowler gave me a violent shove, which sent me sprawling. Now, Snow is a well-built bowler, with strong shoulders, so that poor little me had no chance! I crawled to the crease having lost my bat in the tumble. Snow came and tossed the bat back to me. He did not fling it as reported in the newspapers. In fact, after lunch he came to me and apologised. However, the England selectors dropped him from the next Test as a disciplinary measure. Snow, in any case, looked a tired man after his strenuous Australian tour and was nowhere near his best in the Lord's Test.

Vishwanath went next, given out, caught in the leg-trap with the ball coming off his pads. That was a sad blow, but worse was to come. Dilip Sardesai tried to cut a straight ball from Illingworth and left his stumps open, with fatal results. I got out when a ball from Gifford kicked up from a length, hit my gloves and lobbed to Edrich in the gully. At this moment there was a slight drizzle, and though play continued for a while, the players couldn't come out after tea. India then needed 38 runs for victory, with two wickets in hand. Though the dice was heavily loaded in England's favour, India could also have won if play had continued. Everybody agreed that a draw was a fair result to this thrilling match.

Peter Lever, recalled to the England ranks to take the place of John Snow for the second Test, would be playing on his home ground at Old Trafford, and what a game he had ! Illingworth won the toss again and elected to bat on a wicket so green that, from the players' balcony, it was difficult to distinguish the pitch from the rest of the outfield.

Abid, however, gave the England batsmen a fright, knocking out three batsmen (Jameson, Edrich and Fletcher) in 10 balls in his sixth and seventh overs for 25 runs. At this stage Luckhurst swept at a ball from Venkataraghavan, which got the top edge of the bat and switched away. I was fielding in an unusual position for me—at leg-slip—and started running for it and almost reached it, but couldn't touch the ball. I was told later that Mankad, at deep square-leg, could also have gone for it, since running forward is much easier than running backward. Anyway, Luckhurst escaped and went on to score 78 runs.

As far as we were concerned, however, the turning point of the game came when Illingworth was given 'not out' to a straightforward bat-and-pad catch by Solkar off Chandra-sekhar. This was the third time in three innings that Illingworth had been given a second life by the umpires. I guess there are advantages of being an England captain in England ! Illingworth went on to score 108 runs and with Peter Lever (88 not out) he added 168 valuable runs—a record for the England eighth wicket against India. When we went in to bat we had to face Price bowling very fast in the gloom of the evening. Fortunately for us, the light deteriorated and we ran in to the warmth of the dressing room.

The next day was no better. Price was faster than ever. He just stood around while Lever grabbed the wickets. Actually Price was by far the quicker of the two, but, as it often happens, it was Lever who got among the wickets. The over that Price bowled to me and got my wicket was the fastest spell of bowling I've ever faced. I was out to him when the ball brushed my glove as I was removing my bat out of the way, to offer an easy catch to wicket-keeper Knott. Solkar offered some resistance and the two of us were the only Indians to score over 50 runs. Our innings ended with 212 runs on the board. With a lead of 174, England went for quick runs in their second innings. Solkar injured his hand trying to fasten on to a fierce cut from Jameson, off Abid, and had to be taken to hospital for an x-ray. I was asked to bowl my medium-pace stuff and nearly got my first Test wicket, but Farokh Engineer missed a leg-side catch off Luckhurst. To make things more difficult for us, the weather was extremely cold and our spinners could do nothing as their fingers were numb. Luckhurst helped himself to a century (101), while Edrich got 59. Illingworth declared at tea, leaving us to get 420 for victory. At the end of the day we were 65 for three, with Sardesai and Vishwanath at the crease. We were in a precarious position, but knowing Sardesai and Vishwanath's potential, with the reliable Solkar to follow, we could have saved the game. However, it rained the whole of the last day and we spent the time reading and writing letters while some played cards with the English players. The Test, which looked ominous for us, eventually ended in a draw.

Our main problem was to find an opening partner for me. Ashok Mankad was not successful in the Tests, though he was getting plenty of runs in the County games. Jayantilal was finding it tough playing in English conditions, and Abbas Ali Baig was a total disappointment. Engineer wasn't keen on opening the batting, and so we kept on with Mankad, because, with his determined approach, he was the most likely to succeed.

We went to the third and final Test at The Oval, with an unchanged team, praying for rain-free days and better umpiring. Illingworth won the toss for the third time in the series, but Luckhurst was back in the pavilion in Solkar's first over. The England opener sliced a drive and was caught by me in the slips. Edrich and Jameson then had a fruitful 106-run partnership. Jameson struck some hefty blows and was rather unlucky to be run out for 82 runs. He played punishing cricket and slammed two sixes, which the crowd loved. On this occasion our spinners couldn't do a thing. Earlier, playing for Warwickshire against us he piled up 231 runs in even time. That was an unbelievable innings and left our attack in tatters. After the Jameson-Edrich partnership was broken, England suffered a slight collapse, but Hutton and Knott steadied the innings. Knott made 90 and Hutton 81, and the innings ended at 355, a few minutes before the end of the day's play. It was an entertaining day's cricket for the spectators and they thoroughly enjoyed it.

The next day, the headlines in some of the English newspapers surprised us. One of the newspapers even went to the extent of saying that England could go ahead to an easy victory. Mind you, at this stage we had not even begun our batting; but the English critics were already predicting an England victory. This, more than anything else, spurred us on to do better.

The entire second day's play was washed out by rain. On the third day there was a delayed start, but Price struck the first blow when he bowled Mankad for 10. John Snow, back in the team in place of Lever, bowled me middle-stump, and we were two down for 21 runs. Just before Snow knocked out my middle-stump, a dog had strayed on to the field and play was held up for a long time. The dog came behind me, sniffed and went away. Those who know me are aware that I am mortally scared of dogs, and this one had come and stood so close to me that I was literally shivering, though I tried to make a supremely nonchalant gesture of looking the other way. I am not saying that this was the reason for my dismissal, because it was a good ball that got me. However, I am mentioning this to indicate my state of mind. Let me add that Snow had been bowling with a lot of fire. He bounced his first delivery to me and was really going flat out with his thunderbolts. Perhaps, this time he wanted to give me a 'shove' with the ball! Ducking into one of Snow's attempted bouncers, I broke the chain I wore round my neck as the ball brushed past me. Illingworth at short-leg picked it up and returned it to me saying, "You shouldn't be wearing gold in a Test, lad!"

Ajit and Dilip came together and played some brilliant cricket to offset the advantage that Snow and Price had given England. Dilip was at his best. He had an unproductive tour until then, and badly needed a big score. He chose this Test to mark his return to form. However, he was out after scoring 54 runs, which was marked by the usual 'raid' of the field by some over-enthusiastic spectators. An announcement was made on the public address system asking spectators not to rush to the wicket, just as Ajit was taking strike. This must have disturbed his concentration, because he played a wild slash outside his off-stump, and was out for 48. Vishwanath was bowled for a 'duck' by a ball from Illingworth which Vishwanath played over. Eknath Solkar, however, played a pretty good knock of 44 before he was out. Engineer (59) was out to the last ball of the day, when he played an overhead tennis-like shot at a bouncer from Snow and was caught at mid-on. We were in trouble again.

After the rest day, Abid and Venkataraghavan added a few runs before our innings ended, 71 runs behind England's score. When England began their second innings they were well placed to drive home the advantage. Instead, they found Chandrasekhar at his devastating best. No batsman had an answer to him and he scalped six wickets for 38, with Venkataraghavan chipping in with two for 44, and Bedi taking one for one. Solkar held some incredible catches and Venkataraghavan also took a superb catch to get rid of Luckhurst for 33.

We had a little over two hours and the entire fifth day to get the 171 runs required to win. I was given out leg-before to a ball from Snow, which clearly pitched outside the leg-stump and to which I offered no stroke. But then you don't question an English umpire's decision, do you? They are supposed to be the best in the world. However, I earned the distinction (?) of getting out for a 'duck' for the first time in Tests! Ashok Mankad played determinedly and with Ajit stroking well they took the score to 37 and wore down the England pace attack. Ashok was finally out to Underwood for 11, his highest in the series. But, he had stuck around and denied the pace bowlers a breakthrough. His was an insignificant score, but an immense contribution to the eventual victory. Ashok has a tremendous sense of humour and constantly pulled everybody's leg. After he returned to the pavilion and had taken a shower, he remarked, "At last I can go home and tell them what the English spinners were like." Then when he was told that he had scored just 11 runs, he said, "A pity the Tests are over, I was just getting into my stride and by the fifth Test I would surely have scored 25 runs." Travelling by coach between the Counties, Ashok would keep everybody in good humour with his jokes and singing. At the several official parties and receptions he had to face innumerable people who would come to him and tell him they knew his father and would talk about him and

Ashok would turn around to one of us and say "I am getting to know a lot about my father". He would put on a typical British accent and converse with the people. He enjoyed doing that and with his power of observation he was a terrific mimic.

Well, to come back to the game, Dilip and Ajit played sensibly picking the right ball to hit. On a wicket which was yielding considerable turn, particularly to the crafty Illingworth, Dilip repeatedly stepped out and drove through the covers. To hit an off-spinner on a normal wicket through the covers is difficult but Dilip proved that he could do it even on a turning wicket. Dilip has such quick footwork that the moment the ball is flighted a couple of inches more than normal, he is down the wicket and crash goes the ball. Towards his later years he developed a cross-batted swish against the off-spinners which often sent the ball soaring over the mid-wicket boundary. On that day he employed that shot very rarely because the Oval boundary is a long one. But his stepping out to the spinners, particularly whenever Underwood threw up his slower one, was as good as ever. He was out to an amazing catch by Knott who plucked the edge almost off the bat.

Ajit was his usual calm self and realising how close victory was at hand took the minimum risks, content to nudge the ball away for singles and twos. This was in complete contrast to his first innings knock. Then he had played some thrilling shots with supreme confidence. At the end of the fourth day we were 95 for two.

The next day we were in for an early shock when Ajit was run out, as he hesitated a little in responding to Dilip's call for a run. D'Oliveira's throw was bang on top of the wicket, and Knott had only to whip off the bails. Ajit returned very depressed and after watching the game for a few minutes went off to sleep.

Vishwanath joined Dilip and Illingworth promptly crowded

him with fielders. But Vishwanath was equal to the task. He
was soon playing his wristy shots and the fielders, who had
blocked his tiny figure from our view, were soon dispersed to
the deep to stop his shots. Dilip fell to a brilliant catch by
Knott after he had scored 40, and Solkar followed soon after,
making a half-hearted drive which was well caught by bowler
Underwood. Now the pressure was on. Farokh Engineer dealt
with the situation in his own flamboyant way. He played a
few risky shots, but settled down just before lunch. Illingworth
brought back Snow and Price for a final fling, but Vishwanath
and Farokh were unperturbed. At lunch we were only 29
runs away from victory.

During the morning session, particularly after Dilip's dismissal, I gave up watching the game and preferred to play cards
with Abid, who had padded up, and a couple of others. Abid
too didn't want to watch the game. But, though we were
playing cards, our ears were tuned to the game outside. Both
Abid and I had, on a few occasions, a hand of rummy but, with
our minds more on the game, we did not declare it. After
lunch, Farokh became more aggressive and with only
four runs required for victory, Luckhurst was brought on to
bowl. Vishwanath, who had played patiently so far, tried to
hoist him over mid-wicket for the winning hit, but only succeeded in snicking the ball to Knott, for the wicket-keeper to
take an easy catch. Abid, however, after scooping the first ball
uppishly, square-cut the next for four and we won.

The scene after that was unbelievable. Abid was swallowed
up by the huge crowd of spectators, mostly Indians, who had
rushed on to the field. Farokh, who was at the other end, had
no chance of making it to the pavilion. Both the players were
engulfed by the crowd and they were hoisted on willing shoulders and held high up in the air. Their trousers were stuffed
with money and it was a good ten minutes before they could get
to the dressing room, where there were equally wild scenes.
After all, this was our first-ever victory in England against

England and in the process we had won the 'rubber'—also for the first time in England. The players were shaking hands and embracing the others. Some Pakistani players were also there to congratulate us and we could see that they were really happy. A number of former England players came in and offered their congratulations. After some time, the England players, still in their flannels, joined us in celebrating our victory with champagne. Ajit and Hemu Adhikari were on the telephone receiving congratulations and felicitations from our Prime Minister in New Delhi, the Indian High Commissioner in London, and numerous other well-wishers. Then the crowd below wanted the players on the balcony, particularly Chandrasekhar, Wadekar and Vishwanath. They went out and acknowledged the thunderous cheers with which they were greeted. It was great stuff! Very moving! The celebrations continued after the match. We were entertained to some choice Indian food at a famous Indian restaurant. The Indian High Commissioner also hosted a party for us. Actually, this was just the beginning of the chain of celebrations which followed when the team returned home.

The tour was not over and we played a few games before returning home. Just before we played Worcestershire, an English daily newspaper had published the tour averages of the Indian team. I noticed that I needed 189 runs for making thousand runs on the tour and I was determined to get those runs. Ajit won the toss against Worcestershire and elected to bat. I opened with Jayantilal, but he was out soon, and Ajit joined me. Ajit was also nearing a thousand runs and he played superlatively. I survived two chances before I reached ten but was comfortable thereafter. We two added 327 runs for the second wicket. Ajit was out for 150 runs, during which he passed the thousand runs on the tour. I was 188 not out at the end of the day, needing only one run to complete my thousand. I got my thousand runs and went on to score 194 when I lost my wicket in trying to push the score along. Surprisingly, the later batsmen made no attempt to score quickly. If I had known that there was no need to rush things, I could have played quietly and got my double-century. However, since the instructions were to go for runs, I threw my wicket away.

In the last game, against T.N. Pearce's XI, we won a thriller by five wickets with three quarters of an hour to spare. And, so ended the tour on a triumphant note. Ashok carried his bat through in the first innings for 154 runs and I got 128 in the second innings.

It was time to go home and we heard that there were big plans for our return. The plane was to be diverted to Delhi so that the team could meet the Prime Minister. A red-carpet welcome awaited us at Bombay and numerous functions were being organised all over. But I was to miss all this. I had been invited to play a double-wicket tournament in Bermuda, for which the President of the Cricket Control Board, Mr. A.N. Ghose, had given me permission. Along with me there were Intikhab Alam, Gary Sobers, Rohan Kanhai and Brian Luckhurst. Wes Hall was to arrive directly from the West Indies.

We had a fright when our aircraft was landing in Bermuda. The pilot took off again, just as he was within ten-twenty feet from the runway, which the aircraft had apparently overshot. The plane shuddered and it appeared as if it was going to break into pieces. But we lifted off again and then returned, this time for a perfect landing.

Alma "Champ" Hunt, the President of Bermuda C.A., was on hand to receive us. When we reached our hotel room, there was a basket of fruits and two bottles of Bacardi rum on the table. The makers of this famous rum were sponsoring the tournament. Rohan Kanhai came and took away one of the bottles, knowing that I didn't drink, and left the other one saying, with a wink, "That's a souvenir for you. It's rum and not water".

The tournament was won by Intikhab Alam and his partner. We all had local partners. The tournament was highlighted by a magnificent spell of fast bowling by Hall, particularly to Luckhurst. Luckhurst had decided to share the prize money with the rest of us. This was done while Wes Hall and his partner were in the process of beating Gary Sobers and partner. When Wes was approached by Luckhurst to share his prize money in case he won, Wes flared up thinking this was cooked up by Luckhurst because Hall and partner had beaten Sobers and partner. And so, Luckhurst had a torrid time with Hall, who, knowing he had only three overs to bowl, put everything into each delivery.

11

On the Hop, Down Under

When I returned home from Bermuda, the Secretary of the Cricket Control Board, Prof. Chandgadkar, received me at the airport. He told me that I had been invited to play for 'Rest of the World', which was to tour Australia, instead of the South Africans who had been refused entry by the Australian Government. Prof. Chandgadkar, however, asked me to keep the information to myself, because the Australian Cricket Board had still to announce the team.

The Indian team had meanwhile returned from England to a fabulous reception. At Delhi's Palam airport they were greeted by Punjab's famed Bhangra dancers; while at Bombay it looked as if the entire city had come to receive them at Santa Cruz airport. The team was entertained by the Prime Minister, who presented mementoes to them. Alas, I missed all this, being away in Bermuda. It was fascinating to hear about all this, and I basked in the glory of being a 'hero', though at second-hand. One of my friends told me that even the Pope and Mr. Khrushchev had not received such a tumultuous welcome in Bombay. Later, I saw it all on film and was very much moved by the scenes of adulation. Young and old, male and female were in high spirits. It was terrific and I had to miss it!

Soon after my return I had to go to Madras with my office team to play in the Buchi Babu Tournament. When we reached the ground, which was rather small, I couldn't believe my eyes. The crowd was simply terrific. I was told that the people had come to see me in action and I better not disappoint them. I had to be escorted by the police to the wicket, which I do not think has happened anywhere before. Still, the people would surge on to the field during the drinks interval. I will never, never forget that day and that crowd. And I am glad I did not disappoint them, for I scored 75 runs and the crowd seemed happy enough. The A.C.C. team, for whom I played, won the shield, easily beating the State Bank team from Bangalore.

I had to fly off that evening to Bombay to attend the engagement ceremony of Milind Rege, who is like an elder brother to me. He had kept on postponing the engagement because I couldn't be in Bombay and, even when he had finally fixed the date, I was away in Madras. I managed to be in Bombay later in the evening, and was able to join in the festivities. Milind and I grew up together and started our cricket career at the same time. Though I played for Bombay in the Irani Trophy, he played in the Ranji Trophy before me. In fact, when I made my debut in the Ranji Trophy, he was already an established Bombay player. Though he was selected for Bombay primarily as an off-spinner, his strokeful and aggressive batting often saved the side and also got bonus points. It was unfortunate that illness temporarily halted his first-class cricket, and he has recently made a comeback in club matches with a bang, though strictly as a batsman.

A.C.C. also participated in the Moin-ud-Dowla Gold Cup Tournament at Hyderabad that year, and we lost an interesting game to the State Bank in the final. I had a good tournament though I missed my hundred in the first game against Hyderabad by just six runs. I've never been able to score a century in the Moin-ud-Dowla Tournament, though I've reached 80's and 90's almost every time that we've participated.

The Moin-ud-Dowla was a very popular tournament earlier, but now the interest seems to have waned a bit. The Fateh

Maidan Club could do with a bit of renovation, particularly the rooms where the players stay. These are uncomfortable, to say the least, and the mosquito nets hardly give any protection. The toilet facilities are also poor and so also is the food. The Hyderabad Cricket Association is not to blame as the Club is apparently owned by the Andhra Pradesh Government.

The tournament attracts the cream of national talent and occasionally even overseas players are invited to participate. Also, this tournament is among the first first-class games of the season, which makes it an important fixture, for which the facilities should be improved.

Before I left for Australia, Bombay lost the Irani Trophy to the Rest of India. For the Rest of India, Chandrasekhar bowled devastatingly to rout Bombay, with all its batting array.

On our way to Australia to play for the Rest of the World team, we spent a couple of pleasant days in Singapore, where we joined the rest of the players who had flown directly from England. I had met most of them, except Asif Masood and Prob Taylor. Tony Greig and Hylton Ackerman, who were playing in the Currie Cup, South Africa's national championship, and the Pollock brothers were to join the team from the third Test onwards in the new year.

We landed at Melbourne, where Gary Sobers, who had been playing club cricket in South Australia, Tony Greig and Hylton Ackerman received us at the airport. During the drive to the motel where we were to stay, we were told of a humorous incident involving Ackerman. Greig and he had flown in from South Africa, and were received at Adelaide airport by Gary Sobers and an elderly gentleman. Gary mumbled an introduction and Greig and Ackerman, both tired from the long journey, sleepily mumbled 'hello' and sat down for a cup of coffee, while waiting to go to the hotel,

Ackerman asked the gentleman to hold his overnight bag, while he went to the toilet to freshen himself up. When he returned, he made some polite conversation and then asked the gentleman if he was connected with Australian cricket. The gentleman replied in the affirmative. Ackerman asked him if he had played cricket, to which the reply was again "yes". Since Ackerman had not caught the gentleman's name properly, he asked him, "What did you say your name was?" The answer was "Don Bradman"!

Ackerman was a tremendous bloke. He was the other opener in the team, besides me, and we got on famously right from the start.

My first meeting with Sir Donald Bradman was no less amusing. The 'Don' had come to meet us at the Adelaide airport while we were in transit to Perth for the second Test. He came around asking, "Where's that little fellow from India"? I was chatting with Bob Taylor and Sir Donald joined us. He asked me how the tour was getting on. Gary seeing us together shouted, "Hey, you little blokes must gang up together huh?" Sir Donald turned to me and said, "These big blokes have the power, but we little ones have the footwork, huh?" This was said with a wink, and his charming and modest ways bowled me over completely.

We began with a game against Victoria. I had been warned by Farokh Engineer about 'Froggie' Thomson, the Australian fast bowler; but when I faced him I found him to be erratic. I was meeting the ball well and found that I liked the ball coming on to the bat. In fact, I was enjoying myself when I foolishly repeated the swing off my legs to give a catch to long-leg. Earlier I had swung a similar delivery over the long-leg fence.

The match was interrupted by rain and was eventually left unfinished. The walk from the Melbourne dressing room to the wicket is the longest that I've come across. So, before I opened Farokh jokingly said: "Don't get out for a duck. It's too long a walk back." I didn't, but Farokh did!

We went on to play New South Wales next. After failing in the first innings, I got 95 runs in the second. I was dropped off the first ball I faced in the second innings, when the fielder at gully moved far too slowly. I had another 'life' when a cut was deflected by the wicket-keeper; but at 95 the same fielder at gully took a brilliant catch to his left to get me out. That was to be my highest score in Australia.

We next played Queensland. Rohan Kanhai played a brilliant innings, scoring a century between lunch and tea. For Queensland, Allen Jones, a tall right-hander, played some exciting shots. But the one who impressed me most, because of his correct approach, was Philip Carlson. Carlson was also a good medium-pace bowler and we were certain that he would be selected to tour England in 1972. But so far he has not even got a look-in in the Australian side. In the second innings Farokh scored a century and we shared a century opening partnership. I was stumped off leg-spinner Francke, who had migrated to Australia from Sri Lanka.

Just before we played the first 'International' there was a mild controversy regarding the preparation of the wicket. Clem Jones, who was the Lord Mayor of Brisbane as well as President of the Queensland Cricket Association, had taken upon himself the task of preparing the wicket. It had been raining intermittently, yet the Lord Mayor was there out in the middle in his shorts, trying to get the wicket redone. However, the first day's play was washed out, and we were asked to make up for it by playing on the rest day. We refused and got a fair bit of stick from the Press, which complained that we were interested in pastimes other than cricket.

Australia won the toss and elected to bat. Keith Stackpole

and Bruce Francis opened, and after Francis was out early, Stackpole and Ian Chappell settled down and slammed centuries. Stackpole enjoyed himself cutting and hooking the short stuff, while Chappell played his drives nicely. This was a great demonstration because the wicket was slow and the ball was coming up even slower, but not once did Chappell mistime his drives.

When our turn came to bat, the wicket had rolled out to be hard, with just the hint of moisture on it. I started by cutting the first two balls from fast bowler Lillee for fours; but he had his revenge, for he bowled me with an inswinger which kept low. I made 22 runs. Zaheer Abbas was out early, and then Kanhai joined Ackerman, who had opened with me. Both of them played the lively pace of Lillee and McKenzie with relative ease and went on to score centuries.

In the second innings, Stackpole and Chappell batted well again, with Chappell scoring another century. He hit Bedi for a huge six in the mid-wicket region and showed his quick footwork against the spin of Bedi and Intikhab Alam. It was during this innings that Richard Hutton, a tremendously funny bloke, made that coarse remark to Stackpole, who had hammered Hutton's loose deliveries in the first over for a couple of boundaries. In the second over, however, Hutton struck a length and beat Stackpole thrice with perfect out-swingers. After the third time Stackpole had groped, Hutton walked up to him and said: "Why are you pulling the slip's legs, why don't you edge one for a change." Everytime Stackpole and Chappell hit him, Hutton would invite them to play against him on Yorkshire's green wicket, where, he said, he would be able to move the ball better than on the Gabba wicket.

The match having been reduced to four days, a draw was inevitable. We had just the last two hours of the game to bat, but during that time Dennis Lillee showed what a force he would be before the rest of the series, as well as against future opponents. In a display of blistering speed and late movement off the wicket, he had both Ackerman and myself out, and gave a torrid time to the others, before Ian Chappell rested him. Compared to him, McKenzie looked fast-medium, though the movement he got off the wicket was more than that of Lillee. Suddenly, with Lillee's show of speed, our boys developed a healthy respect for the Australian bowling.

I was rested from the Western Australia game at Perth. Zaheer got a brilliant hundred and another fifty in the second knock. He played some cracking shots on the off-side and his flicks to the square-leg boundaries, off his legs, went scorching the grass to the fence. It was good to have him in form, for he is essentially an attacking player and on his day he can tear any attack apart.

We lost the services of Ackerman before the second 'International' match when he sprained his ankle at the nets. It was a blow to us, because he had scored a century in the first 'International' and on the Perth wicket, the fastest in Australia, he would have been an asset. Besides, he was the only other recognised opening batsman in the side. Farokh was then asked to open with me.

Ian Chappell won the toss and elected to bat. Though Stackpole got 55 and Walters and Chappell made useful contributions, the Australian innings ended at the end of the day's play for 349. The wicket played perfectly, though Gary let slip an occasional quick one which whistled past the nose of the batsman. One of the most unpleasant features of Perth is the number of flies that attack you while you are in the middle. We were constantly spraying ourselves with repellent every second over. In any case, I didn't give the flies much chance to disturb me, because I was caught behind, off the fourth ball from Lillee. This came up from a length, brushed my gloves and that was that! Lillee was just warming up and before starting to let himself go. Farokh was not very comfortable against him and hit back a catch to Lillee. Zaheer and Kanhai tried to repair the damage, but Zaheer was run out. It was then that the collapse started. Lloyd was out, fending a short one, to be caught brilliantly by wicket-keeper Marsh on the leg-side. Gary Sobers lasted just two balls. In trying to protect his chin, he only managed a snick and was caught behind. Tony Greig retaliated in a typically aggressive fashion but after two boundaries over the slips' heads, he was caught off a fierce slash by Stackpole. Bedi didn't last long and the Rest of the World were knocked out for 59 runs, Lillee taking 8 wickets for 29. It was a great spell of fast bowling. McKenzie gave him good support and got rid of the dangerous looking Kanhai. Imagine the World XI batting shot out in less than 2 hours!

We had to follow on and had a few minutes batting before lunch. During this time we lost Farokh again. Farokh tried new tactics against the fast bowlers, going away to the leg-side and trying to slash the ball over the slips. He didn't succeed, and all that he did was to lob a catch to Sheahan in the covers. So Farokh had the dubious distinction of having been out twice in one session. I had got off the mark off the first ball I faced from Lillee, but that was also eventful. I played the ball very wide to the right of gully, where Jenner was fielding. However, he was so far back and the ball was a good 15 yards away, that I didn't even doubt a single would be difficult. But Farokh had not budged from his crease when I found myself almost facing him. In the meanwhile Jenner, who had earlier relaxed in anticipation of an easy single, suddenly found that there was a run-out chance. He tried to hit the stumps as I charged back, but fortunately he missed the stumps and off the overthrow we took three runs. The incredible part was that, though the ball was in the hands of the fielder, Farokh wanted to go for the fourth run.

After Farokh was out he came in and said he had mis-

timed his shot because the ball had stopped. On this wicket
there was no stopping, and everybody in the team ribbed him
for this statement. This, as well as an earlier statement by
Farokh about the India-Pakistan War, which was then going
on, didn't exactly make him 'Mr. Popular' with Bishen and
and myself, as well as the other members of the team. Farokh
was reported to have told an Australian journalist that,
because his house in Bombay faced the sea, he was afraid
about the safety of his wife and daughters and that he was
going to ask them to go '₋ome' to Lancashire. Bishen, whose
parents were in Amritsar, was rightly upset because Amritsar
is close to the Pakistan border. Nevertheless, Bishen had
offered no comments to th Press.

The World XI players, particularly Ackerman, used the
situation to imagine some really funny situations, such as
Intikhab and Farokh facing each other with bayonets; myself
in a fighter plane, with Asif Masood on my tail; and Bishen
and Zaheer trying to run away. We had a good laugh. Though
the Australian players were careful not to joke with us on
this subject, Richard Hutton came up with a typical one
when he said that even if Farokh stabbed Intikhab first with
his bayonet, the Pakistani player would survive as he had so
much of fat to absorb the blow.

I must say that there was no tension at all between the
Indians and Pakistani players, despite what was happening.
Almost every evening we went out for a meal to a restaurant
owned by a Pakistani. The owner would hear reports from
various radio news bulletins and write them down in Urdu
on a paper napkin and give it to Intikhab. Intikhab would
barely glance at it, crumple it up and throw it away.

Coming back to the 'International' match, Kanhai joined
me and what an innings he played! He told me just to hang
on at one end while he would look after the bowlers, and he
really set after them. After a rising ball from Lillee had

With the Dadar Union team.

The author and G.R. Vishwanath
share a joke.

Bowling at a practice session in tropical heat in Madras. Behind him is Ashok Mankad.

The author with his two closest friends. Ramnath Parkar and G.R. Vishwanath (left).

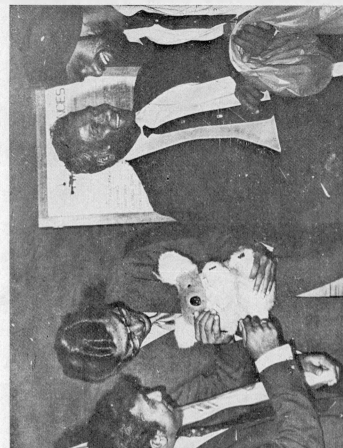

Sunil with Zaheer Abbas, Rohan Kanhai and Bishen Bedi in Australia where he went to play for the rest of the World XI against Australia

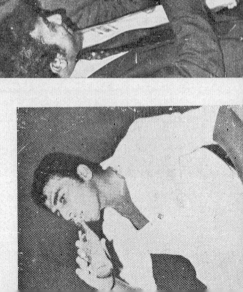

Cooling off after a strenuous game

struck him on the chest, his next shot was a hook to the mid-wicket boundary. I was with him for 100 minutes during which he was well past his 50. When I flashed outside the stumps he would come over and caution me. Watching him bat that day was an education on how to play pace bowling. I got out when I inside-edged a ball from McKenzie on to my stumps. Zaheer then joined Kanhai and together they added 107 runs before Zaheer was out. Kanhai made 118 runs. It was a brilliant innings right through. There was just a bit of resistance from Sobers, but we folded up thereafter against Lillee, who claimed four wickets. We lost by an innings and 11 runs.

We lost to South Australia in just two days, with only Greig and myself being regular batsmen in the side, since the others were either rested or injured. Clive Lloyd's injury took place during this match. Ashley Mallet drove an Intikhab leg-spinner uppishly and 'Hubert', as Clive is called, jumped up to his right and took the catch, falling down in the process. I think that he fell in a wrong position, and the next thing we saw was that the ball had slipped from his grasp, and 'Hubert' was lying prone on the field. He was hardly moving. We rushed to him and he said he was in pain and that he couldn't move at all. A physiotherapist examined him and he was carried off the ground on a stretcher.

At the hospital it was found that he had badly injured his spine. The doctor said even if the bone, which was dislocated, had gone half an inch deeper, Lloyd would have been paralysed for life.

We were all very sorry for Lloyd and to cheer him up for X'mas the Rest of the World team composed a song and booked a call to his hospital room to sing it to him. Imagine our surprise when we were told that he had gone out. Only a week before the doctors were of the opinion that he may not

be able to walk! We were happy, anyway, though he was
obviously not going to play on the tour anymore.

We came in for a lot of lashing from the Press again for our
approach to the game. Even Sobers was criticised for not
practising at the nets with the team. After this, we had a
meeting of the entire team and were told to be more serious to
keep up our reputation.

On the eve of the New Year (1972) the Pollock brothers—
Peter, better known for his fast bowling, and Graeme, the
left-handed batting artist—joined us. The brothers are vastly
different, though obviously attached to each other. Peter, who
is a journalist by profession, is an extrovert. He loves beer
and enjoys a cigarette. He would talk about cricket endlessly,
showing an amazing knowledge of Indian cricket, which really
surprised me.

Graeme, on the other hand, doesn't look as sturdy as his
elder brother. He does not smoke and drinks beer only occasionally. He is the quiet type and would rather smile than
talk. In any case, his deeds spoke for themselves. He, too,
was very much interested in Indian cricket, and recalled with
pleasure his association during the 1968 series with Chandrasekhar. He thought Chandrasekhar was as fascinating as his
bowling.

We had tremendous celebrations on New Year's eve. At
that time the Australian Open Tennis Championships were on,
and many of the boys had the women tennis players as their
'dates'. The next day, however, was the start of the third
'International' and all this celebration wasn't certainly going
to do us much good. It didn't.

Gary won the toss and elected to bat, which surprised many
of us. Because, the Melbourne wicket had the reputation of
playing unusually quick on the first morning than at any other

time during a match. Besides, the history of the Sheffield Shield matches played earlier in the season had showed that the sides batting first had never scored more than 250 runs.

But there we were, Hylton Ackerman, back in the side after his ankle injury, and 'little' Sunil Gavaskar walking the long distance from the Melbourne dressing room to the middle. Ackerman looked and smelt as if he had not recovered from the earlier evening's celebration. As we walked out he made a classic comment, "Dennis Lillee, huh, I'll take care of him". Three balls later Dennis Lillee had taken care of Ackerman, by clean bowling him! But, I suppose, Ackerman had a good reason to be so confident. In the first International match he had scored a very good hundred and, in the second, which was Lillee's match, he was absent owing to a sprained ankle.

Zaheer Abbas also didn't stay long. Bob Massie, who was making his debut for Australia, moved one away and Zaheer was caught behind. This brought in Graeme Pollock, who had begun wearing spectacles the previous season, and there was plenty of speculation in the Australian newspapers about the effect of this on his play. He played the first ball sweetly, off the middle of the blade for two and that removed doubts about his future in the game.

All this while, I was determined to stick around without bothering about the number of runs I scored. After our defeat in the Perth game, as is the practice in Australia, some of the journalists came into our dressing room. One of them pointedly asked me whether I was suffering from a 'Lillee complex', since I was out to Dennis Lillee three out of four times. I was not only stunned by this, but I was determined to prove him wrong. Lillee, however, was bowling not only very fast, but intelligently. He got the wicket of Graeme Pollock when a ball rising from a length just outside his off-stump took the edge of his bat. Graeme took a step as if to walk, but waited for the umpire's decision. There was however, no doubt in the umpire's mind and his finger shot skyward.

As Gary walked up to the wicket, I was wondering if I could have a long partnership with the great man. But Gary was out first ball : a delivery similar to the one that got Pollock out, and Gary edged it to second slip. Gary looked ruefully at the spot from where the ball had come up, smiled and walked away. The Australians were all cock-a-hoop. They crowded round Lillee with broad smiles and were joking away. The crowd too were on their feet though they must have been disappointed to see the great man out so soon. I was watching all this from the other end. Tony Greig came, smiled and said, "Well it's up to us".

We took the score along steadily. Lillee was tiring now and he was replaced by 'Beatle' Watson, who had an action similar to Graham McKenzie's, but he was much slower. Greig, after blasting him through the covers for four, edged his next ball on to his pads and Greg Chappell dived forward to pick up a brilliant catch. Greig, however, had turned his back to the whole thing and pretended to be an innocent spectator of the proceedings. The Australians appealed loudly, but the umpire negatived it. Greig smiled broadly at Greg Chappell, took his stance impssively and carried on with his batting. We were unseparated at lunch and, as we were returning to the pavilion, Greig kept on urging me to stick around with him. We must have looked a sight : Greig in his impressive 6 ft.7 ins and the 'pint-sized' Gavaskar a bare 5 ft 5 ins. I was 33 not out at lunch. Lillee was brought back again, and this time it was sheer over-confidence that was my undoing. Trying to hit through the covers, off the back-foot, I only managed to edge a catch to third slip. As I walked past Greg Chappell, who had taken the catch, I heard him tell something to his brother, Ian, about a 'hot potato'.

Intikhab and Greig added valuable runs and both got fifties.

Intikhab played some awkward-looking shots, but, as far as I was concerned, the shot of the match was played by Bishen Bedi. He put his front foot down the wicket and drove Lillee, with a full follow through, through the covers. Our dressing room erupted at that shot and it put us in a good frame of mind to get at the Aussies. We got the wickets of Watson and Stackpole quickly and there wasn't much resistance from the others, except Greg Chappell.

Greg had not played in the first two games and he hadn't been too successful in the other first-class games he had played against us. But in this game he showed us why he was soon to be acknowledged as one of the greats of the game. He started off by showing Bishen and Intikhab the sight screen and then all bowling came alike to him. He found a useful partner in Bob Massie and they added 97 invaluable runs for the ninth wicket.

Sobers, with the new ball, had Massie caught behind and greeted Dennis Lillee with a bouncer. The ball whistled past Lillee's hair and Gary told Lillee: "We can also bowl this stuff." Lillee was out next ball, wildly hitting into the covers to Bedi. Greg Chappell was unbeaten with 115.

We expected Lillee to open the attack. I had to face much of the bowling and I think Lillee tried too hard to bowl too fast. Unusually for him, he sprayed the ball a bit. We lost Ackerman, however, caught in the gully off Massie. Zaheer joined me and got into his stride right away. He stroked Lillee off his legs to the square-leg boundary and drove Massie to the cover fence. The Melbourne boundary is so long that often one had to run three before the ball crossed over the boundary.

Zaheer was in an attacking mood and he was severe on anything slightly loose. Sometimes he played odd-looking shots. He has a peculiar style, and lifts his bat from point, and then brings it down quickly. He doesn't seem to have a forward defensive shot, but follows through and seldom does the ball stay dead at his feet. For deliveries pitched on his legs he turns quickly and, with a flick of the wrists, sends them past square-leg. This is a remarkable shot because, more often than not, he is only showing part of the face of the bat to the ball. He has very supple and strong wrists and, in spite of his seemingly incorrect technique, plays very stylishly.

The pace attack was seen off by us and the spinners came on. This was the first time in the series that I was playing an Australian spinner. In the Perth game, I had played just one ball from Jenner, got a single off it, and didn't face him again. My ultra-watchfulness against the speedsters came on again as Jenner tossed his 'leggers' invitingly, which I played very watchfully. Then, in Jenner's next over, the ball hit the toes of my stretched left foot, as I played forward with my bat behind the pads, and carried to Ian Chappell at first slip. After a typical Australian appeal I was given 'out'. I was very disappointed, as I was looking forward to playing the spinners well, after being watchful for so long. I had scored 27 runs. Later, some of the fielders in the covers came and sympathised with me on the decision. Anyway, the damage was done. Graeme Pollock, who joined Zaheer, was careful, but he also didn't stay long.

My entry into the dressing room wasn't exactly peaceful and, when I was inside, I gave full vent to my feelings. Gary, already upset by his first innings failure, was fuming, because of the manner in which the Australians had done me in. As Graeme got out, Gary was padding up. At the fall of the next wicket, he picked up his bat saying "We have to show them." Zaheer, who was on 86, was the one who was out. Trying to cut a ball, he edged it high to Ian Chappell at slip.

The innings Gary played has been described by many, including Sir Don Bradman, as the 'greatest ever' since the war. Lillee had his tail up and, no doubt, the bouncer with which Gary had greeted him earlier was fresh in his mind. But, Lillee was an intelligent bowler. He did not pitch it in short to Gary. Instead he pitched it right up outside the maestro's off-stump, but Gary was very watchful. Then, after Gary had been in for about ten minutes, Lillee bowled a bouncer. The ball was hit with such a force that it was at the fence before you could say 'Gary Sobers'. After that Gary just cut loose. Anything pitched up was driven past the bowler and anything pitched short was cut or hooked savagely. Until he reached his 50 there was, seemingly, no footwork. None of the technicalities like the front-foot near the ball, as the bat simply came down from a high back lift and ended with a classic full follow-through. It was exhilarating cricket and it was coming from the captain of our side, who had been smarting under criticism. At the end of the day, Gary was unbeaten with 139, and was his usual, laughing self. Though tired he joked with us and the Australians. Peter Pollock was unbeaten with 28, and had given his skipper excellent support.

During this 'International', particularly in the Perth game, I was feeling a kind of lump around my right eye. I ignored it thinking it was a mosquito bite or something. On the rest day, however, I went to have it examined. It turned out to be a cyst and the doctor advised me to get it off immediately. I phoned up Bill Jacobs, our manager, who asked me to go ahead and get it off. The doctor advised me not to play for one week.

He put a patch on my right eye and so for the day I became a one-eyed 'Jack'. This temporary disability brought home to me the tremendous handicap under which Mansur Ali Khan Pataudi had to play. When I tried to take hold of a glass of water, I would miss it by a foot. It was the same when I tried to do anything on my right side. My admiration for "Tiger" Pataudi grew as a result of my experience. Every little thing I did, like eating an ice-cream cone, found me missing the cone and licking the air instead! I wondered how 'Tiger' played fast bowling, and so well too.

The next day Gary continued to hammer the bowling and with Peter Pollock defending stoutly and attacking in sudden bursts, we were really going strong. Two shots of Gary stood out. First, when he cut Massie to the point boundary, the ball beat the fielder, who was posted wide just for this kind of shot, before he could move even two feet. And remember, Melbourne has the longest boundary in the world. The second one was off Dennis Lillee, when Gary went back and slammed the ball straight back past the bowler and it crashed into the fence. He also lifted O'Keefe for two successive sixes. When he returned to the pavilion the crowd rose to a man in applause.

Peter Pollock went on to score 54 before he was out. It was a disciplined knock and his stubborn resistance made it possible for Gary to launch his magnificent assault. However, his long innings didn't stop Peter Pollock from showing his mettle as a pace bowler. He worked up a lively pace and bowled the bouncer liberally. He confessed that the sight of a batsman in a green Australian cap always spurred him on to bowl that much faster. Watching him from the dressing room, with my one good eye, I admired his lovely run-up and high bowling action. But I missed a tragic moment.

Tony Greig, who relieved Peter Pollock, bowled in his customary steady style, his action showing that he did more with the ball than in actual fact. As he was bowling, his hand brushed against his leg, resulting in the grip being loosened and the ball went through high, but slowly. Graeme Watson tried to hook it, but only succeeded in edging it on to his nose. The impact was hard, because he started bleeding from the cut and, within minutes, his shirt was soaked in blood.

Watson was brought into the dressing room and, when I went to see him, I found that the blood was spurting out of his nose at regular intervals. He was whisked away to hospital in an ambulance. We learnt later that his life was in danger and he had to be given a tremendous amount of blood. It speaks volumes for his courage that within three months he was back in the team for England.

In the second innings Doug Walters played a terrific innings. But, what surprised me most was that Gary never really tested him with any quickies. This is not to take away credit from Walters' innings—he scored 100 in two hours and that too against Bedi and Intikhab. But, I, for one, felt that Peter Pollock, who had pulled a leg muscle, would have really tested him. However, we won the match by 96 runs, to level the score at one-all.

Everybody now looked forward to the fourth 'International' at Sydney. Before this, we played a game against the New South Wales Country XI and another one in Canberra. These games were not much, but we remember them for our tantalising air journey. Newcastle is not very far from Sydney, so we took a shabby-looking Dakota aircraft, which really looked rather ancient. After the plane took off we were sorry that we had decided to fly in it, because it lurched and shook and it was anything but a pleasant journey. The return flight was also equally depressing, and nerve-racking.

Shrugging off all this, however, Graeme Pollock scored his first century. I was his partner in a long stand and one incident stands out in my mind. Graeme uses a very heavy bat—about 3 lbs. in weight. He played forward to a ball and I called out to him to wait. Imagine my surprise when I saw the ball speed past the mid-off fielder to the boundary. Graeme had timed it so sweetly that it had looked like a defensive push and, as he had put no power behind it, I had declined a run. I sheepishly said to him, "Jeezus, that did go, huh"? Graeme replied modestly, "Yeah, sometimes they do!".

We went into the fourth 'International' full of confidence. Ian Chappell won the toss and elected to bat. Peter Pollock was unfit and Bob Cunis was brought back in his place. The morning's play belonged to Bedi. Ian Chappell, who had started well, was lured down the wicket and, as he tried to drive, he found the ball just that much short and was bowled. Next ball, Greg Chappell was brought full stretch forward, with the ball turning sufficiently to bowl him. And, all this, during the first session of play! The crowd went wild, as Bishen bowed down to accept their greetings. After all, though he had got two of their favourite batsmen out, to the crowd Bishen was their 'son-in-law', having married a Sydney girl.

Our batting was, however, rocked by the swing of Bob Massie. He started by claiming the wickets of Ackerman and Zaheer, and Asif Masood came in as night watchman. The next morning Asif, playing the first over from Massie, missed five balls consecutively and, in disgust, hit the next to mid-on. I suffered from a bad decision again when I chopped a ball from Massie down into the ground and was given out caught by Stackpole in the slips. Once again, we were rescued by Greig and Intikhab, and some hilarious hitting by Bedi. He had the crowd on its feet, particularly those one on the 'Hill', who kept on chanting, 'Bedi, Bedi, Bedi.'

In Australia's second innings, Ian Chappell got a hundred (119), but the innings of the match was that of his younger brother Greg. Having been out first ball in the first innings, Greg was naturally cautious at the start, but then played his shots so well that he was unbeaten with 197 runs when the innings ended.

As we walked back to the pavilion, applauding Greg's magnificent innings, we heard him say some harsh words to Lillee. Greg had very cleverly shielded him from Intikhab for long time but, because of a miscalculation, he had taken a run off the sixth ball. This left Lillee to face two balls from Intikhab who bowled Lillee with the first delivery. A prize of 500 dollars was offered to anyone who scored 200, and it was a pity that Greg missed it by three runs. When we asked Greg later in the evening whether the harsh words to Lillee were out of disappointment at missing the 200 runs and the 500 dollars, he smiled and said: "Hell no! I just wanted him to be rearing mad to get at you boys when he bowled." Well, Lillee did bowl really fast for a couple of overs, but suddenly slowed down his run-up. It was the beginning of the back trouble that was to keep him out of cricket for over a year.

Ackerman and I added 155 runs for the first wicket, with Ackerman as the dominant partner. I had learnt my lesson and, after the early part of the tour when I was trying to score runs off every ball and getting out in the process, I had gone to the other extreme and was hardly playing my shots. During this innings, however, I played my shots, but not as recklessly as before, and the result was a good innings.

However, after Ackerman was out there was a 'mini' collapse, during which we lost Zaheer and Graeme Pollock in the same over. Then Gary Sobers was bowled by a full toss from Inverarity. At the end of the day I was left unbeaten with 68 runs, and the World XI had to survive a full day to save the match. Luckily for us down came the rain and the match had to be abandoned as a 'draw'.

By this time I was feeling pretty homesick, though the presence of the Cricket Club of India team, which was touring Australia, lessened the feeling. Since I was a member of the club and knew all the players it was nice to know from them about what had been happening at home.

The fifth 'International' was played at Adelaide and, after my unbeaten 68, I was full of confidence and looking forward to the game. The Adelaide wicket reminded me of the Feroze-shah Kotla wicket in New Delhi. It was absolutely devoid of grass and, like the Kotla wicket, took spin from the very first day. Australia batted first and were able to reach a respectable total (311), thanks to good knocks by Greg Chappell and John Benaud. Greg Chappell scored 85 and Benaud 99. Benaud got out when he flicked a short ball from Intikhab straight to me at short mid-on. I fumbled with the ball, but caught it at the second attempt and poor John missed his ton by one run. I felt sorry for him because he had played some grand shots.

Our innings was highlighted by a classic 135 by Graeme Pollock. On a turning wicket he played so well that I can't remember his being beaten even once. He hit two sixes off deliveries which were barely short of a good length. Zaheer scored 73 runs, but was the victim of 'sledging'. Stackpole, who had been brought on to bowl, would raise his hands or say something to Zaheer after every delivery. Losing his patience and temper, Zaheer tried to hit him out of the ground and was bowled. Earlier, I had scored 18 runs, before uppishly driving O'Keefe to Walters who was substituting at mid wicket.

In Australia's second innings Ian Chappell played a superb, attacking innings. Time and again he danced down the track to Bishen and Intikhab and drove them powerfully through the off-side. His hundred (111 not out) came after a peculiar mix-up, which almost got him run out. He was stranded in the middle but two overthrows enabled him to reach the century mark. The Australian innings ended leaving us just 146 runs to win.

Ackerman was again the dominant partner but I reached my first—50 and simultaneously the 100 of the partnership was raised. However, I was out in the same over in trying to steer wide off the slips, but instead tickled one which stuck in the leg-guards of wicket-keeper Rodney Marsh. Ackerman continued the good work and, when we won, he was unbeaten with 79 runs to his name. We won the series 2-1.

After the match, Sir Don Bradman distributed the various awards and I was thrilled to receive the award for the best fielder of the series. These awards were given on the basis of points scored in every match. Just before Lloyd's injury he was leading me by two points and he was easily the most outstanding fielder on either side, but here I, an average fielder, was walking away with the prize. The only thing in my favour was that I ran and chased the ball on those long Australian boundaries and made an honest effort to save as many runs as I could.

The teams had their usual friendly drinks, and the Australian Cricket Board officials also joined us in the dressing room. Sir Don Bradman spoke to me at length about my batting and pointed out the shortcomings which, he suggested, I should try to remove. He was most encouraging in his remarks, and I was thrilled when he said that a square-drive I had played in the South Australia match was a 'memorable' one. It was a great compliment coming from one of the all-time greats of the game. I felt very happy that he remembered the shot I had played two months ago.

Sir Donald asked me not to be over-anxious to attack, as I had been doing during the early part of the tour, or over-defensive, as I had been later. He suggested that a judicious blend between attack and defence would do me good. It was 'super' hearing "The Greatest" giving you friendly advice and it is ever-green in my memory.

The evening before we dispersed to return to our homes we had a 'team dinner', to which Sir Donald Bradman was invited, since it was he who was largely responsible for organising the tour. He gave his impressions about every member of the side. He spoke in glowing terms about Sobers and Pollock, and offered great encouragement to Zaheer and myself, when he said some very complimentary things about our performance. Then every member of the team talked about his individual experience during the three months we had spent in Australia.

It was all very touching, and nobody really wanted the evening to end.

I said farewell to my team-mates, particularly my 'Partner', as Ackerman called me, and the Pollock brothers who were South Africans and I wasn't sure whether I would ever play with them again. The Pollocks had been extremely nice to me, and I cherish my friendship with them and with Ackerman very much. I hope some day to meet Ackerman again. The Pollocks, I may mention, made sincere enquiries about Chandrasekhar, Bapu Nadkarni and 'Tiger' Pataudi, which showed how much they cared for their friends of former years.

12

Riding on Euphoria

I returned home from Australia with the C.C.I. team and played a game for them at Singapore on the way back. It was, however, all in fun and we were all more keen to do some shopping rather than playing. Everybody took turns to bat and went out shopping.

When I returned home there was more cricket, as the knock-out stage of the Ranji Trophy was still to be played. Immediately, however, I had to fly to Jamshedpur to play in the Duleep Trophy. Amazing, this was to be my first Duleep Trophy match. Imagine playing a Duleep Trophy game only after having played for the Rest of the World! Both Ramnath Parker and I got centuries on our first appearance, and Ashok Mankad also got a hundred. We won the game easily on the first innings.

In the final, however, we were surprised by Central Zone. This was Salim Durrani's game. Apparently, he had promised Hanumant Singh that he would win the Duleep Trophy for Central. Durrani's superb bowling and bold hitting swung in their favour a match which looked like being in our pocket when we led by 79 runs on the first innings. This was Central Zone's first victory in the Duleep Trophy and, indeed, a deserving one.

In between these games a match was arranged between the

victorious Indian XI (comprising members of the 1971 team to the West Indies and England) and the Rest of India XI. The match was to be played at New Delhi in aid of the National Defence Fund. At Jamshedpur I had verbally secured permission from the Board President to skip this N.D.F. match. However, I got frantic telephone calls from New Delhi asking me to come over. My decision to go turned out to be an important one eventually. For, during the game I was introduced by Dilip Doshi, the Bengal left-arm bowler, to Marshniel Mehrotra who, two years later, was to become my wife.

I wasn't particularly successful in this match, because I was troubled by a sore leg-muscle. We were due to play the knock-out and hence I didn't want to aggravate the injury. In the knock-out stage our first game was against Bihar. At the end of the first day I was 200 not out and Solkar was unbeaten with 88. The next day he got his 100 and went on to score 131. I was last out at 282, when Anand Shukla foxed me with a 'wrong one' and bowled me. We, however, had an easy innings victory, but during this game I sustained a hairline fracture of the thumb while catching Ramesh Saxena. Curiously, this didn't bother me in the semi-finals against Mysore. This was probably because I didn't bother the Mysore bowlers, getting out in the first over of the match for 4 in the 1st innings, and for 45 runs in the second innings. I also played in Vijay Manjrekar's benefit match, though the pain had increased during the match.

It was touch and go whether I would play in the Ranji Trophy final against Bengal. Until the eve of the game I was uncertain, as I was getting pain in the injured thumb every time I played the ball. I went through a fitness test on the morning of play and found that the pain had eased a bit. Ajit Wadekar was also keen that I should play and so eventually I did play.

Subroto Guha and Samir Chakravarty, one of our foremost pairs of new-ball bowlers, luckily didn't make use of the moisture on the first morning. After a slow and painful start, I opened out and, at the day's end, was unbeaten with 139. Ajit Wadekar, who scored 57, easily played the better innings and so also did Dilip Sardesai who scored a strokeful 34. Mine was a satisfying innings, however, and Bombay were in a very healthy position, being 280 for three wickets. The next day Guha bowled me middle-stump for 157. He had a fine spell with the second new ball and Bombay slumped to 377 all out.

For Bengal, Gopal Bose and Ambar Roy batted well, before Rege got rid of both of them within minutes of each other. Rege was again proving his usefulness to the Bombay side. Having come in primarily as an off-spinner replacement for Sharad Diwadkar, he had pulled Bombay out of trouble with his hard-hitting batting many a time. His performances as a bowler were never as spectacular as Shivalkar's, but if one is to see through the score sheets, he would see that he had usually chipped in with 2 or 3 wickets. Besides, he was a tremendous fielder at gully and had a powerful throw, flat and straight on top of the bails.

In our second innings, both Parker and I got out cheaply, and there was an outside chance of Bengal surprising Bombay. But, Ashok Mankad played such a terrific attacking innings that the phrase "taking the bull by its horns" immediately came to mind. He was unfortunately run out when he was two short of his 100, but what a grand 98 runs they were!

That was it. Bengal had no chance after that, for Ismail demolished the top half of their batting and the next day they crumbled for 115 runs. Bombay had won the Ranji Trophy for the 14th year in a row. Thankfully the season, which started for me in September 1970, had ended in mid-April 1972. I was glad to lock my kit for a further four months before the new season began. I thought I had had enough cricket for a while and looked forward to a few weeks rest. I really needed to relax.

The 1972-73 season began, as usual, with the Irani Trophy. Earlier, of course, was the Moin-ud-Dowla Tournament, organised by the Hyderabad Cricket Association, which is traditionally the curtain-raiser to the season. The locked-up cricket kit comes out, the boots are given a new coat of white, the leg-guards are brushed, the bat is oiled, and sometimes even the limbs have to be 'oiled' for loosening creaking joints.

Generally, when rain prevents Moin-ud-Dowla matches from being completed, the coin decides the winner. But, fortunately the final is invariably uninterrupted. The State Bank of India team, with its galaxy of Test 'stars', have won this Gold Cup more often than any other side. Vazir Sultan Tobacco Company sponsor a team full of youngsters, with a senior cricketer as captain. Many of today's India players have played for Vazir Sultan Colts. The company deserves compliments for the way it has been encouraging cricketing talent in the country. When I was just out of school I played for the V.S.T. Colts under 'Tiger' Pataudi. It was a great thrill to play under an Indian Captain. 'Tiger', of course, couldn't do much by himself, and the inexperienced youngsters under him, exposed to rain-affected tracks, were no help. U-Foam is another company which is invited to participate and they include a number of Test players as well as Test aspirants in the side. Captained by the evergreen and shrewd Jaisimha, they have made a habit of entering the final.

Spectator-interest in this Tournament in recent years has been disappointing and only the final attracts a decent crowd. The Hyderabad Cricket Association, in spite of this, continues to hold this tournament. Peter 'P.R.' Mansingh, a live-wire, is one of the leading lights of the Hyderabad Cricket Association, and he has tried hard to make Hyderabad cricket a success. He organises tours for the 'Hyderabad Blues', whose players have proved very popular overseas.

The 1972-73 Irani Trophy tie was played at Poona. If that

match proved anything it was that Ramnath Parker had
arrived. Until the end of various seasons, Parker had been in
the reserves for Bombay. He seized his opportunity when five
Bombay players went to West Indies with the 1971 Indian
team and scored two centuries. He also fielded brilliantly in the
covers and saved at least 30 to 40 runs. In the Irani Trophy
match, however, he staked his claim as an opening batsman
for India. He scored 70 runs in the first innings in just 95
minutes, before recklessly jumping out to be stumped off
Bishen Bedi. He learnt his lesson after this and scored 195
runs in the second innings, before he was out following a
doubtful decision. He played all shots to the distant corners of
Poona's Nehru Stadium and didn't spare even Bedi, Prasanna
and Venkataraghavan.

Vishwanath's reply to Parker's 195 was a classic, unbeaten
161 in the Rest of India's second innings. Whereas Ramnath,
who is even shorter and slighter than Vishwanath, hit the ball
with tremendous power, the Karnataka batsman seemed to
caress the ball to the boundary.

Dilip Sardesai, in spite of a bruised forearm, also scored
a century for Bombay. Time and again he proved he was a
champion player of spin as he danced down the wicket and
drove and lofted the bowlers who didn't know where to pitch
the next ball.

I failed miserably in this match and the next two games of
the Ranji Trophy didn't ease my worries about my poor form.
I was batting reasonably well until I got 20 or 30 runs and
then got out.

When I went to play for the Board President's XI against
the visiting M.C.C. team, their opening match of the tour, I
was hoping to strike form. Ramnath Parker opened with me
and we added 100 runs, before Parker was out for 59. He
clinched his place in the Indian team with this innings. Though

I was certain of being picked as the other opener, I wanted runs behind me before the first Test.

I thus batted slowly against the tight M.C.C. attack and was content to wait for my runs. When I was in my 70's I had an attack of cramps in the right leg. At 80 I tried to take a cheeky single but turned slowly because of the cramped right leg and was beaten by Amiss's direct hit at the stumps. It was disappointing to miss the century, though I was fairly happy that I had been able to regain my usual concentration.

For the M.C.C., openers Amiss and Denness batted well and they too were trying to get acclimatised with Indian conditions. The others, however, didn't last long and we had to bat out the last session of the match, when Tony Lewis declared at the tea-time score.

Tony Greig opened the M.C.C. attack and his second ball, a huge in-swinger, got me leg-before. So I was to back to square one! As I packed my kit-bag to get to Delhi for the Test, I was hoping for a break in the run-famine. I consoled myself with the thought that everything would click in the Tests.

We reached New Delhi a week before the Test started. Except for the few who were engaged in playing for their Zonal team against the tourists, everybody was there and we had a good work-out. My form at the nets was satisfactory, and I felt very much elated. Normally, I don't worry about my form at the nets. Invariably, when I have batted well at the nets, I have batted badly in the match. If, on the other hand, I've batted badly at the nets the result is that I am able to concentrate better in the match and I find that it helps me to score runs.

Ajit Wadekar, who led India in the first Test, was lucky with the toss, and Parker made his Test debut with me as my partner. This must surely be one of the rare occasions when the same players open the batting for their Club, State, Zonal and National teams. The wicket looked a beauty, though there was a hint of moisture, which is always the case at Ferozeshsh Kotla. Geoff Arnold opened the attack for England, while Bob Cottam bowled from the other end. England had decided to feed Ramnath Parker with short deliveries, knowing his tendency to go for the hook shot. Accordingly, Arnold, trying to get more bounce, overstepped the mark thrice in succession and off the third delivery had Parkar caught on the deep fine-leg fence by Pocock. The umpire had failed to call no-ball on all the three occasions and, thus a wicket, which should not have fallen, had gone. Ajit Wadekar came in and, after a couple of overs, was late in coming down on the ball and had his off-stump knocked out of the ground.

At this stage what was needed was caution because Arnold was bowling well and, with two wickets behind him, was rearing to go. I thought if I attacked he might be taken off. So when he bowled short outside the off-stump, I went to cut, but only managed to edge the ball and saw Tony Greig leaping up at second slip to catch the ball. I doubt if anyone else in the M.C.C. team would have reached the ball, but there it was. A rank bad shot, and a deserving fate. And so, back to the pavilion for me.

Vishwanath and Sardesai held on till the lunch-break. At lunch Dilip, in his characteristic way, promised to make a hundred. In the West Indies, and often for Bombay, whenever Dilip made a promise he generally kept his word. This time, however, Arnold got through his defence and bowled him without addition to his lunch score. We were soon in trouble, because Solkar also didn't stay long. Abid, however, struck back boldly to get runs and we reached a total of 173.

Now, the only way of saving the match was to get England out cheaply. Chandrasekhar bowled a terrific spell and got

eight wickets, beating the England batsmen by his spin and
bounce. Only Greig defied him to a certain extent and
remained unbeaten with 68.

We had, however, to ensure that our batting clicked in the
second innings and we got enough runs to make it a stiff target
for the Englishmen. This time Parker scrupulously avoided his
favourite hook shot, but played some lovely shots off his legs.
I was given out, caught by Greig, after the ball had come off
my pads. The poor umpire got foxed by Greig and wicket-
keeper Knott, who began applauding the bowler with such
gusto that he declared me 'out'. When I met Greig in our
dressing room in the evening, he laughed in characteristic
fashion and started pulling my leg. I, however, swallowed all
the choice bad words I had thought of, because, with Greig it
is a love-hate relationship. On the field he makes you hate
him; but off it he is a wonderful chap, who doesn't bear you
any grudge. He believes that whatever happens on the field
should be left there and should not be allowed to sour one's
friendship.

Throughout the tour Greig made use of his knowledge of
Hindi expletives which he learnt from us and the Pakistanis
during the Rest of the World's tour of Australia. Often,
he did not even know the meaning of what he was
saying, but the rest of the members of the Indian team were
certainly surprised to hear his Hindi vocabulary. His pronun-
ciation was not perfect, but the meaning was clear. More than
anyone else, Farokh and Ajit suffered, because they often
played long innings during the series. Yet, when the M.C.C.
left, all our players agreed that he was a likeable guy, off the
field.

To come back to the Delhi Test, Farokh Engineer and
Eknath Solkar tried vainly to put us back in the game but,
when we were finally all out, the M.C.C. were left to score
only 210 runs for victory. They scored 95 of these runs, losing
three wickets on the fourth evening. The last morning we had
to get a breakthrough to stay in the game. Though we got

Barry Wood at his overnight score of 45, Tony Greig and Tony Lewis played sensibly and England notched up their first victory of the series easily.

Ajit Wadekar said after the Test that it was a Christmas present to Tony Lewis and he hoped that Tony would give him a New Year's gift in return! The second Test was to be played at the Eden Gardens in Calcutta. The ground can accommodate about 65,000 people, but with a little squeezing 70,000 people can be crammed into the stands to enjoy their cricket. The Test, which was a real thriller right from the first morning to the last day, kept a huge crowd agog with excitement. When India won their joy knew no bounds and the scene after that had to be seen to be believed.

Ajit Wadekar must have used a 'lucky' coin, because he won the toss again. To us, the Bombay players, it was a common sight to see Ajit come in after the toss to announce with a shrug of his shoulders that he didn't mind losing the toss, so long as he won the match. Well, this time he came in to announce that we were to bat. Geoff Arnold, who had set us on the road to defeat at Delhi, was unable to play due to some stomach trouble. I am sure he must have eaten some tinned food brought from England! Chris Old, making his Test debut, opened the bowling, and I got off the mark with a boundary to square-leg off the first ball. I wonder what Chris Old thought of starting his Test career like that. Parker was playing well and we safely negotiated the new ball. Derek Underwood was brought on and he got my wicket immediately. A delivery popped up from a length, hit my glove and landed in the direction of silly mid-on, where Chris Old, diving to his left, took a good catch.

Wadekar, the next man, ducked in to a short ball from Greig and had a bad crack on the ribs, which compelled him to retire. Vishwanath didn't stay long, and Parker, after playing well, was caught behind off Old for 26. Our innings was again in the doldrums. Durrani failed, and so did Solkar. Engineer played a lone hand, scoring 75 runs.

England fared no better and though Greig was looking dangerous we got him out and secured a lead of 36 runs. The start of our second innings was a disastrous one. I tried to a shortish delivery from Old, missed it completely and was leg-before for two runs. Ajit was sick and so Durrani came one wicket down, and began to clout the bowling. Parker in the meanwhile had been caught behind off Old. But Vishwanath played a lovely innings of 34.

Salim Durrani, who had injured his leg while fielding, took me as his runner. But, there was precious little running I had to do for Durrani, who seemed to concentrate on hitting boundaries. Once, after the crowd chanted that they wanted a 'six', Durrani swung a ball from Underwood into the noisiest stand at mid-wicket for a huge six. While the ball was being returned, I walked from my square-leg position and congratulated Salim for the shot. I also wanted to caution him, because our position was not secure as yet. Salim's reply typical of him: "I wanted to show him (Underwood) who is the boss." He scored 53 before he fell to a brilliant diving catch by Fletcher in the slips. He had, however, played his part well. With useful contributions from Engineer and Abid, England were left to score 261 runs for victory.

Abid bowled Barry Wood with a lovely leg-cutter and then Bedi chipped in with three victims, and England had slumped to 4 for 17. Greig and Mike Denness, however, held on and towards the close both played some confident shots that set us thinking. The next morning, Chandrasekhar struck. He had bowled indifferently the previous evening but, on that morning, he was right on top. Denness was out leg-before, and Greig followed in the same manner, when he missed a dipping full toss. Typically, Greig stood his ground and looked unhappy for the entire world to see. After the game,

however, he was again laughing, and admitted that he was
plumb lbw. In desperation, Alan Knott tried to swing
Chandrasekhar, but succeeded only in skying a catch to Durrani at mid-on. Durrani held on to the ball as if for dear
life, because he would have been in trouble if he had muffed
it. Earlier in the morning, before the match started, Salim had
made some gestures to the crowd under the huge scoreboard,
showing his annoyance because they had booed him for dropping catches during practice. The crowd was thus properly
steamed up, in spite of his earlier innings and if Salim had
dropped Knott, then his life would not have been worth a
'paisa. To relieve the tension, I went up to Salim, raised his hand,
and the crowd roared back signifying that it had understood.

Chris Old put up unexpected resistance and clouted a
'six' over long-on. He and Cottam took the score to within
28 runs of their target before Cottam padded up to a googly
and was leg-before wicket. Underwood was brilliantly taken
by Wadekar diving to his left. For a man running a tempera-
ture, this was truly a magnificent catch and after that our
victory was a formality.

As we sprinted to the pavilion we were engulfed by the
crowd, which was delirious with joy. Some people had hoisted
us on their shoulders. The stumps, of course, had vanished
and, if we had not taken the precaution of leaving our caps
behind, those too would have disappeared.

Long after the game was over huge crowds were waiting
outside our hotel to catch a glimpse of the players. Calcutta
crowds are terrific and the players are treated like heroes. The
players I think feel unnecessarily that there is danger to them
physically. True, the enthusiasm of the crowds can be a little
too much, but it is well meant. The enthusiasm of the Calcutta
crowd is terrific and I, for one, would rather play before a
Calcutta crowd than at Lord's where the applause is strictly
limited to three or four claps.

Tony Lewis, remembering Ajit Wadekar's words after the first Test, said that, as Ajit had wanted, he had given him a New Year's present, and he hoped that there were no more Indian festivals to follow. What Tony Lewis didn't know was that the 'Pongal' celebration would be on in Madras around the same time as the third Test.

Between this and the Madras Test I got 160 runs against Gujarat in the Ranji Trophy and was quite pleased to be among the runs. My four innings in Tests had got me a meagre 40 runs: 20 in the first Test and 20 in the second.

The third Test at Madras started off with Ajit Wadekar losing the toss, and Lewis had no hesitation in electing to bat. Abid Ali had been dropped and Eknath Solkar shared the new ball attack with Sunil Gavaskar. The only over I bowled in the Test proved uneventful and disheartening. I tried to bounce one, but the ball wouldn't get up at all. Wadekar took me off and gave the ball to Bedi and I said to Ajit, "I had just warmed up." But then Bedi proved his skipper right by having Wood caught. Soon, England were in serious trouble, with Chandrasekhar striking repeated blows. Amiss became his 100th victim in Tests when he snicked one to Farokh Engineer, and Lewis followed when he gave an easy catch to Solkar. All the while, Keith Fletcher had survived precariously against Bedi at the other end. Fletcher, always a nervous starter, kept pushing out his leg-guards along with the bat. More often than not the ball hit his pads. Slowly, however, the ball started hitting the bat with a regularity which was disconcerting to us. In spite of the uncertain start, Fletcher's knock was a classic example of how to build up an innings. Towards the end he was so confident that he smote three 6s into the stands. However, he was left stranded at 97, but his innings had saved England from utter rout. We had two overs left to play out before draw of stumps; and

Chetan Chauhan and I survived the overs and we were four for no wicket at the end of the day's play.

The next morning Chauhan, who had returned to the Indian team for the first time since 1969-70, was caught behind, off Arnold, for a duck. He sparred at one leaving him and paid the penalty. Chauhan's failure in Tests continues to surprise me, for he has a good technique and a voracious appetite for runs. One has to just glance at his Ranji Trophy record to see how prolific a scorer he has been. Though he doesn't have many shots, it's his determination that gets him runs. I don't believe that he lacks big-match temperament. I think he hasn't got on well at the Test level, because he has not been lucky. He has invariably fallen to a good ball or a brilliant catch. In any case, he can hardly complain for he has played five or six Tests without much success.

Wadekar joined me and got quickly into his stride. Arnold was bowling well as usual; and Old was working up a good pace. One of his deliveries reared up from a length, and he hit me on the thumb and then my shoulder. Later, I discovered that I had a hairline fracture of the thumb and also a badly bruised shoulder. Tony Greig once again got me out. I played defensively forward to Norman Gifford and the ball again went off the pads to Greig who promptly began a war dance with Knott, and there was Gavaskar once more making his way back to the pavilion. I had made 20 runs and had been looking forward to many more. Wadekar scored 44 and Durrani again hit a huge six on demand from the crowd in his 38. But the innings of the Test was Pataudi's 73. Having missed two series against the West Indies and England in 1971, it was thought by many that his career as a Test player had ended. 'Tiger', however, got a 100 for South Zone against the M.C.C. and was picked for the Madras Test. He confessed later that he had been out second ball in the match, but the umpire had negatived the appeal for leg-before and he went on to score a century. In the Test he didn't need any such luck as he middled the ball sweetly and sent it to the far corners of the Chepauk ground. He hit three sixes and, in trying to hit another, was caught on the boundary.

England's second innings was a shambles right from the start. Only Denness put up some resistance in scoring 76, before Solkar took a brilliant catch off Prasanna, who finished with a tally of 4 wickets. We were left to score only 86 runs to win and everybody was relaxed. Since I was nursing a bruised thumb, Farokh Engineer opened the innings with Chauhan. Chris Old, however, shattered our complacency by having Engineer leg-before wicket. Farokh who, during the series had never once played off the back-foot to the fast bowlers, as far as I can remember, was given out as he characteristically danced down the wicket. The decision not only surprised him but all of us, too, for he was as far down the track that it looked as if he was going to shake hands with the bowler.

Wadekar, who followed, edged Chris Old low to Greig at second slip and was caught. Ajit, however, had missed seeing the ball and therefore had no idea of the direction the ball had travelled and he waited for the umpire's decision. To this day I can't fathom why umpire Mamsa didn't give him out there and then, but had to consult the square-leg umpire. While Mamsa walked to speak to his colleague, all hell seemed to break loose. Greig ran forward with the ball in his raised right hand, Alan Knott flung his glove in the air and the other England players rushed in from where they were fielding, to confront the umpire. At this stage, Tony Lewis came in from mid-on to calm his players and asked them to get back to their position while the umpires conferred and then Mamsa declared Wadekar 'out'. Lewis deserves full marks for the way he handled the explosive situation. Luckily, this happened in Madras, where the crowds are the most disciplined and I shudder to think what would have happened if the game was at Kingston, Jamaica.

We asked Ajit Wadekar why he waited for the decision. He explained that he had not seen the ball after he edged it and then when he heard Tony Greig appealing and, knowing his ways, did not walk. Whatever it was, we were 1C for two!

The next morning we lost Chauhan and Durrani, who smashed 38 quick runs. During this innings he survived a confident appeal for leg-before and Gifford, the bowler, said something, and Durrani promptly hit next delivery for a six. We lost Solkar too when he was caught at cover. Vishwanath was bowled by a beauty from Pocock. The ball curled between his bat and pads and took off his bails. At 72 for six, I walked in with my thumb strapped up. I had not opened the innings and when I went in I was the last recognised batsman left. However, I had to do precious little, except to play out an over from Gifford. 'Tiger' Pataudi got the runs off Pocock and the scores were level when Gifford bowled a 'no ball' to give us victory. I was not out without scoring, and my aggregate in the fourth Test was only 20, and a total of 60 in three Tests.

I don't subscribe to the view that if we had to chase a target of 150 runs, we would have lost. I am sure that if the target had been that much the players would have batted with greater concentration. As it is, in spite of our losing wickets regularly, the atmosphere in the dressing-room was relaxed, knowing that victory couldn't elude us.

Just before the Test, an English journalist complained that Farokh Engineer led a chorus of 45,000 people when appealing. This allegation was carried in an Indian newspaper. This shut up Farokh effectively because he had to consider his prospect in English cricket, and thereafter he rarely appealed. It set me wondering that if Farokh was appealing what was Alan Knott doing? He wasn't opening his mouth as a part of the exercises he performed ! As a matter of fact, Alan Knott appealed almost as much as Farokh. And it is hardly Farokh's fault that Indian crowds love their cricket so much that they have to take vocal part in the Tests. As I have said, I'd rather play before a vocal crowd, rather than have the spectators sit mournfully watching a match, as they do in England.

All through the tour this English critic did nothing but criticise the conduct of the Indian players and spectators. If this was his idea of encouraging the Englishmen or lifting their drooping morale, he was sadly mistaken. As far as he was concerned, everything the Englishmen did was pardonable, and the Indians were always wrong.

According to this English journalist, whenever the Indians appealed, it was pressurising the umpires to force them to give a decision against England. It's funny how the English critics come up with all kinds of arguments to cover up their own team's weakness. If an Australian quick bowler runs through an England team, invariably the British Press will damn the bowler as a 'chucker'. If the bowler's action is scrupulously fair, then he is accused of overstepping the bowling crease, but he is not being 'no-balled' by the umpires, If all else fails, the bowler is accused of using abusive language towards the batsman. All in all, it is any kind of stick with which to beat those who 'dare' to beat England in their own game. So much for the 'fairness' of English cricket writers!

In India, the complaint is not only against the manner of our 'appealing', it is the condition of our wickets also. It is alleged that Indian wickets are invariably tailored for our spinners. True! Absolutely true! We would be fools if we did not prepare wickets to suit our ace spinners. When we go to England, we cannot distinguish the wicket from the outfield. And, aren't English wickets prepared for the advantage of their own bowlers? But, of course, it is all right for England to do so. The British are fair, but we are not.

The M.C.C. team itself was friendly off the field except for a couple of players, but then there will always be some 'rotten apples' in any group. What made the Indian players all the more determined was the patent bias of the English critics and their comments. John Snow had declined to come to India, preferring to play for a Melbourne club in Australia. From that distance he had passed a judgment that it was absurd to call a Test in India a Test, because "the spinners come on in the third over and, therefore, the Test is a farce". I suppose it was a typical fast bowler's lament. But then I wonder what one calls a Test in England, where the spinners are seldom called upon to bowl. The Indians don't call that a 'farce', do they? And, passing judgment from thousands of miles away is just rubbish!

The fourth Test at Kanpur ended in a draw. This was inevitable on a wicket which was perfect for batting. Batting first, Chauhan and I put on 85 runs. I finally managed to score more than 20 runs, and when I reached 21, I had scored 1,000 runs in Tests. Later I came to know that it was the fastest (in 11 Tests) by an Indian batsman. But, from 774 in the first four Tests I had played in the West Indies in 1971, it had taken me 7 more Tests to score 226 runs. I was eventually out for 69, being Jack Birkenshaw's first Test victim. I pulled a short ball straight to Tony Greig at square-leg, who took the ball well up. I cursed my luck for trying to clear the tallest Test cricketer. Greig had now caught me four times in four Tests. The fact that twice it was off the pads doesn't alter what's in the record books.

During my innings there was a funny incident when I survived a leg-before appeal off Arnold. Greig walking past me at the end of the over remarked, "It was close, wasn't it?" I replied. "Yeah, sure. But the umpire is my uncle!" Greig then asked what his name was. I said "Gothoskar, but he had changed it, or else he would never get to be a Test umpire". Within minutes word had gone round and I was asked with much consternation by quite a few people whether umpire Gothoskar was really my uncle.

Ajit Wadekar got to 90, before Greig got him caught by Fletcher, who had to dive to his left to reach the ball. 'Tiger' Pataudi got 54, before being leg-before to Arnold. When England started their innings they had a new opening pair in Denness and Roope, both of whom were dismissed by Chandrasekhar. Knott batted well for his 40, and so did Fletcher who was a completely different batsman after his 97 not out in the Madras Test. He was confident from the start and played some crisp shots. All these innings were, however, overshadowed by Tony Lewis's maiden Test century. Showing beautiful footwork, he stepped down the wicket repeatedly and played some fine lofted shots. His confidence, I'm sure, must have increased with the knowledge that the ball wouldn't turn on this wicket. It was a very fine innings.

With India trailing by 40 on the first innings and about three hours to go, the match was doomed to be a draw. Our careless batting, however, led to an exciting finish. We had lost five wickets for only 75 runs, and still there was more than an hour of play left. Vishwanath and Solkar, however, batted sensibly and avoided an embarrassing situation. Vishwanath remained unbeaten with 75 which saved the innings. Just imagine that he was on the verge of losing his place in the side!

Towards the end, with Prasanna defending stubbornly, Chris Old bowled him five consecutive bouncers. It was a blatant attempt to injure one of our star spinners. Prasanna, who, over the years, has played bowlers faster than Chris Old returned unbeaten to the pavilion with his usual broad smile. Like all renowned bowlers, Prasanna takes his batting seriously and nothing makes him happier than a good innings. He has saved India often by resisting solidly, while his partner has got the runs.

I was still being troubled by the broken thumb and so the West Zone selectors left me out of the game against the M.C.C. at Ahmedabad. Wadekar was rested and Sardesai led West Zone. He, however, did not use this last opportunity to win back his place in the Indian side. It was known that he was retiring at the end of the season. Parker also didn't enhance his chances by failing in the game.

For the fifth and final Test at Bombay, Chetan Chauhan was dropped from the side, and Farokh was to open with me. This was my first Test before my 'home' crowd at Bombay. But I began badly when Chris Old bowled me through the 'gate' for only four runs. When I made my way back to the pavilion I was booed by the huge crowd in the C.C.I. stands. It was an unnerving experience. Farokh, however, went about merrily and Ajit, who was magnificently consistent in the series, added over 220 runs with him. Just as they looked like going on and on, Lewis brought on Birkenshaw. His second ball, a full-toss, got the wicket of Ajit, who tried to hit him over mid-wicket, but ended by giving a catch to the fielder there. Ajit had again missed his century, this time by 13 runs. Ajit has only one Test century to his credit, having been out in the 80s or 90s on six occasions.

Farokh also got out to a Birkenshaw full-toss for 121 runs. At this stage he was getting runs off almost every ball and playing some shots which were not in the coaching manual. Before the day was out Pataudi was yorked by Underwood, and he too was booed by the crowd. Vishwanath and Durrani carried on as Wadekar and Engineer had done earlier. Salim had been dropped for the Kanpur Test, and there was a big outcry in Bombay, where posters appeared saying "No Durrani, no Test". The posters also condemned the Chairman of the Selection Committee for leaving out Durrani, and there was considerable public support for Durrani's inclusion in the team for the Bombay Test. And Durrani did not disappoint his fans. Once again he hit a six when the crowd asked for it. Trying another one, he got out for 73.

Vishwanath, however, was a different sight. All elegance,

he caressed the ball beautifully to the boundary. When he
scampered for the run that got him his 100, he became the
first Indian to score another 100, after making a century on
Test debut. Tony Greig, who has the uncanny knack of the
right gesture at the right time, picked the 'puny' Vishwanath
up and rocked him like a baby. The crowd roared in laughter
and clapped in wild appreciation for this sporting gesture.
From that moment, Greig was the most popular member
of the England team.

Tony Lewis was bowled first ball, off his chest, when
England batted, and Roope was brilliantly caught by Abid
Ali at leg-slip when he hit a full-blooded shot off Chandrasekhar. So, Abid had a hand in the eventual dismissal of
both the openers. Knott then played a strokeful innings to
get 56, and Fletcher and Greig were left to ward off our
spinners, who had scented blood. Fletcher once again showed the way to build up the innings. To the keen youngsters
in the crowd, here was a fine model. He started off by pushing the ball away for singles and twos, and, only after he had
passed his 30s, did he venture to play his shots. Greig, on
the other hand, played freely and was first to reach his
hundred. At close to play, he was way ahead of Fletcher,
who had been dismissed in the last over of the day for 113.

The next day, however, Greig was never the same player as
on the previous day, and he prodded and pushed at the ball,
until he was dismissed for 148. Some merry hitting by Geoff
Arnold and Birkenshaw took the England total to 448. When
England's innings finally ended at 480, the visitors had a lead
of 32 runs. We had two hours' batting before the end of the
day, and we had to make certain that there was no more
careless batting, because there was a whole day's play left.

Farokh was confidence personified after his first innings
century and went into his stride straightway. He was lucky to
see Knott fumble a stumping chance off Pocock. Pocock bowled

very skilfully that evening, but the bowler who spelled danger
was Underwood. He had found a rough patch caused by
Solkar's follow-through just on the off-stump and, from there,
he made the ball jump, turn and, at times, shoot through low.
I got my fifty off one such ball which turned, took the edge
and went past Fletcher at slip for a four. It was not the most
satisfying way of getting a 50, but then my form in the series
had been such that I was glad anyway. Farokh was unbeaten
with 47, and our total at the end of the fourth day stood at
102 for no loss. The next morning both Farokh and I were out
in quick succession. I was caught and bowled off a slower
ball from Underwood, for 67. I drove too soon at the ball
and ended up by giving a simple catch. In the next over
Farokh, who had resumed with a runner, was bowled for 66.
Durrani, however, was again in the mood to oblige the crowd
and when they asked for a six he gave one to them. Some
days, he says, he is going to write a book entitled "Ask for a
Six."

Vishwanath, not content with his first innings century, was
also batting well, and when he was two short of 50, fell to
an excellent catch down on the leg-side by Knott, off Greig.
Pataudi came in for a lot of booing from the crowd for his
laborious innings of five runs in 90 minutes. When he went in
he found Underwood making the ball 'talk'. He even survived
a popped-up chance to Greig in the gully and barely survived.
But the crowd, whose appetite had been whetted by Durrani's
big hitting, couldn't understand Pataudi's crawl, and started
barracking him. Towards the latter half of the innings I
think 'Tiger' deliberately patted the full-tosses back to the
bowler, to snub the crowd. Typically like 'Tiger'!

Wadekar didn't declare till tea and when the curtain came
down on the Test, England had lost two second innings
wickets for 67 runs. Abid kept wicket, instead of the injured
Farokh Engineer. Incidentally, Abid had started his
career as a wicket-keeper and, though obviously not in

practice, he 'took' the unpredictable Chandrasekhar well. Interest in England's second innings centred around Chandrasekhar, who required to take one more wicket to beat Vinoo Mankad's record of 34 wickets in a Test series. I am glad he got Knott's wicket with a beautifully flighted ball, and had his name inscribed in the record books! He deserves the honour.

At the end of the match the England players ran a lap off the ground and were cheered lustily by the crowd. This last gesture of theirs touched the hearts of the spectators and made the team more popular than before. Tony Lewis had done a magnificent job as captain. When he came to India he had yet to play a Test, but it was apparent how much the players liked him. His charming ways also won over the crowd and went a long way in making the M.C.C. team a popular one. Tony Greig, of course, was the most popular player, but Tony Lewis wasn't very far behind.

The season had not ended for us yet, because the Ranji Trophy was still on. I went with the Bombay team to Indore for the quarter-final against Madhya Pradesh. We had travelled by rail and a huge crowd was waiting at Indore station to greet us. When the train stopped people swarmed all over the train and some, more daring than the others, climbed to the roof. We had no alternative but to wait in the train because we just couldn't get out. Normally the train was to halt at Indore station for about twenty minutes, but this time it was well over an hour before the huge crowd could be cleared and the train could steam off. Additional police reinforcements were called in, before we finally got off, amid much back-slapping, pushing and jostling. The enthusiasm of the crowd was truly remarkable. The cricket lovers of Indore had erected a huge bat made of concrete to commemorate India's victory over England in 1971. The names of all the players were inscribed on the bat, with the autograph of skipper Ajit Wadekar on top.

Looking back on that animated scene, I am reminded that, when we lost to England in 1974, the same bat was smeared with tar and defaced. I suppose, if we beat England in the home series in 1976, the bat will be cleaned and repaired, and our image as victors will be restored!

In the Indore match I got a century against Madhya Pradesh. As I returned at the lunch interval, Syed Mushtaq Ali, one of India's all-time greats, came down the steps of the pavilion and congratulated me on my innings. This was one of my most cherished moments for I have not been so fortunate with some of the former Test greats in my own home, Bombay. And, here was one of India's most popular players ever, coming down the pavilion steps to offer his felicitations! I was deeply touched by this sporting gesture. Bombay won easily. Incidentally, this was during the Holi festival and many of the players were splashed with colour every time they chased a ball to the boundary.

In the semi-final we met Hyderabad, one of the strongest sides in the Tournament. With a century from me and brisk knocks by Sardesai and Wadekar, we were through to the final.

Our trip for the final against Tamil Nadu at Madras started eventfully. Sandwiched between the semi-finals and the final was the Inter-Office Tournament in Bombay. This left us little time to make the journey down south by train and, the Bombay Cricket Association, ever alive to the interests of the players, agreed to send the team by air to Madras. We landed at Madras with a bang, the worst I've ever experienced. At one moment the wing-tip on my side almost touched the runway, and we very lucky to get out in one piece. Some of us thought that this was a good omen for us and we were destined to retain the Ranji Trophy.

The five-day final lasted just one ball bowled on the third

day. On a wicket, which one can only charitably call a cricket pitch, we were shot out of 151. It was obvious that, if the Bombay batsmen were unable to cope with the viciously turning ball, the Tamil Nadu batsmen would do no better, particularly in view of Bombay's excellent close-in fielding. This is exactly what happened. From the overnight score of 50 for two, Madras were all out for 66. Their spinners Venkataraghavan and Kumar again bowled well to get us out for 113. As wickets were tumbling I was watching the game from the stands and the crowd around me, expecting a Tamil Nadu victory, were laughingly asking me what I thought Bombay's chances were. Poor ignorant souls! They should have, instead, been worried about Tamil Nadu's chances of pulling through. With just 171 runs to get for victory, Madras lost 9 wickets for 61 runs at the end of the second day. One ball on the third day, and Bombay were the champions again—our 14th victory in a row.

Dilip Sardesai, who retired from first-class cricket with this match, was given the honour of leading the side back to the pavilion. The crowd gave him a standing ovation and, I thought, I saw tears in Dilip's eyes which showed how moved he was. Dilip had come into the side in 1958 and since then and until the 1972-73 season Bombay had never lost the Ranji Trophy. He kept on repeating this, and said, he hoped that Bombay would continue in the same winning streak.

The long season had ended, and we were looking forward to the monsoon for a period of rest and relaxation.

13

Sour Sri Lanka

The 1973-74 season once again opened with the Irani Trophy game between Bombay, the Ranji Trophy Champions, and the Rest of India. The match was played at the new stadium of the Karnataka Cricket Association in Bangalore.

After the 1972-73 series against England, Wadekar had once again lapsed into his usual habit of losing the toss. The Irani Trophy match also started with Ajit calling wrongly, and conceding first use of the wicket to the Rest of India. On a wicket which gave no help to the bowlers, the Rest team piled up runs. Gopal Bose got 170. Jayantilal, Vishwanath and Brijesh Patel all got runs. Chasing a total of 444, Bombay started disastrously. Parker was bowled by Amitava Roy for 2, Ajit fell to Chandrasekhar and I was run out for 24 when Mankad sent me back. I thought I had reached the crease and was most disappointed about the decision. I confess I was so upset that I showed my disappointment and surprise by glaring at the umpire, which was an absolutely silly thing to do. I realised as soon as I was in the pavilion that my action was unworthy of a sportsman. In future I only hope my frustration doesn't cloud my judgment, as on this occasion.

Milind Rege (67) and Sudhir Naik were the only players who resisted, but we could not avoid the follow-on. In our second innings we struck the kind of form we should have in the first innings. Parker and I put on 83 runs, before Parker

was out for 50. Then Naik, who had scored 58 in the first
innings, was promoted to No. 3 and I shared another fruitful
partnership with him. I eventually got my first century in the
Irani Trophy. Over the years, I had been consistently failing
in this annual fixture and my century, though too late to be
of help to Bombay, was satisfying. Naik scored another 50.
He was wonderfully consistent that season.

The Indian team was due to leave for Sri Lanka for a six-
week tour in early January next year (1974). It was pretty
well known that our main spinners would not go to Sri Lanka,
as the tour to England was to follow in April. Before the
team to Sri Lanka was picked, North Zone created a sensation
by winning the Duleep Trophy. 'Wooden spooners' till then,
they surprised everybody by beating West Zone in the semi-
final and Central Zone in the final. Central had earlier
shocked South Zone, which was yet another upset in the
Duleep Trophy.

Before the start of the season I was pleasantly surprised
and honoured to be appointed Ajit Wadekar's deputy in the
Bombay team. Ajit couldn't play two of the league games
and I led Bombay for the first time.

The Deodhar Trophy for one-day limited-over games
between the Zonal sides was started this year. In the final
between the West and South Zones, I had to face the most
embarrassing incident of my cricketing career. Our captain Ajit
Wadekar split a finger in trying to catch Jaisimha in the slips
and went in for medical attention. For a minute or two there
was complete confusion as to who should lead the side in his
absence. Being Ajit's deputy for Bombay, I took charge and
led the side for three overs, before the 12th man came in and
told me that the senior-most player in the side, Ashok Mankad,
was to act as captain.

'Kaka', as we called Ashok, was most apologetic about it,

but took command. For me, however, it was most embarrassing to be told to hand over charge to another player in full view of more than 20,000 people who must have seen the 'change'. Even to this day I cannot help shuddering whenever I remember the incident. I feel that a vice-captain should invariably be appointed or the senior-most cricketer should be authorised to take over automatically in case something happens to the skipper. An almost similar situation occurred when I was appointed deputy to 'Tiger' Pataudi in the Bangalore Test against the West Indies in 1974-75. Fortunately, I was told before the game that I was the vice-captain and so there was no trouble on the field once I announced that I was to take charge.

My form was atrocious and, but for the century innings in the Irani Trophy and a score of 84 against Saurashtra, I had not been among runs. Against Baroda also, I led the side in Ajit's absence. After this match a journalist from one of the national news agencies came to interview me. When he had called me up I had told him that I would only speak about our just-concluded Ranji Trophy match against Baroda. He agreed and so I invited him to our hotel. Somewhere during our talks the topic turned to the forthcoming tour of Sri Lanka. He wanted to know what my team would be. I said I was not competent enough to select a team and, in any case, I didn't want to say anything on the subject. He, however, reverted to the composition of the team to Sri Lanka again. But this time he wanted to know my view, which he assured me would be treated as being "strictly off the record". I said then that, may be, our main spinners should be rested for the England tour and some of the others should be given a chance. I also said that the main batsmen should, however, be there to go to Sri Lanka. A few days after my return to Bombay a news item appeared in the newspapers quoting me as saying that younger spinners should be taken to Sri Lanka, which was all right. But the journalist had mentioned the names of some of these spinners, which I had not done. In any case, our talk about the Sri Lanka tour was "off the record" and the journalist had no business to use it in his report.

The next thing I knew was that the President of the Cricket Control Board wanted to see me about this matter. I explained the position to him and he very kindly accepted my word. I was furious anyway with the journalist. Later, I came to know that this journalist had heard from some other friend that, at a private dinner, I had mentioned the names of these promising cricketers who, I thought, deserved a chance and rushed off to make it appear as if I had personally suggested the names of those players when he met me.

As expected, all our main spinners, except Venkataraghavan, were rested, and a number of young players were selected for the Sri Lanka tour. It was to give them a chance of staking their claims for the England tour a few months later.

Sri Lanka had been trying to get full membership of the International Cricket Conference for some time. In this they had the backing of Pakistan. In order to strengthen their claim for grant of Test status, Sri Lanka were anxious to notch up a victory against India. For this reason they attached a great deal of importance to the Indian team's visit. I was happy to Tour Sri Lanka, where I was very successful with the Universities team in 1970. I had made a few friends there and I wanted to renew those friendships.

Leo Wijesinghe, Harold de Andrado and Eddie Melder had looked after me well during my last visit and I was looking forward to meeting them again. All three of them are not only cricket-mad, but also keen students of the game, and we had spent a lot of time talking cricket. I also had friends in the Sri Lanka team.

We started the tour with a game against the Sri Lanka Cricket Board President's XI. Within an hour of the game an accident robbed us of the services of Vishwanath. Chasing a ball, he tripped over the boundary rope and injured his right knee again, which developed a swelling and he had to be taken off the field, assisted by Salgaonkar and Madan Lal, two hefty young men who were to serve us so well on the tour. Though the knee looked bad, we were all shocked to learn that Vishwanath was going to be sent back home, apparently on instructions from the President of the Indian Cricket Control Board. The ridiculousness of the decision was apparent when Vishwanath was practising with the boys on the day of the first unofficial Test against Sri Lanka. By this time his replacement, Partha-sarathy Sharma, had arrived in Sri Lanka and, though the Sri Lanka Cricket Board very generously agreed to bear Vishwa-nath's expenses if he stayed with the team, he was asked to return.

The journey from Colombo city to the airport takes longer than the air journey from Madras to Colombo. Solkar and I went to see Vishwanath off at the airport and I've never seen the good-humoured Vishwanath so upset as on that day. As we were driving to the airport he did all the physical exercises one can think of excepting standing on his head to prove that there was nothing wrong with his knee. Vishwanath is tremendously popular, and we were all disappointed that he had to go away and particularly since he was fit to carry on.

I started off the tour well with a century against the Board President's XI at the Colombo Oval. I was hoping to have as successful a tour as my earlier visit to the Island with the Universities team. Our first four-day 'Test' was also at the same venue. We elected to bat on a greenish wicket and lost three wickets. Ashok Mankad held on and gave the innings some respectability. The chief wreckers were Mevan Peiris and Tony Opatha.

When Sri Lanka batted it soon became obvious to us that it was useless asking for leg-before decisions. Anura Tenne-

koon, their skipper, survived even a caught behind decision
off Venkataraghavan and went on to score a century. He
played some lovely shots but, time and again, he was rapped
on the pads by the spinners who shouted themselves hoarse,
appealing to the umpires. When he got his century there were
a couple of our boys who didn't clap and the Sri Lanka newspapers raised a furore about it. Commenting on the appeal
for caught behind, which was turned down by the umpire, the
newspapers said that Tennekoon would have 'walked', because
he was a gentleman. In effect, it amounted to calling us cheats.

In our second innings, Gopal Bose and I shared an opening
partnership of 194 runs, when I was out for 85 runs. Gopal
went on to score a century and we saved the match easily.

In the one-day matches we beat Sri Lanka with ridiculous
ease. It was rather funny that, prior to these matches, the Sri
Lanka newspapers were calling their team 'World Champions'
in one-day cricket. This claim eventually turned out to be a
big joke, and we proved to the hilt how ridiculous such self-
praise can be. As it happened, we beat them without a bead of
sweat on our brows. Our players also made no secret of their
feelings. Quite frankly, the crowds and the newspapers were
terribly biased, and it gave us perverse pleasure in seeing the
crowds go back dejectedly.

By this time Sri Lanka were desperate. They badly wanted
to beat us to prove to the International Cricket Conference
that they were good enough for official Tests. But this was not
to be and their fondest hopes were shattered. In the second
Test, our batsmen came into their own. Gopal Bose got 50,
Ajit Wadekar, who was a doubtful starter, made 89, Parthasarathy and Mankad got 60 and we piled up a total of 344.
When Sri Lanka batted Salgaonkar and Madan Lal skittled
them out for 121 runs. Both bowled with tremendous
fire and, for the first time, we were standing a good 20 yards
behind the wicket in the slips. Salgaonkar, in particular,

achieved great pace and, what is remarkable, he sustained it throughout his long spell.

Having been asked to follow on, Sri Lanka did little better and were quickly in trouble against Salgaonkar and Madan Lal who didn't seem tired after their first innings effort. Anura Tennekoon, however, played a captain's innings. He suffered a bad blow on the elbow from Salgaonkar, but he kept going with determination. At the end of the Sri Lanka innings he was unbeaten with 169, a truly magnificent innings. We should, however, have dismissed them earlier, but for some atrocious umpiring decisions. I am specially reminded of one such perverse decision. Ajit deSilva popped up a catch off his gloves to the wicket-keeper, but the umpire negatived it. All this, while the batsman was wringing his hand in pain and, after the over, took off his gloves to inspect the damage !

As the Sri Lanka innings ended I was reported by the newspapers to have clapped the umpires to the pavilion. This was yet another example of tendentious reporting because I do remember applauding our bowlers, but surely not the umpires. Madan Lal was walking behind the umpires and I applauded him as he walked along with the umpires. Certainly not the umpires! I read about this later somewhere and I thought that I really should have applauded the umpire for having given the last man run-out. So what, if the batsman was a good two yards out of his crease, as long as he was in his half of the wicket, and could have easily been given 'not out'. But horror of horrors, the umpire actually gave him out. Surprises never cease! I should have known that the umpires were actually practising raising their fingers for the time when we would bat. True enough, I played forward to Pieris and there was the finger sticking up its signal for me to go back. We, however, won the match in the 17th of the 20 mandatory overs; not because of the umpires, but in spite of them.

Right then I thought I would never tour Sri Lanka again,

certainly not as a cricketer. Most of my team-mates also agreed with me after that tour. I must add, however, that the relations between the players of both the teams were excellent. In fact, all of us made a number of friends on the tour, though the crowd never got used to the idea that we were the better team. One can understand the 'patriotism' of the crowd, but the spectators were positively hostile and our players were barely applauded for their cricket.

My feeling is that the Sri Lanka journalists, in their enthusiasm to secure official Test status for their country, got carried away; and the average man who read these reports got the impression that we were an unsporting bunch. And, thus the hostile attitude to anything we did on the field.

From this tour Salgaonkar and Madan Lal emerged as India's new-ball hopes and Gopal Bose staked his claim for the opener's berth. The success of the tour was Ashok Mankad. He seized the opportunity afforded by Vishwanath's absence and scored heavily. Eknath Solkar was, however, a failure on the tour. But, it must be added that he suffered terribly at the umpire's hands. He was given out leg-before in almost all his innings. This prompted Vishwanath later on to remark that Eknath had gone through a 'pad patch' and not 'bad patch'. Parthasarathy Sharma also made runs in the few innings he played. One man for whom the tour proved a disappointment was Karsan Ghavri. He just didn't get a chance to play in the 'Tests'.

To compensate him for this, Ghavri met his future wife on the tour, and returned to Sri Lanka a year later to get married to the girl. Thus, the Sri Lanka tour was not completely futile for this hard-working and talented cricketer!

Back home, I once again plunged into cricket, with the Ranji Trophy Tournament still on. In the Ranji Trophy knock-out match Bihar almost surprised us. They got us out for 200 runs and took a first innings lead of 72 runs, thanks to a century by Tilak Raj. His innings was a mixture of some superb shots and a good bit of playing and missing the ball. In our second innings we scored runs mainly through Parker, Naik and Mankad. Amid mounting excitement we got the Bihar batsmen out in the second innings and managed to scrape through to the semi-finals, with a 59-run victory. Shivalkar bowled superbly, accounting for most of the wickets.

The semi-final against Karnataka started sensationally. Ismail's first ball, an out-swinger, was edged by Vijay Kumar straight to me. I fumbled with the simple catch, but luckily the ball stuck in my lap. Vishwanath let go at the next ball but, off the third delivery, he played back, missed and was hit on the pads at ankle height. Surprisingly, the umpire gave him 'not out'. Thereafter Vishwanath simply blasted our bowling all over the ground. We couldn't get him to commit a second mistake, until he was 162. If ever an umpiring decision changed the complexion of a match, it was the one when Brijesh Patel was let off when he was 16. Patel went on to score a century and Vishwanath took a heavy toll of our bowling to take the Karnataka total to 385.

At one stage, Bombay were 200 for two wickets, and Wadekar and Mankad were batting untroubled against Chandrasekhar and Prasanna. Ajit, however, ran himself out, and, despite Naik continuing to get runs, we started losing wickets. We were all out for 320 and with only a day's play left. We were out of the Ranji Trophy final for the first time in 15 years. It was a sad blow for Bombay. In the other semi-final also, there was an upset when Rajasthan got Hyderabad out cheaply in their second innings. Karnataka eventually went on to lift the glittering Ranji Trophy, for the first and only time in their career. It was a proud moment for Prasanna when he received the Ranji Trophy, as captain of the victorious team.

So, Ajit Wadekar as the captain of Bombay had lost the Irani Trophy, the Ranji Trophy, and the Duleep Trophy. In a few months, he was to lose a Test series for the first time, and concede a 3-0 victory to England!

The author cooling
off on the balcony
of Lord's. The
Treasurer of the
1971 team, Mr. Ram
Prakash Mehra, is
in the background.

Ajit Wadekar leading the West Zone out to field in a Duleep Trophy match. Sunil Gavaskar (extreme left) running in to join the team.

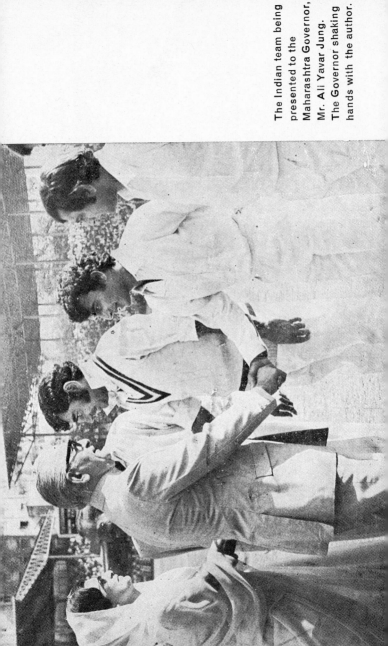

The Indian team being presented to the Maharashtra Governor, Mr. Ali Yavar Jung. The Governor shaking hands with the author.

A warm welcome at home after the 1971 W Indies tour.

The Gavaskar 'Family Score-board' to record the fabulous prformance of Sunil in the West Indies (1971).

14

Back to Blighty

The team to England had more or less picked itself and there were no surprises. However, a mild flutter was caused by the omission of Salgaonkar, particularly after his lion-hearted bowling in Sri Lanka. The experience of English wickets would have done him a world of good. After he was left out of the team to England, a number of cricket lovers collected funds to send him to Alf Gover's Coaching School in England. Unfortunately, while in England, Salgaonkar fell ill and couldn't play much cricket. As a result, when he returned to India, he had put on a lot of weight but his stamina was the same and he could bowl for long spells. He can still work up a lot of pace and if he seriously applies himself, he can hope to play for India.

We left for London, in defence of the 'rubber' we had won in two successive series, after the usual round of farewell functions. As our plane circled over London in bright sunshine, I told those of us who were having their first view of England, to take a good look, because they might not see the sun again! As it happened, for the next month and a half, in fact right through our lightning tour, the sun came out to dispel the gloom only for a week or ten days.

The start of the tour could not have been more miserable for us. In our first match, against D.H. Robins' XI at East-bourne, John Jameson 'caned' our attack for a century before lunch in 85 minutes. He was helped quite a lot by the extremely cold weather. None of the fielders dared to put their hands out to stop his hard-hit shots. It was bitterly cold for that kind of bravado! Dennis Amiss notched up 152, and the home team's total reached 402. Then, in the last hour of the evening, we lost two wickets to John Lever. However, Brijesh Patel somewhat redeemed us with a knock of 107.

That certainly wasn't the end of our troubles on that day. We were invited that evening to dinner by an Indian family. At the dinner there was a serious and furious argument between Ajit Wadekar and Bishen Singh Bedi. Without going into the rights and wrongs of that verbal battle, it is sufficient to say that, for the younger members of the side, it was a terrible thing to see two of India's senior-most cricketers squabbling in an unseemly manner, specially in a house where we were guests. Sure, on a tour there are always minor disagreements but, what happened on the day of our first match on the tour was more than a mere 'disagreement'.

When we returned to our hotel, I could see that the younger members had been shocked by what they had seen. Though the whole thing was patched up by the players concerned the next day, there was a lot of tension still left. This continued throughout the tour. Now, Bishen was a very popular member of the team and, Ajit also, in his own way, was liked by everyone. Besides, he was also the captain.

Ajit and Bishen are men of different stamps. Bishen is an extrovert who joked and 'fooled' with the boys, never once letting the younger members feel that they were with a great bowler. Ajit, on the other hand, has a dry sense of humour, and is always prepared to help the junior colleagues in all their difficulties. However, towards the end of the tour I found Ajit a little more withdrawn, and he preferred to spend his time alone with his worries. To the credit of both, however, it must be said that whatever their differences, these did not interfere with their trying their best on the field. However, their best, as well as the team's, was just not good enough to beat England that year.

Jameson, who must be the only player in the world to rate the Indian spinners as his favourite target of attack, once again scored a whirlwind century. In the little time left Gopal Bose stroked 59 runs.

Our second game against Worcestershire proved to be an exciting one. Madan Lal, in a great spell of bowling, captured 7 wickets for 95 runs. Vanburn Holder then ran through our side. He bowled real quick on that track and the light drizzle kept the pitch fresh for his seam bowling. Norman Gifford, 'The Pink Panther', as he is called, declared Worcestershire's second innings closed, giving us 195 minutes to score 221 runs to win. It was a very sporting declaration, as the mandatory 20 overs were also to be bowled in the last hour. After we had lost two wickets, Vishwanath joined me and we carried the score to 150, before 'Vish' played on to Inchmore, off the last ball before tea. Abid and Eknath Solkar kept up the chase with me but, at 203 for six, we had to put up the shutters. I was run out for 88, when I slipped while turning for a second run. It was an exciting game, mainly owing to Gifford's declaration.

The weather still wasn't getting any better. We almost always played in cloudy conditions and in terribly cold weather. However, the match against Somerset saw Brijesh in good form, and it ended in a draw. We played another drawn match against Hampshire at Southampton, before taking on Leicestershire.

Ajit Wadekar must rank Leicestershire's Grace Road as his favourite ground. On the 1971 tour he had got a century here and, in the course of the innings, scattered the people at the bar when his sweep for a six, off Birkenshaw, crashed through

the glass panes and shattered them. The section of the crowd in
front of the bar was full of Indians who remembered this feat
and were demanding a repeat. Ajit, however, preferred to
play himself into form and he did just that with a century. He
overshadowed Eknath Solkar who scored 75. A ball from
Holder had struck me a painful blow in the ribs during the
Worcester game, which began to give me a lot of trouble, and I
found that it greatly hampered my movement. So I was rested
from the Yorkshire game during which I learnt that a blood clot
had formed and would require heat treatment.

The Yorkshire match was the beginning of Geoff Boycott's
failures which were to climax in his eventually losing place
in the England side. As if to compensate for this, the game
marked Chris Old's advance as a batsman and he scored
his first century in a first-class match to rescue Yorkshire. To
show he was not to be ignored as a bowler, Old took five
wickets to send us reeling to 102 all out. Only Madan Lal, with
a defiant, strokeful 48 not out resisted him. Madan was
developing into a fine all-rounder. He was playing the quick
bowlers comfortably, relishing the short delivery. In the Hampshire game he had belted Andy Roberts' bouncers all over the
place to score an unbeaten 79. So, his subsequent failure in
the Tests and his repeated dismissals off the short ball came
as a big surprise, and we were extremely disappointed.

Boycott had fallen leg-before to Abid Ali in the first innings
for 15, and Solkar got him in the second for 14. But, after
losing two more wickets, Yorkshire were saved by an attacking
innings from Barry Leadbeater and Peter Squires, both of
whom got fifties. Set to score 265 for victory, we ended
the game on 144 for five, Wadekar playing brilliantly for
his 47.

We travelled to Manchester to take on Lancashire, the
traditional rivals of Yorkshire. In this match we tried Solkar
as my opening partner, since Gopal Bose had not been shap-

ing well and Sudhir Naik was still recovering from a hand injury. Solkar batted well against the pace of Peter Lever, Peter Lee and Ken Shuttleworth and at lunch on the first day, I was the only batsman out, with over 100 runs on the board. At lunch, Solkar, who was on 48 and batting confidently, cheerfully predicted, "You saw my technique, now see my strokes." After the first two balls bowled on resumption, he was back in the pavilion, grinning sheepishly. However, Solkar had helped Ajit to put on 93 runs for the second wicket before he was out. We lost two quick wickets, those of Vishwanath and Ashok Mankad, before Wadekar and Brijesh Patel steadied the innings with a 57-run partnership, when Wadekar was out for 82. When Ajit gets going his partner can never hope to match him. So was the case with Brijesh. After Ajit went, Brijesh took over to play some lovely shots off Lee. When he got his second century of the tour, and was unbeaten with 104 runs, Wadekar declared.

For Lancashire, David Lloyd scored a century, showing very good footwork against the spinners; and Clive Lloyd scored 55 runs, in even time. But the innings the crowd enjoyed most was that of Frank Hayes. At times Hayes was halfway down the track to drive our spinners. He reached his century with two thrilling shots. At 91 he suddenly rushed out to loft Bedi deep into the stands at long-off for a six. Of the next ball he clouted him for another six. This time the ball kept going on and on and landed on the roof over the scorer's box. This is the longest hit sixer I've seen. Hayes didn't let up after reaching his century but went on to score 187, and eventually fell to a catch by wicket-keeper Kirmani off Bedi. All the Lancashire batsmen made merry at the expense of our attack.

Surprisingly Lancashire did not declare. Unlike Gifford, whose declaration enlivened the Worcester game, David Lloyd continued to let his batsmen go on and, by the time our turn came to bat, there was no hope of a positive result. At the end of the game we were 187 for no wicket. I had scored my first century of the tour and was unbeaten with 104, while Eknath again showed his ability as an opener with 69. During our partnership we had to run often between the wickets, because the ball just wouldn't travel on the grassy outfield. In one over from Lee we took 3, 2, 3, 1 and 3. At this stage both of us were completely out of breath. So, in order to get back my breath I pretended that my leg-guards had come loose and I took my own time to adjust it. Solkar, who was leaning heavily on his bat at the other end while I finished adjusting my pads, had not recovered his breath, so he took off his gloves and began tightening his boot laces. Peter Lee's last ball of the over was a slower half-volley, but I just didn't have the strength to put it away and patted it back to him.

Now came the mini 'Test' against M.C.C. at Lord's. Boycott fell to Solkar again edging a drive to me at second slip. Then Eknath got Amiss caught by Patel at cover. Harry Pilling was caught by Vishwanath off Bedi. This catch went *via* the bat and pad to Vishwanath who would normally have taken this easily, but not being accustomed to the forward short-leg position, he had to lean forward to reach the ball. In the process he lost his balance and toppled over, but held on to the ball. We were roaring with laughter. Vishwanath calmly dusted his flannels and announced he had better lose weight by scoring runs. Mike Denness and Fletcher scored lovely centuries; Denness in particular was most impressive. Fletcher suffered in comparison, but was still very good. Greig fell in the chase for runs before the M.C.C. declared at their overnight score of 305 for eight.

Arnold got Eknath out quickly and then Edmonds picked up a flick from me, which should have gone for four runs instead of sending me back into the pavilion. Ajit Wadekar and Vishwanath counter-attacked only as they can, with stylish strokes all round the wicket. Engineer made a brisk 44.

We were all out for 231. In M.C.C's second innings Solkar got again Boycott, caught by me. As Geoff was making his way to the pavilion Solkar came running around gesturing to him how he had made the ball move away to take the edge of Boycott's bat. I dropped Amiss, off Solkar, low down to my left, just before the day's play ended.

Next day there were to be no more wickets for us for a long time. Amiss showed the kind of form that was to make him such a prolific scorer against us later in the Test.

Harry Pilling, who is as short as me, if not shorter, scored 81 not out and Edmonds, promoted just for a slog, was 29 not out. There was no question of us going for the runs, so we settled down to some batting practice. I got 57 not out and Ashok Mankad played an attacking innings to remain unbeaten with 50. He hit Edmonds for four successive fours in an over, all brilliant shots.

On the last evening of the game, we were entertained at an official dinner by the M.C.C. Ajit made a bright, humorous speech and so too did Manager Lt. Col. Adhikari.

During the dinner Bishen Bedi was collecting autographs of the great names in cricket who were present at the function. He approached Geoff Boycott who turned around and told him "I'll give you my autograph only if you bowl me a full toss first ball". Bishen quipped : "Yes, provided you last out our seamers." In a newspaper article a few days later Boycott wrote, "Everybody's talking about the great Indian spinners and many have asked me what I think about them. But, where have I played them? I am getting out before these famous spinners come on to bowl."

In the next game against Northamptonshire, Vishwanath struck form to get 103 not out. Against Essex in the next match, Sudhir Naik touched splendid form to score a cen-

⁺ury. Though slow at times his innings showed that he was ᵖʳᵉᵖared to stay at the wicket and wait for the runs to come. Again, in the second innings he played patiently to score 42 not out. Wadekar got 50s in both innings and Madan Lal scored 64 not out.

We had so far played ten matches and all of them had ended indecisively. There were only two games left before the first Test and it was essential that Farokh Engineer should strike batting form before we took on England. Unfortunately, against Surrey he failed again, rushing out to Intikhab and was stumped. I got my second century (136) of the tour, playing for the most part with one hand, particularly the seamers, as a ball from Jackman had hit me on the right thumb early on. It was a beautiful wicket and Ajit Wadekar showed his appreciation by banging ten boundaries in his score of 57.

Surrey were skittled out for 85 by Abid Ali, who took 6 wickets for 23 runs. On such a beautiful batting track it was great bowling by Abid, who kept the ball up, moving it both ways and had everybody in trouble. Following on, Surrey did a little better in the second innings scoring 265, Roope (64) and Intikhab Alam (56) being the main scorers. Intikhab Alam used the long handle effectively, while Roope played a patient innings. Farokh Engineer, who opened with Naik, slammed 32 out of the 37 runs needed for victory. We had finally won a match after ten drawn games.

During the Surrey match I had strained a thigh muscle badly and had not fielded in Surrey's second innings. The muscle was not responding to treatment and I had to drop out of the next game against Derbyshire, which was to be our last County fixture before the first Test.

Abid, continuing to maintain good form, bowled Lawrence Rowe first ball, and went on to take five wickets. Only Brian

Bolus, who played as many balls with his pads as with the bat, survived. He scored a century. Farokh at last got into form with a bustling century, and Ashok Mankad played a patient innings for his 66 not out. Bolus left us 155 minutes to score 197 runs to win. With Naik playing strokefully and Engineer treating the seamers with scant respect, we won the match at the cost of only two wickets. Naik with 76, and Engineer with 55, remained unbeaten.

With two victories under our belt and centuries from all our recognised batsmen, we went into the first Test with confidence. Our bowlers had also bowled well in adverse conditions. There was only one major problem and that was Ajit Wadekar's fractured finger. He had broken it while fielding in the Surrey match. I passed the fitness test on the morning of the Test and Ajit, too, decided to play. He did not, however, field in his customary position at first slip.

The Old Trafford wicket of Manchester looked green, so much so, that it could not be distinguished from the rest of the field. And, it was cold, really cold. Mike Denness won the toss and elected to bat. It was so cold and we were swathed in four sweaters each. Boycott and Amiss began confidently. Abid opened with a wayward over, but then settled down to bowl a good length. Soon we had to turn off the field as it started raining. After the interval, Abid brought one back to trap Boycott leg-before for 10. The decision was given after due deliberation, but there was no doubt about its correctness. Edrich was bowled round his legs by Abid, and Denness was bowled off Bishen's faster delivery. During the tour Bishen had practised this delivery and he got plenty of wickets trapping the batsmen either leg-before, or bowling them as they expected the slower, flighted delivery.

Abid was bowling superbly and he brought one back off the seam to trap Fletcher on his back-foot. Our appeal was,

however, negatived by the same umpire who had given Boycott out to an identical delivery. Boycott had been hit on
the front foot as he shuffled across, but Fletcher was on his
back-foot, and he was perhaps more palpably leg-before
wicket than Boycott. May be, the umpire didn't like Boycott
very much! Dennis Amiss, who had survived three chances,
got his 50 and then pulled Chandrasekhar straight to Madan
Lal at square-leg. Underwood came in as night-watchman
and survived the last few overs.

The next day Fletcher went on his methodical way, unlea-
shing all of a sudden a slashing cover-drive. Greig came and
attacked the bowling straightaway. By this time, the weather
was really turning bad and our spinners could hardly grip
the ball in the cold. Chandrasekhar was constantly blowing
into his palms to warm them up. In the slips we stood with
our hands in our pockets till the last possible second when
the ball would be delivered. There wasn't a fielder whose
nose wasn't running. Fletcher and Greig, taking advantage of
the situation, added 103 runs for the sixth wicket. Greig eventually fell trying to force the pace, to give Madan Lal his
first Test wicket. Two balls later, Madan Lal trapped Knott
leg-before. Fletcher reached his century in the company of
Bob Willis, who pushed his front foot down the wicket to
smother the spin. Denness declared at 328, giving us half
an hour's batting before the close.

That season there was a new provision in the playing conditions for the series. If more than an hour's play was lost it
would be made up by playing after 6.30. So we had to play
till 7.30. Bob Willis worked up a good pace and Hendrick
bowled well. Hendrick got a wicket with his second ball
when he had Solkar taken low down by Willis in the gully.
Venkataraghavan, who had come in as night-watchman,
was yorked by Willis, and at that stage play ended for the
day with India on 26 for 2.

Rain delayed the start the next day till half an hour before lunch and we lost Ajit Wadekar during that time. Driving at a ball leaving him he was caught by Hendrick, off Chris Old. Vishwanath joined me looking like a round, white ball wearing three sweaters. Right from the start he was meeting the ball in the middle of the bat, and a square-drive by him rocked the fence at point, in spite of the heavy outfield. After lunch we carried on cautiously and Underwood, brought on to relieve the fast bowlers, got a wicket. He made a ball turn almost at right angles, and knocked out Vishwanath's off-stump. It was a ball which could have got anybody out and it was Vishwanath's bad luck to get it. This was like a shot in the arm for the England bowlers, coming just when the initiative was slipping away from them. Patel opened his Test career, driving a four to mid-on; but he fell to Willis who was brought on after Vishwanath's dismissal. I was doubtful if the ball had carried to Knott, who was standing behind, but Brijesh walked without waiting for the umpire's verdict. Farokh Engineer came in to a grand ovation from his 'home' crowd, who expected fireworks from him. He, however, disappointed them, being yorked by Willis for a 'duck'. First ball after tea, Hendrick bowled Madan Lal, when his off and leg stumps were knocked down, but the middle stump remained standing. Abid, who came in to take his place, made his intentions quite clear as he started attacking the bowling with great gusto. When Greig came on to bowl his off-spinners he was carved to mid-wicket twice in succession. As I neared my first Test century in England, Abid got his fifty. Abid is a very fast runner between wickets. He loves to take singles from under the very noses of the fielders, but gets carried away by this and so is a poor judge of a run. What he doesn't take into account is that the other man may be a slow runner. We, however, struck a good understanding and took many singles by just tapping the ball away.

When I was on 97 the umpire wanted to know if we wanted to go in as the light was getting bad. I didn't want to, because both of us were right on top of the bowling and there was no sense giving a respite to the England bowlers. So, we opted to carry on much to the delight of the crowd, which was loving the fight we were putting up.

I got my century off a ball from Underwood, which I lost sight of as it left his hand. I only saw it at the last minute pitching short outside the off-stump. I cut it away past Willis for three to get my century. It was a great moment and very satisfying to get a century in those difficult circumstances. I was engulfed by a large number of Indian spectators who swarmed on to the field. One of them put his scarf around my neck and, if Mike Denness had not put his hand through, I may have been strangled. My elation had turned to shock. Abid came and drove the intruders away.

Bob Willis was brought on by Denness in the fading light, but I was destined to be run-out. After Abid hit the ball a little wide off Denness, we hesitated a fraction of second before taking the run. Denness, who is an outstanding fielder, hit the stump directly, with myself just failing to make the crease. Abid carried on, shielding Chandrasekhar from the bowlers, and was last out for a rousing 71. It was a knock which put hope into our hearts again. Abid had not only shown defiance, but also rattled the England players with his attacking batting.

This Test saw a unique record created. I normally don't wear a cap while batting, and even on this windy day, I wasn't wearing one. The breeze often blew my hair over my left eye, obstructing my vision somewhat as the bowler delivered the ball. Instead of asking for a cap, I asked umpire Dickie Bird if he had a pair of scissors with him. Dickie replied that he had a razor blade and I requested him to cut off the offending locks of hair. He was taken aback at first, but then cheerfully did the job muttering, "What things the umpire has to do these days". Keith Fletcher who passed by during the hair-cutting operation, remarked to Dickie Bird that, what he needed was not a pair of scissors, but a pair of shears. Keith was no doubt influenced by my thick curly hair, which over the years had thinned considerably. I have taken to wearing a cap now while batting and the 'hairy' problem is no more there. I am happy to hold this unique record of a hair-cut in the midst of a Test match, and that in the middle!

It was England's turn to bat out the last hour and Solkar got Geoff Boycott's wicket again, caught brilliantly by Engineer. It was amazing to see Boycott 'fish' outside for such an innocuous ball. Make no mistake, Boycott is a great player. Only that morning at the nets he had shown his ability, tackling Willis and Co. who were outstepping the mark and really letting the ball go. He played them all with time to spare and once contemptuously called to Willis not to bowl spinners.

However, Amiss and Edrich thwarted our spinners. There was no purchase from the wicket. The rain also saw to it that our bowlers never got a good grip on the ball. Edrich, particularly, played some lovely shots. Two of them, both lofted ones, stand out in my memory. A ferocious square-cut, off Abid, rammed into the fence. Amiss was eventually out to a beautiful piece of bowling. Bedi brought him forward twice and had him groping for the ball as it turned away from the bat. Before he bowled the next one, I was asked to move from mid-off to first slip. The next ball was a beautifully flighted delivery. It pitched on the middle-stump, lifted a bit as it turned and off the shoulder of Amiss's bat, the ball curled to me for an easy catch. Venkataraghavan, who had been fielding at slip all this while and had just moved to gully so that I could take up my position at first slip, turned around and said, "I field here all morning and nothing comes and you turn up for one ball and end up with a catch."

Denness came in and pushed the score along in order to declare. Edrich was exactly 100 when bad light stopped play. It was a grand comeback by John Edrich, who was playing a Test after two years. Denness declared first thing next morning. No doubt, he wanted more runs behind him, but the previous evening's rain had upset his plans. It was a decision which showed his boldness. He gave his bowlers a whole day to get us out. At the same time we needed just two good partnerships to win the match.

Solkar started by sending Willis' first ball for a six over deep fine-leg. Both of us were going on well when Derek Underwood got Solkar out to a brilliant catch by Hendrick, who had to dive to his left to take it. Ajit was never very comfortable due to his fractured finger. He tended to slice his drives and, in trying to cut Greig, was caught behind by Knott.

Vishwanath and I were then concerned in a fruitful partnership. I was past my 50 when a ball from Old stood up and lobbed off my bat gently to Hendrick in the gully. I was batting well and had hoped to get a few more runs. Vishwanath cut and flicked his way to 60, before he was declared caught behind as the ball flicked his shirt-sleeve. That was the beginning of the end. Abid was caught by Boycott, who ran a good twenty yards for the catch, and Engineer fell to Hendrick. We were all out for 182, leaving England winners by 113 runs.

We could have saved the match, because we lost the game only in the 13th of the 20 mandatory overs. Abid and Farokh played totally irresponsible shots when the situation cried out for watchfulness. It was a good win for England, but to a large extent we had made their task easy.

We next played at Oxford, against the Combined Universities, and won an exciting victory in the last over of the match. The outstanding performance of the match came from the Pakistani cricketer Imran Khan. He got a brilliant century in the Universities first innings, in addition to taking four wickets. In the second, he led the counter-attack, which put them in a winning position, but after his dismissal, there was a collapse and we won. On our side, good performances came from Solkar and Sudhir Naik, both of whom got centuries in the second innings. Bose batted well in both the innings and so did Mankad. Bose had a good match, taking four wickets in the first innings with his off-spinners.

We continued our successful run against the Counties by beating Gloucestershire by five wickets. Nicholls and Stovold added 95 runs for the first wicket with Stovold as the dominant partner. Mike Procter failed in the first innings, being bowled by a Chandrasekhar googly. The wicket was not of much help to the South African Mike Procter as he came bounding in and bowled off the wrong foot. He bowls sharp in-swingers and, for variety, goes round the wicket. The odd ball that goes straight through often yields a snick. That is how he got my wicket when I was 61. Abid was 54 not out to boost our score to 281, before Ajit declared the innings.

Procter batted well in the second innings, hitting two huge sixes off Bedi in his 51. Set to score 195 runs to win, Naik and I put on 58 runs before I was declared caught by Knight, when the ball actually hit my foot as I danced down to off-spinner Graveney. Naik also played well, including an unforgettable shot, when he crashed a Procter bouncer through the covers. Ajit Wadekar made the issue safe for us, with a commanding 76. Just as in the first Test, we were going to the second Test with two successive victories.

Ajit Wadekar lost the toss which wasn't unexpected, Dennis Amiss and David Lloyd, making his Test debut, put on 116 runs before Solkar dived in front of him to catch Lloyd off Prasanna for 46. That was the only wicket to fall that

day, as Amiss and Edrich plundered runs on a beautiful
track. Amiss played some great shots. His cover-drive was
magnificent and he was 187 at the end of the day's play,
with Edrich on 96. Erapalli Prasanna struck a big blow for
us when he got Amiss leg-before for 188 and, from the other
end, Bedi dealt similarly with Edrich, who missed his century
by only four runs. His impetuosity got him out as he tried
to pull a ball which was not short enough for the shot. Fletcher, the first Test 'centurion', fell to Bedi, but that was the
end of our success for a long time. Mike Denness and Tony
Greig scored centuries and added 202 runs. Denness walked
down the track often to play the spinners, whereas Greig,
with his height, did not need to do so. During the Amiss-
Edrich partnership of 221 runs we had lost the services of
our trump card, Chandrasekhar, who injured his thumb trying to stop a hard drive from Amiss, when he was just beginning
to bowl well.

Funnily, during the massive Denness-Greig partnership,
Bedi continued to flight the ball unnecessarily. The batsmen
either stepped out and drove him or lay back and cut and
pulled him. Ajit should have taken him off but he persisted with him and the batsmen made merry. Bishen has said
that he will not stop giving the ball air, just because the
batsmen are attacking. However, the situation was such
that he should have bowled tight. There was no question of
buying the wickets, and England were all out for 629, leaving
us an hour's batting.

Farokh, who had kept wicket all through the innings,
opened with me and typically went on the attack. The way
he batted in that last hour gave the impression that he wanted to score those 630 runs in an hour. To the crowd it was
thrilling. To me it was horrifying. We survived the hour
and were 51 without loss at the end of the day.

The next day Farokh reached his 50 in a flash. He was

batting responsibly this time, though still playing his shots. I reached 49 and then was frustrated when Farokh refused easy singles thrice in an over. When Farokh is at the non-striker's end a quick single is out of the question. Even after the bowler has delivered the ball he is near the stumps and does not bother to back up a few yards down the wicket. For a cricketer who plays limited-overs cricket in England regularly, this is an unpardonable habit. When he is batting, he is always looking for quick singles, but when he is at the non-strikers end his attitude is one of indifference and inertia.

In my frustration, I tried to turn a ball from Old down to third man, but the ball moved a fraction and I succeeded only in edging it to Knott. I was out for 49 and our partnership had yielded 131 runs. Farokh carried on, driving and pulling the England bowlers but at 86 played too soon at Old and gave Denness at cover an easy catch. Vishwanath scored 52 and Solkar 43. The rest didn't offer much resistance and we were all out for 302. Chandrasekhar, despite his injured thumb, went in to bat, which was quite unnecessary. There was no question of avoiding the follow-on. We were only exposing our main bowler to the risk of further injury. In the one over possible after being asked to follow on we were two for no loss.

The next day we were entertained to lunch by the Lalvani brothers who are great cricket fans and always entertain visiting Indian teams and present them with wonderful souvenirs. They came to England when they were very young and are extremely successful businessmen and are highly respected in London. During the lunch, which the whole team attended, the topic was only whether we could avoid an innings defeat and force a draw. There were still two more days of play left and a draw would have been a great achievement. All this speculation was fruitless, as the events of the next day were to prove.

Arnold started with two huge out-swingers, followed by an in-swinger which hit Engineer on the pads as he played forward. Farokh stands a fair bit outside the batting crease and then he had stretched forward, so it must have required tremendous eyesight to give him out. Later Farokh claimed that he had even got a faint edge. Wadekar was bowled by Old and Vishwanath was out to a beauty which Knott snapped up in front of first slip. Patel got one which lifted and brushed his glove on its way to the wicket-keeper. Eknath received a bouncer from Old, which he tried to hook, but which bounced off his head. He hit the next bouncer over the deep fine-leg boundary for a six. At the end of the over, Solkar came down the wicket to ask me to stay and help him save the game. That was not to be as I was leg-before to an Arnold break-back. By the time I had removed my leg-guards, Madan and Abid had joined me in the pavilion. And, before you knew it, we were all out for 42. England had won the Test by an innings and 285 runs, and with that the series.

Lots of theories have been advanced about our being skittled out for a paltry 42 runs, when on that same wicket England made 629 and India 302 runs. The simple answer is that Arnold and Old bowled five good balls which got our top five batsmen out. After that there was no resistance from the tail-enders. We were skittled out before lunch, and champagne was flowing in the English dressing room to celebrate England's victory in the series.

The day after the Test we were supposed to attend the Indian High Commissioner's party. We were also invited to a party to bid farewell to the State Bank of India's London manager and to welcome his successor. Our team consisted of at least eight players who were employed in the State Bank and so we accepted the invitation to the Bank's function, which we were supposed to attend from 5.45 to 6.15 p.m. and then go on to the High Commissioner's party. As we came down the elevator to gather in the hotel lounge before leaving, we saw our Manager, Lt. Col. Adhikari, talking worriedly over the telephone. His conversation went on for about half an hour. We had no idea of the reason for his agitated look and the numerous telephone calls he made then. Finally, instead of leaving at 5 o'clock we started for the Bank function at about 5.40 and reached the function around 6. But, before we left the coach, we were told to stay at the function only for ten minutes and leave for the High Commissioner's party.

At the Bank function a few London-based Indian journalists came to ask us the reasons for being out for 42 runs. When we explained that it was a game they turned round and accused us of having had fights amongst us, and of being drunk and various other misdemeanours. A few players ignored these accusations, but others gave a verbal lashing to the journalists. I was watching all this quietly. I heard two of the journalists say, "We'll see that these chaps are brought down. What do they think of themselves?" As we were leaving the Bank function there was the usual cluster for group photographs and this went on for about ten minutes. The resident Indian journalists also couldn't resist the temptation of being photographed with the cricketers.

By the time we got into the bus it was already 6.30, the time we were expected to be present at the High Commissioner's party. Fortunately, the Manager and Treasurer, Mr. B.C. Mohanty, had gone there earlier to explain to the High Commissioner that we would be a few minutes late. Normally the distance between the venue of the Bank function and the High Commissioner's residence takes about 15 to 20 minutes by car. Our coach got delayed in the traffic and we reached the entrance of the Kensington Gardens around 7 p.m. The entrance was too narrow for the big coach to go in and all of us had to get off and rush past a few houses until we came to the High Commissioner's residence. Ajit, Venkataraghavan and Farokh had rushed in, while Vishwanath and I were, as usual, last in the line. When Ajit had gone in we were still in the driveway of the house. By the time we reached the porch, Ajit was returning, crestfallen and looking grim. When we asked what the matter was, Ajit replied, "He has asked us to get out." We realised that Ajit was referring to the High Commissioner, so we all trooped back to the coach which was waiting outside. I will never forget the look of astonishment on the face of Derek Allen, our coach driver, who said : "Don't tell me it's the bloody wrong address!"

There was a lot of excited conversation going on, with everybody wanting to talk at the same time. It was in the coach that I learnt what had really happened. Some of the boys said that we should not go in for the party. By this time Lt. Col. Hemu Adhikari had rushed into the coach and was exhorting the boys to return to the party. Some of the senior players tried to explain that since the host had asked us to 'get out', there was no question of our going back. The others felt that since the captain had been insulted, nobody should go back. All this while, Ajit sat around calmly smoking a cigarette. Meanwhile, somebody from the High Commission came and said that the High Commissioner was sorry and had requested the boys to come back. None of us was however in the mood to comply. Lt. Col. Adhikari was in tears and he resorted to 'ordering' the players to go back to the party. Still, no one budged. Finally, it was Venkataraghavan who said that we should go back to the party. After a few minutes everybody got up and went back. The High Commissioner embraced Ajit and apologised to him for losing his temper. This time I was among the first to get in, because I didn't want to miss this part, as I had missed the beginning. The resident Indian journalists were straining their ears near the High Commissioner to hear what he was saying to Ajit.

Donald Carr and Tony Lewis were also at the party and the boys spoke to them more than the others around. Though very few accepted the snacks that were being served, most of us accepted something to drink. The incident was another opportunity for the Indian journalist 'friends' to pass comments. They sent back reports that we had insulted the High Commissioner, and refused to take any drinks and refreshments served at the party. I suppose, having to stay in London, they couldn't afford to write against the High Commissioner. Also, the fact that they had been snubbed by some of the players barely half an hour ago was too fresh in their minds. And, hence the vengeful tirade against the Indian team.

I really wonder how we could have insulted the High Commissioner. True, we were late by about 40 minutes and for that deserved a rocket, whatever the reasons for our delayed arrival. As a matter of fact, Ajit's first words to the High Commissioner were, "We are sorry for being late." And, how can one stay at a party where the host himself asks us to get out? The High Commissioner could have given us a ticking off later on. After all, in his position he has to tackle so many problems, that he ought to be able to keep cool, whatever the circumstances. Actually his blowing up came as a surprise because, when he had visited us during the Manchester Test, he looked extremely mild and keen on cricket. As for the accusation that we didn't accept the drinks or snacks, it is a blatant lie. I know for a fact that almost everybody accepted a drink. A lot of the boys left the party later without sipping the drinks, but the newspaper reports said that the entire team had refused refreshments.

Poor Bishen Bedi was reported to have said uncomplimentary things about the High Commissioner in the coach, while all Bishen said was that, "If we had won, even if we had turned up late there would have been no problem. But, just because we've lost, we get the stick." All said and done, it was a sad affair and got a lot of unhealthy publicity. Later on, the players agreed that the High Commissioner was after all human and so blew his top. When we met him at another function later he was his usual jovial self and there was no tension at all between him and us.

What we didn't understand was why the manager kept on telephoning, in spite of knowing that it was delaying our departure for the two functions. The mystery was solved the following day. We were due to play the Indian Gymkhana in a one-day friendly game which was unfortunately washed out. During the lunch interval Lt. Col. Adhikari called us solemnly and announced that Sudhir Naik had been accused of shop lifting and he had made efforts to hush up the matter, but it had still unfortunately appeared in the evening newspapers. That was the reason why he had delayed the coach's departure for the State Bank function and the High Commissioner's reception, while he spoke to the various authorities on the telephone.

This came to us as a bolt from the blue and suddenly the reason for Sudhir's absence at the previous evening's function became clear. Some of the boys insisted that he should be sent back to India. Yet, others, like myself, wanted to hear his story and then decide what to do. In any case, the manager had spoken to the Cricket Control Board authorities in India and was going to be told the course of action to follow.

I have known Sudhir Naik ever since we played against each other in shorts in tennis ball 'tournaments' between teams of young boys living in the different blocks of buildings in our locality in Bombay. I was shocked and was positive that this was all a mistake. I didn't ask him at all about what had happened but later he told me his story, and I had no doubt in my mind that he was innocent.

He had gone out shopping on that fateful afternoon in London, while a few of us had gone to see a movie. Some of the players had given money to buy some underwear, toilet goods and other things. Before he had gone to the Marks and Spencer Department Store on Oxford Street, he had bought two pairs of slacks from a Boutique, and was carrying them in a paper bag with a handle. From there he went to the Department Store and selected about 20 pairs of socks, put these into the paper bag and moved on to the counter to the sales girl to pay for the socks which he gave to the girl to pack for him. Suddenly he remembered that four of the players had asked him to buy underwears for them. He went to another counter to buy these items, where the sales girl put his purchases in a paper bag and gave it to him. Now, Marks and Spencer don't give paper bags with handles and Sudhir had to hold it in his other free hand, when he went back to the socks counter to pay for them and take delivery of the socks. Since he couldn't possibly hold it in both his hands, he requested the sales girl to put the parcel of socks in the paper bag. While doing this, the sales girl noticed a pair of socks under the slacks he had purchased from the Boutique. Sudhir told me that when he took the socks from the shelf he had put all of them in the bag along with the slacks, and had taken them out to put them on the cash counter when he went to pay for the socks. In doing this two pairs of socks had apparently slipped under the pair of trousers and was overlooked by him. It was this pair which he was accused of having 'stolen'.

In any case, it is difficult to believe that a man can pay for 20 pairs of socks and not pay for two pairs. The Department Store authorities were adamant and wouldn't listen to his explanation. It was at this stage that Sudhir was given, what I think, a bit of wrong advice. He was asked to plead guilty before the Magistrate on the assurance that the case would be over, and due care would be taken to ensure that the matter received no publicity at all. If he pleaded 'not guilty', the case would go on and who would bear the expenses ? The attitude of those concerned should have been, "to hell with the expenses, we'll go ahead and get our man a good lawyer for his defence". But then Sudhir was not given a chance even to think and he was hustled to plead guilty and in the process got a black mark, which will be difficult to erase. In cases like this, the contracts which the player signs with the Cricket Control Board to keep 'mum' is a severe handicap. There was thus no way in which Sudhir could explain the true facts through the Press, though the newspapermen were very sympathetic. The result of this was that he was not able to clear doubts in the minds of people in England and at home.

I asked Lt. Col. Adhikari to let me allow Sudhir to share my room for the rest of the tour. Col. Adhikari agreed, even though the practice was not to have players from the same State sharing a room. But in this case he made an exception. I intercepted a number of anonymous telephone calls to Sudhir, obviously from people who were out to 'give him hell'. Sudhir confessed later that because of the stigma attached to his name, even though it was entirely wrong, made him contemplate taking his own life. But, when he saw on Television the former U.S. President, Richard Nixon, cheerfully waving after the Watergate scandal, he thought to himself, "If this man can take so much, why can't I? Particularly because I know that I am innocent."

It speaks volumes for Sudhir's concentration and determination that he got runs after this traumatic experience. In the game against Nottinghamshire he got 73 and 68, Vishwanath scored a century, and Mankad and Abid batted well. His consistency earned Sudhir Naik a Test 'cap', and Mankad was brought into the side in place of Brijesh Patel to bolster the middle-order batting for the third and last Test of the series at Edgbaston (Birmingham).

Ajit won the toss and elected to bat. However, rain washed out play on the first day, but when the game got going it began disastrously for India. Geoff Arnold's first ball to me pitched outside the off-stump and cut back in sharply. I tried to withdraw my bat, but the ball seemed to be drawn by a magnet, hit my gloves and went to wicket-keeper Knott. For the first time I was out to the first ball in a Test match and also found a 'duck' against my name for the second time in a Test! It was an extremely disappointing way to get out.

Farokh was the only one who offered some resistance, and was 64 not out in our score of 165. Any team that bats for less than three hours doesn't deserve any piece of luck, so was our case.

Amiss and David Lloyd ground us down before Amiss played what appeared to be an uncharacteristic uppish drive to be caught for 79. David Lloyd and Mike Denness then rubbed the salt in with a vengeance. Lloyd remained unbeaten with 214, Denness and later Fletcher also contributed handsomely. David Lloyd swept and drove well while Denness played elegant shots off the front-foot.

I was on a 'king pair' when we had to follow on 204 runs behind England. However, I met the first ball in the second innings bang in the middle of the bat, which was reassuring. I pushed one to cover and got off the mark. It was a tremendous relief. I was, however, not destined to stay long. A ball from Chris Old moved sharply away, nicked my bat and, of course, it was useless hoping for that Knott would drop such a simple catch. And he didn't. I had scored four runs, three runs short of the 1,000 runs on the tour mark. I cursed my luck because this was the last first-class match of the tour, and I would never make it. How unlucky, you can be!

Sudhir Naik played well after an uncertain start and so did Ashok Mankad. They added 87 runs for the fifth wicket, out of which Sudhir got 77, before he was surprisingly given out leg-before. Engineer scored a defiant 33, but it was hopeless and we lost by an innings and 76 runs, to lose the three-match series 3-0.

When I was out first ball, I had gone without looking at Bill Alley, the former Australian cricketer, who was making his debut as a Test umpire. Later on, he came and jokingly scolded me for walking. "My first Test, my first decision off the first ball, and you don't give me the opportunity to raise my finger. You walk!" He also had the distinction of giving a decision off the last ball of the Test, when he declared Farokh Engineer out leg-before.

It was a totally disastrous series and the tour was one of the worst I had made. There was no such thing as "team spirit". Instead there were a lot of petty squabbles, which didn't do anybody any good. The incidents which gave the team such a bad name didn't help. It was all extremely frustrating.

We had still to play two one-day 'International' matches. In the first we scored a record 275, which England overtook losing only seven wickets. Ajit and Brijesh Patel scored fluently, after Naik and I had put on 44 runs in the first seven overs. John Edrich led the England chase with 70 runs, but his innings was nowhere as good as Brijesh's; yet, he was given the 'Man of the Match' award. In the next game we were beaten by 6 wickets, with Fletcher getting the 'Man of the Match' award.

These defeats completed our tale of woes. There were reports from Bombay that Ajit's 'home' had been stoned. This was difficult to believe as Ajit lives in an apartment on the top floor of a high building. But we were really concerned and unhappy when we learnt that the concrete bat erected in Indore following our victories in the West Indies and England in 1971 had been defaced. We sensed that the mood of the people back home would be ugly. We had left for the tour with high hopes, and cricket-lovers in the country were expecting us to do well. Fortunately nothing untoward happened on our return and we were received well by a small number of people.

15

Again the Windies

The West Indies were due to tour India in the 1974-75 season and everybody was keen to have a couple of months' rest before beginning to train and get fit for the series. I had to delay this process because I was getting ready for one of the most important events of my life. On September 23, 1974, Marshniel Mehrotra became Mrs. Sunil Gavaskar and overnight I was well and properly 'hooked'. Meanwhile, Bombay began the quest to regain the Ranji Trophy with a match against Saurashtra at Porbandar. I told the Bombay Cricket Association that I would be unavailable for the quarter-finals of the Duleep Trophy.

Unknown to me a lot of dramatic events took place during my week-long honeymoon. Firstly, Ajit Wadekar was dropped from the West Zone team for the Duleep Trophy. The reason given for this apparently was that he was not in form and didn't deserve a place. Imagine an India captain only six weeks before the new season began being dropped from the Zonal side. One could understand the decision to strip him off his captaincy, but to drop him from the side altogether was ridiculous. Ajit was among the two top batsmen in the country then, the other being Vishwanath. Understandably this was a blow to Ajit and to avoid further embarrassment he announced his retirement from first-class cricket and earned a 'benefit' match. Actually, he had been in correspondence with the West Indies Cricket Board since 1973 for a 'benefit' match. The 1971

team to the West Indies, led by Ajit, was a very popular one
and the Windies Board agreed to play two one-day fixtures for
Ajit Wadekar's benefit.

The mantle of captaincy for the West Zone team for the
Duleep Trophy matches fell on Ashok Mankad. We won the
quarter-final against East Zone by virtue of the first innings
lead. I played my first match of the season in the semi-finals
of the Duleep Trophy against Central Zone at Nagpur. In a
low-scoring match we won by 64 runs and earned the right to
clash with South Zone at Hyderabad.

The South Zone team is an extremely well-balanced side
and one has to play twice as well to beat them. In this case,
on a spongy wicket, Chandrasekhar, Venkataraghavan and
Prasanna ran through our batting. By the time South's turn to
bat came the wicket had improved considerably. The story was
repeated in our second innings and Venkataraghavan once
again won the Duleep Trophy for South Zone.

For two seasons I had been Wadekar's deputy for Bombay
and I naturally expected to be asked to lead the side after Ajit
announced his retirement. Imagine my shock when I learnt
that I had been passed over by the same Selection Committee
which had only a month ago appointed me vice-captain
for the season. Ajit retired after playing only one game and,
when the Selection Committee met, the Chairman's casting
vote put me out after there was a stalemate between the four
selectors. It was hard for me to understand the logic of this
decision, especially after I had led Bombay to outright victories,
admittedly against comparatively weaker teams.

Captaining a Bombay side is one of the easiest things in the
world. Everybody knows exactly what he is expected to do.
Besides, the camaraderie that exists between the players has to
be seen to be believed. Yes, there are occasions when the
team is in trouble, but these instances when the captain has to

really face problems are pretty rare. More important, most of the members of the team are captains of their respective Club sides, and there is no lack of experienced players to give advice when the occasion arises.

Thinking back now, my disappointment was mainly due to the fact that I had been appointed vice-captain earlier. Of course, there have been numerous occasions when the vice-captain had been bypassed for another player. Ashok, who got the job, was more senior to me and had longer experience as a captain. I am sure he must have been disappointed when I was appointed Ajit's deputy in the first place. I have always believed that the team comes first and I did not allow my personal feelings to interfere with my batting. The important thing was to see that Bombay regained the Ranji Trophy, which we had lost the previous year after winning it for 15 years.

The West Indies team came to India with an awesome reputation. Leading them was Clive Lloyd, who had with him Andy Roberts, the fastest bowler in the world then. The visitors opened their tour with a game against West Zone at Pune. Though they lost Fredericks first ball, Lloyd, Richards and Greenidge showed their appreciation of the wicket by scoring plenty of runs. Richards got a century (102 not out), while Lloyd missed his by only four runs. However, the start was electrifying. Fredericks was surprised by Salgaonkar's pace and the West Indies opener fell to a gloved catch to me at second slip. Then, Rowe was also deceived by Ghavri's pace and fell on his wicket trying to hook. Both the batsmen were out before scoring. Greenidge showed his aggression by hitting Salgaonkar for three boundaries, but when Ghavri pitched one short he skied a hook to square-leg where Solkar, running from leg-slip, failed to take the catch. He went on to score 66. We had just half an hour's batting and Andy Roberts showed his pace in his four overs. Naik, however, drove his way to 22 runs.

Next day I found the ball going sweetly off the bat. When

Roberts pitched short, I hooked him for a six. This shot went almost parallel to the ground, hit the cement wall and rebounded back half way on to the ground. It was a great thrill, for everything I did clicked, right from my footwork to the timing of the shots. When Boyce bounced one at me, I was in position and again cleared the boundary, this time the ball just brushing Roberts' fingertips on the boundary. When the spinners came on, it was like butter which I love so much and, in trying to get this butter, I was run out when Naik cut the ball and called for a quick single.

Kanitkar carried on in his calm, unhurried way, while Naik played some polished shots. After Naik's dismissal, Ashok Mankad picked up the threads and scored 69. In the hope of making the match interesting Ashok declared 24 runs behind the West Indies, but there was no response from Lloyd and the Windies used the time for batting practice. Only when Naik who is not a regular bowler, came on to bowl that Lloyd declared, leaving us two hours' batting. My left thigh, which had been bruised by a scorcher from Roberts, prevented me from opening the innings, but Naik used the opportunity to score 68 not out after being dropped off the first ball he received. He displayed his ability to stand up to pace and score runs. It was an impressive innings.

There was a bombshell just before the Selectors met to name the team for the first Test. The President of the Board of Control asked the Selectors not to consider Bishen Singh Bedi for the first Test for disciplinary reasons. Bedi's offence was reportedly a Television appearance in England after our team had left. Let me say quite frankly that Bishen certainly wasn't on top of my popularity chart, as well as on a lot of his other team-mates on the 1974 tour. His behaviour towards the captain, to put it mildly, wasn't exactly respectful. Bishen was generally impatient and intolerant with the rest of the boys. Despite this, the Board President's action was shocking. Apparently Bishen had not replied to about 17 letters and cables sent to him to appear before the Inquiry Committee that had been set up. So, without waiting for Bishen's explanation, the President had asked the Selectors not to consider him for the first Test.

This was a big let-down for Indian cricket because there is no doubt that Bishen is the best left-arm spinner in the world today. To go into the first Test of the series against such a formidable team as the West Indies, without one of our ace bowlers, wasn't exactly a boost to the morale of the team. To top it all, Padmakar Shivalkar, who must be the second-best left-arm spinner in the world, was overlooked, and Rajinder Goel was selected. Year after year Shivalkar has been taking an average of 40 wickets in the Ranji Trophy and the only thing that stood between him and a Test Cap was the presence of Bishen Bedi. However, with Bishen Bedi out of reckoning, it was expected that Shivalkar would be selected. Despite this, we went into the Test with high hopes because the Bangalore wicket was not expected to be very helpful to the West Indies fast bowlers. On the eve of the match I was told by the Selectors that I was the vice-captain. But, for some reason, I was asked to keep the news confidential. This surprised me very much because I didn't understand why I should have been chosen vice-captain, if the matter was kept 'confidential'. I am afraid this cloak-and-dagger business did not make any sense to me.

At the introduction ceremony preceding the first day's play, too, I was asked to go down the line and not stand next to 'Tiger' Pataudi, the captain, as I should have done. This hurt me because I don't believe that a vice-captain has to stand next to the captain. Yet when in the bustle of the match I did so, I was asked to go elsewhere. Frankly, Vishwanath and I love standing last in the line for the introduction ritual. We've always done that. So even though Vishwanath knew I was the vice-captain he laughed when I came and stood next to him at the end of the line. With a grin he asked me, "Demoted?"

Yes, I was, just because there was nobody with the guts to say: "Right now, he's the vice-captain and he should stand next to the skipper". So, there I was.

Heavy overnight rain delayed the start of the Test until 22 minutes before lunch. Pataudi, back in the saddle after five years, won the toss, but asked the West Indies to bat. Solkar should have got a wicket in his first over, but Prasanna dropped Greenidge before he had opened his account. Fredericks retired hurt as he twisted his ankle in trying to pull a short one from Chandrasekhar. Kallicharran took his place and looked confident right from the start. Greenidge, however, had another 'life' when Prasanna dropped a hot return catch. Both the batsmen scored at run-a-minute and batted with complete freedom, until a misunderstanding between them caused Greenidge to be run out. I was fielding at short mid-on and anticipated the shot and was already starting for the ball. Seeing this Kallicharran refused to run but, expecting that the ball could still beat me, went on. Greenidge was not, however, ready and when he decided to make a dash for it, I had picked the the ball up and returned it to the bowler and Greenidge failed to make it. So the first wicket fell at 177 and Greenidge missed a century in his first Test innings by only seven runs. Richards was out soon afterwards, when he drove Chandrasekhar straight to Prasanna at mid-off, and this time Prasanna made no mistake. Lloyd and Kallicharran, however, carried the score to 212 for 2 at the end of the day.

Play began again after lunch on the second day, and Venkataraghavan and Chandrasekhar used the wicket splendidly to dismiss the West Indies for 289. Kallicharran 64 overnight added 60 runs out of a total of 77 runs scored. It was batting of the highest class and he fully deserved his century (124). With the ball turning and popping, Kallicharran gave an object-lesson in batting. The ball dropped dead at his feet when he played defensively forward. But when he hit the ball it invariably went to the boundary. A six off

Chandrasekhar showed his quick reflexes. He was preparing for a defensive shot when he heard the no-ball call from the umpire and he changed his shot to swing it over the mid-wicket fence.

With 75 minutes of batting left, we had to face Roberts on a damp wicket, which was not a pleasant proposition at all. I got two boundaries in his first over—a cover-drive and a hook to the vacant long-leg position. In his next over Roberts made a ball rise awkwardly, hitting me very painfully on the wrist. The numbness was acute and I was not able to flex the wrist again. Anyway, I wasn't very lucky. I flicked Holder hard, the ball hitting Richards on his thigh and bounced away, but Richards showed amazing reflexes and dived to his left to take a catch inches off the ground. The ball, after ricocheting off his thigh, was almost on the other side of the wicket. I couldn't believe my eyes when Richards came up with the ball. Instead of getting four runs I had lost my wicket! That was Richards' second catch. Earlier he had caught Engineer off Roberts at the same position. Hemant Kanitkar was making his Test debut and the first ball from Andy Roberts, which was a real scorcher, hit him bang on the gloves as he played defensively. To this day I wonder how nothing happened to his fingers. The blow was sickening even to me, at the non-striker's end, but Hemant carried on as if nothing had happened. He batted really bravely in his first Test innings, despite the punishment he received. When he came in, his chest was black and blue from bruises he had received. He also survived a run-out after being stranded at the same end with Vishwanath. How he beat the bowlers' throw to the wicket-keeper beats me. But he was there and when he returned to the pavilion his face was as expressionless as ever.

The next day Kanitkar added 89 runs with Vishwanath, who fell leg-before to Lance Gibbs for 29. Kanitkar was batting with 64 at lunch. But with the first ball after the interval Barrett had him stumped when Kanitkar went down the track to play

the bowler on the half-volley. Our middle-order batting caved
in after this, and only Abid with a bright 49, and Prasanna with
a cheeky 23, enabled us to end 29 runs short of the West
Indies total.

Murray opened with Greenidge and got a 'pair', being leg-
before to Abid. Greenidge and Kallicharran, however, were
equal to the task. Greenidge who hit Chandrasekhar for a huge
six out of the ground was the dominant partner. However,
Kallicharran and Richards fell in quick succession, but the turning point of the game came when Lloyd pummelled his way to
a glorious 163. In spite of being an 'opponent', I couldn't but
admire the superb batting of the tall, gangling 'Super Cat' as he
swept and swung away merrily. Greenidge also got the century
he had missed in the first innings. During this partnership, we
lost Farokh Engineer, when he was hit above the eye by a
ball from Prasanna, which bounced unexpectedly. Boyce came
in with the intention of blasting our spinners but, in trying to
hit Venkataraghavan, he skied the ball to Pataudi who brought
off a good catch, but dislocated his ring finger and had to
leave the field.

I was fielding on the mid-wicket boundary at the time and
I was already rushing in to congratulate Venkataraghavan for
taking Boyce's wicket, when Pataudi left the field. The captain
did not say whether he was coming back immediately or not;
but I told Venkataraghavan that I was in-charge, and took
over the task of setting the field. At the end of the over,
Rajinder Goel came out to inform me that 'Tiger' would not
be returning immediately, and that I should take charge.
There were only a few minutes left before the tea-break. After
tea Lloyd was out to a superb catch by Eknath Solkar and
soon after the West Indies captain declared at 356 for six,
leaving us to make 386 runs in 390 minutes to win. When we
began our second knock I sparred at an out-swinger from
Boyce, snicked the ball to the wicket-keeper and was out for
a 'duck'. It was terrible that I should begin my career as Test

:ipper, even though a mere substitute, with 'duck'. Eknath olkar was also out to a rash shot. And our innings ended aree minutes before lunch with Engineer and Pataudi being nable to bat. Vishwanath and, to some extent, Brijesh Patel ffered some resistance. Holder and Roberts were the wreckers--chief. We lost the Test by 267 runs.

As Pataudi was unfit for the second Test I was appointed to ake his place. When the news came, I was too stunned to elieve it. Of course, I had ambitions of leading India, but I ever expected it then. Imagine me as captain! I was in a weet daze. Leading one's country, even if it was only for ne Test! I started preparing myself mentally for a Test kipper's job, which doesn't begin and end on the field. Since had to lead India at Delhi, the country's capital, I had a lot f homework to do.

Before the Test, however, Bombay were to play Maharashtra the Ranji Trophy Tournament at Nasik, but I was nly thinking of the Delhi match. Ismail started Maharashtra's lide in the first over itself, getting Chetan Chauhan caught ehind for zero. Maharashtra were 19 for 4, but a fighting entury by Yajuvendra Singh and a good knock by Vithal oshi took them to 222. We had about 80 minutes batting left efore the close and Pandurang Salgaonkar and Anwar haikh bowled some hostile overs. Salgaonkar bowled real uick, making the ball get up from the matting wicket. His irection was not so good and he wasted a lot of his energy owling bouncers, which went too high to do any damage, hysical or psychological. Shaikh, on the other hand, bowled steady length trying to make the best use of the new ball. nwar was desperately unlucky not to get higher honours. Ie is a fine bowler who can not only bowl for long spells but ne who never gives up. A fighter to the core.

I was facing Salgaonkar most of the time and, in trying to

put down a ball just short of a length, I was hit on the glov
when it kicked. I knew instantly that I had broken a fing
and, as I crossed over for a single, I told the umpire
my injury. He wanted to know whether I wished to continu
and I said I wanted to, since there were only 40 minutes le
and Salgaonkar was likely to be encouraged if I retired.
held on till the end, playing with only one hand for most
the time. Luckily for me Madhu Gupte didn't bring on
spinner, which would have put me in a lot of trouble since
was playing with only one hand. The injury certainly wasn
Salgaonkar's fault. It was just my luck that my finger g
jammed between the handle and the ball. After the x'ray,
rang up the Secretary of the Cricket Control Board, who aske
me to come to Bombay immediately the next day. I didn
want to leave, because our position was not secure. The ne:
day Salgaonkar and Anwar didn't bowl half as well as on th
previous evening, but we lost three wickets in the morning an
slumped to 103 for 4. Solkar who batted, despite high feve
and Karsan Ghavri put on 156 runs for the sixth wicket ar
we had taken a first innings lead. With the match safe, I le
for Bombay the next morning.

My worst fears were confirmed when the doctors in Bomba
told me that I couldn't play for at least three weeks. Dr. Aru
Samsi was very sympathetic, but he ruled out my playing
the Delhi Test. I was a little put off because Dr. (Mrs.) Nadkar
in Nasik had diplomatically told me not to worry and sh
had not given me any idea of the nature of the injury. How
ever, they were very nice people and their prompt treatmen
and care helped to heal the injury very fast. But I had lo
a golden opportunity of leading the country in a Test.
decided, however, to go to Delhi to watch the match.
Delhi, I couldn't get hold of any official of the Delhi & Distri
Cricket Association, and, but for the fact that Sudhir Na
and Vishwanath obliged me with a ticket, I would have had 1
watch the match on T.V. When I did meet a senior offici
of the D.D.C.A. and told him of my predicament, he told m

You are famous, you don't need a complimentary ticket."
That was some consolation, even if I did not get a ticket!

Before I went to Calcutta for the next Test, I had a
work-out session at the nets. As I didn't feel too bad, I
went to Calcutta. There somehow I found that I couldn't even
hold the bat in comfort, and I had no alternative but to rule
myself out for the Calcutta Test too. During my three days'
stay in Calcutta I noticed a singular lack of interest in getting
my finger treated. Amalda, who was, however, most helpful
and turned up regularly, found that the doctors at the clinic
were also busy watching the Test. I decided to return to
Bombay for treatment instead of wasting my time in Calcutta.
I left on the second day of the Test and so missed seeing
Vishwanath's magnificent fighting century that put us on the
road to victory.

I went to Madras for the fourth Test full of hopes of being
fit for the Test. I had fielding practice on the first day and
there was no trouble with the finger. Next day, the first ball
I faced at the nets from Karsan Ghavri hit the same finger
sickeningly and it ended my chances of playing the Test
the next day. Within minutes the finger had swollen, even
more than the first time I was hurt at Nasik. Once again I
had to seek medical assistance and renewed my acquaintance
with Dr. Ahmed who had treated me when I fractured a thumb
playing against the M.C.C. at Madras. Then it was the
ointment he gave me which enabled me to play in the Kanpur
Test ten days later. And when I got runs there he sent me a
cable congratulating me for playing with the bat and not with the
thumb. Once again his calm, methodical manner helped me a
lot, as did the ointment. But I had missed three Tests. I did
not want to take any more chances, so I got a special rubber
padding put on the batting gloves and went to the nets. Fortunately, nothing happened at the nets, and I was in the team
for the Test at Bombay.

The Test was played at a new venue, the Wankhade Stadium, which had been constructed at an amazing speed and was ready in time for the big event. It was a magnificent sight when the curtain went up on the fifth Test in the New Year. The atmosphere was electric. If there is one crowd I positively love to play in front of, it's in Bombay. The average man in the home of cricket knows a lot more about the game than anywhere else in the country. This is especially true of the spectators in the North stands, occupied by Bombay's club cricketers who are always quick to appreciate and applaud a good game. For this reason, I lay great stress on the reactions of people in this particular part of the stands. Their praise or criticism is based on knowledge and experience of the game, which is of immense value to a cricketer. For the Bombay crowd good cricket is important and it does not matter whether it is from the home team or a visiting side. The applause will be there only for good cricket. At other places, there may be sections of people who will applaud only the home team, but they are a minority here. Bombay crowds are also noted for their sense of humour, which is not evident at other centres in India.

I was happy to be fit to play in the decisive Bombay Test. The series was level at this stage and the enthusiasm in the match was tremendous. Gerry Alexander, the West Indies Manager, lodged a protest on the eve of the Test, that the wicket was under-prepared and unfit for the Test. This was a serious allegation, but some people in Bombay, who were disappointed that the Brabourne Stadium was no longer the venue, were happy about the protest. I do not know how Gerry Alexander came to the conclusion about the wicket because 1,000 runs were scored after both sides had completed only one innings each.

Roy Fredericks set the tempo for the West Indies batting by blasting a century in under three hours. Unfortunately we had lost the services of Bedi within minutes of the start. Bishen had been troubled by a bad back and, though he said he was 'fit', he had to leave the field. However, when he returned, he was on the spot and got rid of Fredericks for 104. But he was not completely fit and it told on his bowling. Kallicharran made 98, before Vishwanath in the slips took a fine low catch off Ghavri. Lloyd, who was missed thrice, was unbeaten with 64 at the end of the day and the West Indies were 309 for 3.

In the first over of the next morning, Solkar let a ball slip through his fingers and Lloyd got another 'life'. Nobody could make much impression on the West Indies captain thereafter and he went on to score a double century. In the process he hit two huge sixes into the Garware Pavilion. When Clive reached his double century an enthusiastic fan chased by a lot of policemen ran on to the field to congratulate him. The policemen caught him and handled him pretty roughly. This was the signal for the crowd to voice their protest, and slogans were raised against the minions of the law. Soon tempers rose and good sense seemed to vanish, as the crowd started tearing up benches and the fence. A part of the stand was set on fire which, however, was quickly brought under control.

There is no doubt that the police action against the lone enthusiast had provoked this outburst. What I can't understand is why the policemen rushed on to the field in such large numbers to apprehend a solitary intruder. In any case, there was no way he could have escaped from the stadium. The police could have waited for his return just inside the boundary. Yes, if a large number of intruders had invaded the field then, I suppose, the police would have been justified to move in to disperse them. But, in this instance, it was wholly unnecessary.

The flare-up occurred during tea and there was no prospect of further play that day. Murray was not out with 91 and the next day his partnership with Lloyd was worth 250 runs. Lloyd remained unbeaten with 242 at the declaration, which came at 604 for 6.

Farokh Engineer was out for a 'duck' to Julien in the half hour before lunch, when we batted a second time. Thereafter, Eknath Solkar batted confidently to support me in a 168-run stand. I was out for 86, with just five minutes' play left. It was an innings that gave me great satisfaction, because I had my doubt whether I should have played in the Test at all, since I hadn't played first-class cricket for about two months after my injury. Surprisingly, I had fifteen fours in my innings. I got a bit bogged down after my 50 and suffered from cramps in my left forearm after tea. Still it was good to be among runs in Test cricket.

I don't look at the scoreboard when I am batting nor do I look at the time. However, I do have a general idea about my score. On this occasion I was misled by a shout from the stands, for a six and I thought that I was on 94. Being aware that there was time only for one or two overs and seeing the vacant space between extra-cover and point, I thought I had room to cut the ball through the gap, but missed and was bowled.

Eknath went on to score his first Test century the next day after giving all of us some terribly anxious moments in the 90s. Vishwanath was again among runs and was out when he was 95. With Anshuman Gaekwad unbeaten on 51, we were 373 for 6 wickets, needing 32 runs to avoid the follow-on. Anshuman went in the first over and 'Tiger' struggled, but Karsan Ghavri and Bishen Bedi avoided the follow-on and we were all out for 406.

With a lead of 198 runs the West Indies unleashed some super shots and thrilled the crowd. Lloyd, in particular, played a hurricane innings of 37 and Vivian Richards played some incredible shots to score 39 in 30 minutes before Lloyd declared at 205 for 3.

Our second innings started on a disastrous note with Farokh edging a ball on to his wicket to get a 'pair'. Andy Roberts, bowling at a furious pace, got one up off a length to get me caught off the shoulder of the bat for 18. Our biggest hope, Vishwanath, was bowled by a beauty from Holder, and at the close we were a hopeless 53 for 3.

Seventy-five minutes after lunch the next day the West Indies won the Test to clinch the rubber. Gaekwad again batted very stubbornly for 42 runs and Brijesh Patel scored a sparkling 73 not out. Apart from Holder's bowling the only thing of interest was a girl running up to Brijesh and, in spite of his best efforts to avoid her, planting a kiss on his cheek. Brijesh had a very interesting story to tell after that, but I won't mention it here because I do not want to deny him the pleasure of recounting his story if he ever writes his autobiography. The Windies also played two one-day games before leaving for Sri Lanka and Pakistan.

I now turned to concentrate on Bombay regaining the Ranji Trophy. With the finger troubling me again, I was never in form and struggled for runs until the final against Karnataka, to whom we had lost in the previous year.

Ashok Mankad and Ramnath Parker were in top form and Ashok especially was batting superbly. Before the final he had hit three successive centuries. Prasanna, who seems to have a knack of winning tosses, chose to bat on a wicket which looked a bit green. Karsan Ghavri worked up a lively pace and only Vishwanath was able to stand up to him with confidence. I have a sneaking suspicion that Vijay Kumar was testing my ability as a slip fielder. I had caught him in the slips in almost every match we had played. This time, instead of a snick, he tried to swing Ghavri away to leg, but only gloved the ball behind the wicket-keeper, and I had to run back a few steps to catch it. Vishwanath was out the next morning, without adding to his overnight score of 144. The ball had, however, gone off his thigh and was not an edge, though the umpire thought so. Karnataka's score of 240 didn't look impressive at all.

In the hour before lunch, we scored 52 without loss, but the last ball before lunch from Chandrasekhar was disastrous for me. It popped up from a length and struck me on the index finger which I had broken twice earlier in the season. That was enough to cause it to swell, but I was fortunate that, this time, I did not suffer a fracture even though the swelling was enormous and it was very painful.

I delayed going to the hospital and within an hour we lost four wickets for 129. And I walked out to bat again. Ashok Mankad came up and said he would try and keep the strike as much as possible, so that my injured thumb was not further damaged. But, at 147, he was out when he mistimed a pull and was caught at square-leg. Karsan Ghavri, who followed him, was most uncomfortable against Prasanna, but showed great determination to stay at the wicket. We added 97 runs, during which I was hit on the finger three times more, all by Chandrasekhar's googlies which were jumping off the pitch. But, both Prasanna and Chandrasekhar began to tire towards the end of the day, and we ended just five short of the Karnataka total. There were innumerable interruptions during the day's play, because after every boundary stroke the crowd invaded the field. This was most annoying as we required every bit of concentration against the guiles of Prasanna and Chandrasekhar.

The next day, though we lost Ghavri, Tandon and Bandiwadekar early, Abdul Ismail kept me company. Ismail has a most ungainly stance, but, like all bowlers, he hates to lose

his wicket and he stubbornly resisted Prasanna and Chandrasekhar. Once, after being rapped on the pads several times in one
over, he swung Prasanna over mid-on for a six. Prasanna and
Chandrasekhar, however, didn't have other bowlers to back
them up, while one of them rested. In sheer desperation,
Prasanna brought on Lakshminarayan, who got Ismail and
Shivalkar with his leg-spinners, leaving me stranded four short
of a century. Bombay were all out for 305.

When Karnataka batted again, Solkar, bowling his seamers,
got rid of Vishwanath with a ball that kept low, but Brijesh
Patel attacked the bowling with his usual gusto and reached 50
in as much time. At that score, Eknath Solkar, bowling spinners
this time, made one pop up and turn prodigiously and wicket-
keeper Bandiwadekar took an excellent catch to dismiss him.
The Karnataka batting collapsed and they were all out for 215.
Set to score 115 to win, Ashok and Ajit Pai added 98 runs for
their unbroken fourth wicket stand, to bring the Ranji Trophy
back to Bombay. Once again the Bombay team made a happy
picture holding aloft the Ranji Trophy. The new stadium at
Bangalore had brought luck to Karnataka the previous year
and with it the Ranji Trophy. The new stadium in Bombay
had been equally lucky for us, and the Ranji Trophy was back
with us for the 25th time in 40 years.

In six matches I had failed to score a century and this was
the second successive year that I had not reached three figures
in a single game in the Ranji Trophy.

16

On the Mat

My injury prevented me from participating in the trial matches
to select the team for the first-ever Prudential 'World Cup',
scheduled to be played in England in June 1975. Venkataraghavan was appointed captain and I was to be his deputy.
Since Venkataraghavan had to leave for England in April to
play for Derbyshire in the County championship, I was in
charge of the nets at the Wankhede Stadium in Bombay. We
had five days at the nets, before our departure for London on
May 25. We had only six players at the nets, since five
members of the team were already in England and Mohinder
Amarnath, Vishwanath and wicket-keeper Kirmani didn't
report until the day before the last day of the nets. We, however, had some help from the local cricketers, who bowled to
us at the nets. Arrangements had been made for us to stay at
the Wankhede Stadium; but, as I was a 'local' player, the
manager allowed me to go home for the night. As the weather
was extremely hot in Bombay at that time, we used to begin
practice at 9 o'clock in the morning, and finish at 11,
followed by a second session beginning at 3.30 in the
afternoon.

One morning I turned up at the Wankhede Stadium and found
the Cricket Control Board President, Mr. P.M. Rungta, having
breakfast with the boys. When he saw me he wanted to know
whether I was staying at the stadium or going home. I told
him I was going home for the night. He rebuked me saying,

"Why do you think arrangements have been made for the team to stay here. Team spirit has to be developed and you must also stay here. You are the vice-captain and you should set an example." I replied that I had sought the manager's permission to go home at night. I don't think Mr. Rungta was listening, because he turned to ask Eknath Solkar whether he too was going home for the night. Eknath replied that he was staying at the stadium. This was a lie and everybody around knew that Eknath was spending the night at home. But, seeing the Board President's attitude, he did not dare tell him the truth. I don't understand why Mr. G.S. Ramchand, the manager, who was present, didn't accept responsibility for allowing us to go home.

Mr. Rungta's argument that by staying together we were going to develop 'team spirit' was, to say the least, laughable. There were just six of us at the camp, which was held only five days before we left. According to Mr. Rungta's thinking, six of us were going to develop 'team spirit' as never before.

Eknath's defence of himself by lying hurt me more, because I couldn't understand the need for it. The manager had allowed us to go. Moreover, why a Test cricketer, particularly one of the calibre of Eknath Solkar, should be afraid of a mere cricket administrator, is beyond my understanding. So what, even if the 'administrator' was the Board President himself! Eknath had the manager's permission to go home and he should have said so. This show of inaction by the manager should have made me realise that, for self-preservation, the buck would be passed on to the boys. I was to learn the lesson more bitterly in the next few days.

In London, all the teams were staying in the same hotel and, on the eve of the tournament, all the participating teams were presented to the Queen at Buckingham Palace. It was terrific, especially meeting players, many of whom one had only heard of, but never seen. I was keen on renewing my acquaintance with the Pakistani boys, particularly Zaheer Abbas and Asif Masood, with whom I had so much fun in Australia. The Queen and Prince Philip chatted with the players, and then we were to go to Lord's for some photographs to be taken. There everybody was less formal and mixed freely.

We were to play in the inaugural match of the tournament against England at Lord's, on a wicket that became slower during the day. Playing in 'Group A' of the tournament, England ran up a record total of 334 runs in 63 overs, with Dennis Amiss contributing 137 runs. Fletcher and Chris Old threw their bats about with purpose and England lost only four wickets in the process.

Off the second ball I faced from Geoff Arnold, I got a very faint nick in trying to cut, and was surprised when nobody appealed for a catch. I mentioned this to Greig and the news must have reached Arnold, because in the very next over he bowled to me, I went for a cut, missed the ball by almost a foot, and there was Arnold yelling an 'appeal' to the umpire. John Snow, who was back in the side after a long lay-off, bowled a tight length, while Arnold, Old and Lever bowled short of length. After one cross-batted swipe I found I was unable to connect my shots. Now, England bowlers are a very professional lot and the few loose balls they bowled I hit them straight back to a fielder. At this stage a section of the crowd started banging beer cans together, causing an awful din. I didn't realise then that they were showing their displeasure at my batting. I thought, may be they were just doing it for the heck of it. I was finding it difficult to play any shots and to try anything funny against the fast bowlers was inviting trouble.

At tea, which was taken after 25 overs, I was asked by the manager to look for ones and twos, since I was finding it difficult to score. This was in response to my question whether I should throw away my wicket. Somebody suggested that I should drop anchor at one end, while others scored at the other.

The England field placing, in spite of their big score, was not very attacking, and it was not easy to pick even ones and twos. As I waited for the bowler to run up and bowl, my mind used to be made up to have a shy at the ball, but as soon as the ball was delivered, my feet would move to a position for a defensive shot. The awful noise made by the crowd didn't help my thinking; but only made me confused as hell. Right from the start we knew that the chase was out of the question. Even my attempts to take a single and give the strike to the other batsman failed. There was a complete mental block, as far as I was concerned.

It was by far the worst innings I have ever played. There were occasions when I felt like moving away from the stumps, so that I would be bowled. This was the only way to get rid of the mental agony from which I was suffering. I was dropped thrice, off fairly easy chances too. I was in a curious position. I couldn't force the pace and I couldn't get out, even when I tried to. Towards the end, I was playing mechanically. I can understand the crowd's reaction and I am genuinely sorry for spoiling their day. What I can't understand is the accusation that I played out 60 overs to preserve my average. I also can't stomach the argument that I scored 36 runs in 60 overs. I didn't play 60 overs myself, that's obvious. Excepting Vishwanath, nobody else tried to do anything much about the situation. It was ridiculous even to say that my batting dampened the approach of the other batsmen noted for their attacking batting. Admittedly, my batting wasn't in conformity with the norms of limited-overs cricket, but then even in local cricket I have sometimes found it tough going to attack.

The manager formally asked me to explain the reasons for

my dismal batting, which I did. Apparently he was satisfied by my explanation, because when I sat around with him and Venkataraghavan to pick the side for the next match not a word was spoken about my earlier innings. I should have been disciplined then, if at all. But I wasn't and that was that!

Our next match was against East Africa, who were the rabbits of the tournament, and we had no difficulty in beating them by 10 wickets. For a change our medium-fast bowlers, Abid Ali, Madan Lal and Mohinder Amarnath, got all the wickets that fell, except one that fell to Bedi. They were all out for 120 runs in 55.3 overs. Farokh and I then made 123 runs in 29.5 overs, without being separated. My personal contribution was 65 not out.

We took on New Zealand at the Old Trafford ground at Manchester for the right to enter the semi-finals. Batting first, we could muster only 230 runs in 60 overs, Abid Ali top-scoring with 70 runs. It seemed a fairly respectable total, which would give us a fighting chance against the Kiwis. But we had not reckoned with the gifted New Zealand opener, Glenn Turner. Spearheading the assault on the Indian bowlers, he remained unbeaten with 114 runs, when New Zealand won the match in the last over. It was a near thing, and we could have won, but for Glenn Turner's magnificent effort. So, we failed to enter the lists to take a tilt at the 'World Cup' in its inaugural year. As far as my own performance was concerned, I had an aggregate of 113 runs, twice not out, and an average of 113. Incidentally, I had scored the largest number of runs for India.

I had almost forgotten about my first experience of 'instant cricket' when I just couldn't get going against England at Lord's. It was only a bad nightmare. However, I wasn't allowed to forget the episode. When I returned to India after a month's holiday in Europe I got a letter from the Cricket

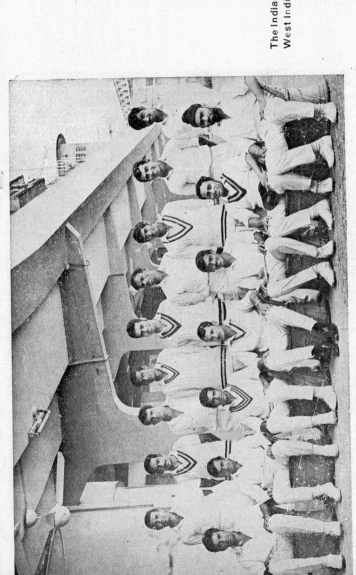

The Indian team to the West Indies, 1971.

Gavaskar completes a double century in the second innings of the 5th Test against the West Indies at Port of Spain (1971) after having scored a century in the first innings. M.L. Jaisimha walks down the pitch to congratulate him.

The Indian team leaving the field at lunch on the 3rd day of the match against Trinidad, 1971.

Batting in the Old Trafford Test (1974)
against Derek Underwood. Tony
Greig and John Edrich (back to
camera are the close-in-fielders.

Control Board President, again asking me to 'explain' my batting in the England match. It seems the manager had reported that I had deliberately played slow cricket, contrary to the interests of the team. The manager, I was told, had also reported that, when I was asked by him to go for runs, I gave some excuse and persisted in playing slow and dull cricket. This, the manager alleged, had a demoralising effect on the younger players, and was also against the country's interest. It now transpired that the explanation given by me to the manager in England was not satisfactory. All this was a great shock to me.

If my explanation to the manager was not satisfactory, why didn't he say so then, and take action against me? What, however, hurt me even more was the report of the manager who accused me of not performing my duties as vice-captain, and of keeping myself aloof from the other members of the team, instead of giving them encouragement.

I can be all things but never 'aloof' from my team-mates. And, as for not encouraging the players and not mixing with them, I suggested that any eight members of the 14-member team be called and if they said that I was 'aloof' and didn't offer encouragement I would retire from the game. But then that was not to be because I had already been adjudged 'guilty' until I was able to prove my innocence. A strange way of doing 'justice'! And how can one call for disciplinary action for performance on the field? If that is so, if a bowler gets slogged he will have to explain his failure. Or, if a fielder drops a catch he has to explain it. What a ridiculous state of affairs! And if my performance was so poor, what about our bowlers? They should have been sent to the gallows for allowing the England batsmen to score at will to pile up a record total of 334!

Mind you, I am the first to admit that I deserved to be censured for my slow scoring to get 36. But, to say that I deliberately played slowly was not true and entirely unfair. How does one prove that I did it deliberately and how does one say that the others didn't? The whole thing made terribly bitter, and I couldn't bring myself to really believe that such things had happened. We weren't schoolchildren to give an explanation in writing to the school master. Bishen was asked to do that after the 1974 tour and I was put on the mat after the 1975 tour.

I was told that my explanation was not satisfactory, but I was given the benefit of the doubt and the 'proceedings' against me were dropped. That was the wisest thing that could be done by the Cricket Control Board. But all this left a very bad taste in the mouth, and did precious little to spur our players to do better in future.

17

A Fruitful Season

Leaving all the unhappiness of the past behind, I decided to concentrate on the new season. I was feeling downcast and was disinterested in almost everything. However, when I was appointed captain of Bombay unanimously, it put new life into me. I started practising with a will, because I wanted to prove that those who were saying that the captaincy would affect my batting were absolutely wrong. I felt really sorry for Ashok Mankad who, in spite of winning the Ranji Trophy in the 1974-75 season, was discarded. But then that's how the ball rolls! I knew, however, I could depend on his cooperation, and he didn't let me down.

In our first Ranji Trophy game, we had a tough time getting Gujarat out, but we eventually succeeded on the second morning when Gujarat had scored 245 runs. In reply, we batted well, and I got a century, and Sudhir Naik contributed 65 runs. We were 240 for two at the end of the day. I knew our only chance of an outright win was to take advantage of the wicket in the morning, before the batting became loose and so I declared immediately after taking the 1st innings lead. My hunch proved correct, because Gujarat were all out for 101, our seamers doing most of the damage. We had to get 99 runs to win, which we got. The victory gave me tremendous confidence, as I had taken a calculated risk and our bowlers had proved me right. Besides, the captaincy made

me concentrate harder while batting, and I avoided playing
all or most of the seemingly dangerous shots.

The Irani Trophy match against the Rest of India at
Nagpur was my next job. This was the match where Dilip
Vengsarkar made his name a household one in India. He
scored 110 runs in only 85 minutes off 80 balls, but the manner
in which he hammered Bedi and Prasanna on a turning wicket
was unbelievable. Young Vengsarkar started by hitting
Prasanna straight over the sight screen and then didn't spare
Bedi either. In all, he hit seven sixes, all of them perfectly
timed. I was having a rub-down when he reached his 50, but
I stopped the massage and went out to watch this young
batsman hammering India's famed spin bowlers. It was a
magnificent sight. There was no wild slogging, the sixes were
brought off with perfect timing and the ball sped to the region
from mid-off to mid-wicket. And to think that he would have
been in the reserves if Eknath Solkar had been fit, Eknath had
split the webbing between the thumb and forefinger and he
had to drop out.

Dilip Vengsarkar didn't get to bat in the first innings in the
Ranji Trophy match against Gujarat, so I promoted him to
one-down in the first innings of this match, while I dropped
to no. 5 in the batting order. Dilip got a good ball and was
leg-before for a 'duck'. When he came back to the pavilion,
he was disconsolate and worried whether he had made a hash
of his opportunity. I tried to reassure him by recounting the
names of some great cricketers, who had been out for a 'duck'
on their first-class debut, but had gone on to do great things.
I told him about my own debut in the Ranji Trophy,
which was similar to his, and added, "See, today I am the
Bombay captain." I don't know whether this convinced Dilip.

Dilip Vengsarkar's innings at Nagpur reminded a lot of
people of the late Col. C. K. Nayudu, and Dilip promptly

acquired the nickname of 'Colonel'. We have, in the Dadar Union side, a Marshal, a Major and now a Colonel!

The next Ranji Trophy match against Maharashtra saw the 'Colonel' playing a different game. He rarely lofted the ball and played mostly along the ground. I got 190 in the match. Maharashtra always have a good opening attack and it was good to get runs against them. Without Shivalkar, who was ill, we couldn't force an outright victory in spite of getting them out cheaply in the first innings.

The Sri Lanka team was in India then to play three four-day unofficial 'Tests'. In the first 'Test' at Hyderabad I got 203, but it was Vishwanath, who made 117 runs, that stole the spectators' hearts. Vishwanath had caught up with me in the 60s and we went neck and neck till the 90s when, in one over from D. S. D'Silva, I hit three boundaries through the covers to reach my hundred first. Vishwanath got his century in the next over. Often, after I played a particular shot, Vishwanath would repeat it in the next over, and more elegantly. I enjoyed batting with him, especially because it was one of the rare occasions when we had a long partnership. The Sri Lanka team had no answer to Vishwanath in this mood and we added over 200 runs for the third wicket. Vishwanath then 'walked' when he thought he was bowled by D'Silva. I was the non-striker and I know that the ball dislodged the bails only after rebounding off the wicket-keeper's pads.

All along in Hyderabad, I often got near the century mark, but never got a 100, because I used to get out in the 80s and 90s. So, I had made up my mind that when I did get past my 100, I would go on to score 200. I had to fulfil the promise I had made to myself and I was happy when I realised my ambition.

The Sri Lanka bowling wasn't penetrative, only Opatha operating with the new ball needed careful watching. The

other bowlers were most ordinary. Much was made of D.S.
D'Silva, who was supposed to be Sri Lanka's Chandrasekhar,
but he looked mediocre. The only good point about him was
his never-say-die spirit. This was the only game I played
against the visitors, because I was dropped for the next two
'Tests'. Bishen jokingly told me in the evening: "You know,
Indian batsmen are not supposed to get a double century.
You have scored one, and so you have been dropped!"

My good batting form continued in the Ranji Trophy and,
batting at no. 5, I got 171 runs against Saurashtra. But, where
I should have got a big score I didn't. That was in the Duleep
Trophy semi-final against North Zone. I got only 40 runs
and West Zone lost to North Zone on the first innings. In
the second innings on the last day of the Duleep Trophy
match, I was batting with more than 50 runs to my
name. While I was walking to resume my innings after tea,
Chetan Chauhan told me, "Watch out, I'm coming on to
bowl." I was 84 and looking forward to a century when
Chetan was brought on. His first delivery pitched on a length
and, as I went forward to it, the ball went straight through
to bowl me. Chetan was delighted but knowing how anxious
I was to get a century in the Duleep Trophy he was most
apologetic when we met in the evening.

I had three centuries in three Ranji Trophy matches and
was keen to score another in the last match of the league
against Baroda. That was, however, not to be, because Dilip
Vengsarkar and Sudhir Naik raised a 200-run opening partnership, before Vengsarkar, who got his first Ranji Trophy century,
was out. Once again, I was to bat at no. 5 and, when I went
in, Anshuman Gaekwad claimed the second new ball. It was
a shrewd move, for the wicket was full of runs and the new
ball was more likely to get wickets than the old one which
the spinners were operating.

Narayan Satham, a fine bowler with the new ball and who
is nippy off the wicket, rapped me on the pads from where the

ball flew to second slip. I was given out caught, though the Baroda players had appealed for leg-before. They were sympathetic later on, but the damage was done. Anshuman Gaekwad's fighting knock saved Baroda from outright defeat.

Just before the captain was selected for the twin-tour of New Zealand and the West Indies early in 1976, there was a controversy about Bishen Bedi. Apparently Bishen had said some harsh things to the officials of the Vidarbha Cricket Association about the board and lodging arrangements made for the players at Nagpur. So, again Bishen had to appear before an Inquiry Committee to explain his conduct.

Bishen must hold the record for the number of inquiries he has had to face, in camera or otherwise. The Selectors were, however, told that there was nothing that could be held against Bishen and they promptly appointed him captain for the twin-tour. If Bishen holds the record for inquiries, I must rank a close second. Perhaps, by this token I was made the vice-captain of the team. And, we had the battle-scarred Polly Umrigar as manager, and Balu Alaganan as treasurer.

There were only two seamers in the side, Madan Lal and Mohinder Amarnath, with the versatile Eknath Solkar also to bowl his seamers.

We assembled in Madras before leaving for Auckland, on the first leg of our twin-tour of New Zealand and the West Indies. The two days there were hectic, with travel arrangements to be worked out, the outfitting to be looked after, and a lot of other things to attend to. It was all a mad rush, and we wished we had more time to get things organised before leaving on a protracted tour covering several thousand miles.

Just before we left for the tour, I had completed my part in a Marathi film called "Premachi Savli". How I came to be a film actor is another story. One evening, after the Bombay Net, Mr. P.D. Reporter, who is a first-class umpire, came and asked if I was interested in acting in a movie. My reaction was negative at first, but I wanted to wait and watch further developments before taking a final decision. Mr. Reporter's sister, Madhumati, who is a well-known dancer and has appeared frequently on the Indian screen, and her husband, Manohar Deepak, were producing this film. At the time the offer came I was inactive, after being dropped from the last two Tests against Sri Lanka. I had a bit of free time at my disposal. I was assured that the shooting of my part in the film wouldn't take more than three days, which induced me to accept the invitation to appear on the 'silver screen'.

It was a novel experience for me, even though I had appeared in a few commercials earlier. However, appearing in a full-length feature film was very different. I confess that I never got used to the glare from the reflectors, which made me feel terribly uneasy. The film, I understand, is due for release soon, and I wonder how my screen debut will be taken by cinema-goers. Anyway, I am keeping my fingers crossed and am hoping for the best.

18

Umpiring Aberrations

We landed at Auckland after a tiring air journey and were told that there would be no overnight halt, because we were to play at Napier.

We started off by coach for Napier and, at about midnight, we had a flat tyre. While the driver worked to change the tyre, with the help of the sleepy-eyed boys, I entertained the team with the song that had been picturised for me for the film in which I had appeared. Judging from the enthusiastic response of the boys, the song should be a hit!

The flat tyre, however, added to our woes. What we needed most was rest after the tiring air journey. Instead, we were made to travel by bus. I wish the people responsible for making travel arrangements would travel like this and find out for themselves whether it is pleasant or not. When we reached Napier in the small hours of the morning, we didn't have strength even to tie our shoe laces.

It rained and rained and it looked as if our first match of the tour against the Central Districts would be washed out. Luckily, on the last two days the rain stopped and though the outfield was soggy we could start the match. The Central District team was skittled out for 152. I was given out caught behind, off the second ball of our innings. The ball had hit my pads and then bounced off, when the wicket-keeper, diving forward had taken it and appealed. I was surprised at the decision, but thought I had been given out leg-before wicket. It was a disappointing start to a four-month tour. Mohinder Amarnath, Parthasarathy Sharma and Brijesh Patel played well and we won the game pretty easily by six wickets. It was, after all, a good beginning.

The next game against Northern Districts, which we played at Hamilton, also ended in a victory for us, by the comparatively narrow margin of 141 runs. Brijesh Patel (71) and Madan Lal (101 not out) in the first innings, and Surinder Amarnath (59) in the second, batted well. For the home team, Roberts scored an unbeaten 104 in the first innings. It was during fielding practice at the ground before the match that Bishen Bedi pulled a leg muscle badly and was ruled out for the first Test to follow at Auckland. As vice-captain I had to lead the side and found myself as the leader of a national team for the first time in my cricketing career. Though I was sorry for Bishen, I don't mind confessing that I was happy at the honour that had come to me purely by accident.

On the eve of the Test, I went, along with a couple of senior members of the team, to have a look at the wicket. The groundsman came charging at us when we tried to lift the covers to see what the pitch was like. It was a bright day with not a cloud in sight. When I requested the groundsman to allow us to look at the wicket, he ignored me and went back to his rolling. I was furious and so were the others. Surely we were entitled to have a look at the wicket on the eve of the Test! John Reid, the former New Zealand captain, who was there, spoke to the groundsman and only then did he remove the covers off the wicket, but with great reluctance. The wicket looked a beauty and we reckoned our spinners would be able to turn the ball by the third day.

Dilip Vengsarkar reported a strained leg muscle in the morning and I had to wait till the doctors reported him fit for the game. In the meanwhile Glenn Turner, who was also captaining his country for the first time, had come into our dressing room to ask me to go for the toss. I requested him to wait for a few minutes. But the few minutes turned to be pretty long for me. Glenn came a number of times, but, at my request, went back again to the New Zealand dressing room.

When we finally went out to toss I said to him, "What a way to begin a Test captaincy!" The coin really rolled after landing and it went from one end of the wicket to the other with both Glenn and I chasing after it. Glenn took one look and triumphantly said, "Bad luck pal, I've won it." As we returned to the pavilion I was reminded of Ajit Wadekar's dictum, "I never mind if I lose the toss, so long as I win the Test."

Glenn, who opened the New Zealand innings with Morrison, was not successful with the bat, and in Chandrasekhar's second over he was caught by me off bat and pad. I had to dive to my right to catch it. I was fielding there because Eknath Solkar had fractured his little finger and was not playing. When I looked towards the dressing room, there was Eknath clapping in approval.

Bevan Congdon and John Morrison, however, batted sensibly, though not too confidently. Both survived confident appeals for lbw, which were turned down. Incidentally, we had been warned by some of the Indian players who had toured New Zealand in 1968 not to waste our breath appealing for lbw decisions. Prasanna, who was one of them, shrugged and said, "Well, we've got to bowl them out, isn't it?"

Chandrasekhar was, meanwhile, becoming unplayable, and after he caught Morrison off his own bowling, a landslide started, which was checked only by a partnership between wicket-keeper Wadsworth and Dayle Hadlee. Wadsworth, who had survived a bat-pad catch appeal, stepped down the track again to play Prasanna, and I took the edge off the pads. Wadsworth waited for a decision but was given out. He was also out of his crease when I took the catch, so I could have got him run out, too, but I was confident that this time the umpire had heard the snick. Fortunately for us, he had! New Zealand were all out for 226 runs. In the two overs left before draw of stumps we made 16 for no loss.

Dilip Vengsarkar was out in the first over of the second morning, when he was trapped leg-before by Collinge. In his first Test innings Dilip was out for seven. Surinder Amarnath, another Test debutant, joined me at this stage. He started shakily, surviving a slip chance to Turner off Howarth's first ball, but settled down to play a fine attacking innings. Howarth was really unlucky because he dropped me off his own bowling twice. Having seen his catching of Ashok Mankad off his own bowling in Bombay in 1969, I counted myself very lucky indeed, to have survived. I had another life when Bevan Congdon failed to hold a return catch. Surinder also escaped being caught by Howarth, when he played a ball back to the bowler. It certainly wasn't Howarth's day.

Surinder, whose nickname is 'Tommy', reached his century daringly. At 93 he swung O'Sullivan over long-on for six and then patted the next ball and scampered for a single to reach his first 100 in Test cricket. In scoring a century on debut, Surinder had emulated his father, Lala Amarnath, who had also scored a century on his debut, against England at Bombay in 1933-34. Our partnership was worth 204 runs, when Surinder was out to the second new ball. He was caught behind, off Hadlee, when he had scored 124 runs. Vishwanath also fell to a catch by wicket-keeper Wadsworth off Hadlee, before he had opened his account. The ball had actually nicked his pads, but the loud appeal by Wadsworth and Co. was upheld.

I was in the 80s when Brijesh Patel joined me. We trudged

along cautiously against the new ball. I despatched a short ball from Collinge over the square-leg fence and followed up with a cut to the third-man boundary. With these shots I had reached my century, my first against New Zealand, and in my maiden Test against the Kiwis. It was certainly not the best of innings, because I had to really struggle to get the runs. This was to be expected, because my form on the tour wasn't too good before the Test and I had to fight hard to get into three figures. On the other hand, Surinder's was a free-stroking innings, thrilling, no doubt, but at the same time it was obvious that on wickets with a little more grass and movement, he would be in trouble.

Venkataraghavan came in as night-watchman. Of our spinners, he has the best credentials as a batsman, and has even scored a century in the Ranji Trophy and 51 in a Test. But 'Venkat' has never succeeded as a night-watchman, due, I think, to the fact that in the last overs of the day he goes for attacking shots, instead of playing out time. This is exactly the opposite of what a night-watchman should do. This time too he paid the price and was out to a brilliant catch by Congdon in the gully. Then came the turning point of the match—the partnership between Mohinder Amarnath and Madan Lal. Their 93-run partnership for the seventh wicket, which ended on the third day, gave us a valuable 148-run lead, which was to prove decisive.

The New Zealand second innings started with Morrison being brilliantly caught by Vishwanath, jumping up at short mid-wicket; then Madan Lal, who was at mid-wicket, ran back to hold Glenn Turner. Congdon and Parker, who put on 122 runs for the third wicket, survived mainly because the umpires refused to give them out. Bat-pad catches were smilingly turned down, and lbw appeals by us might have been stupid, the way the umpires looked at us. Once when I took a bat-pad catch and found it negatived, the entire team was stunned. Shouts from the stands saying "Home rules apply, boys", didn't sound funny. At the end of the day New Zealand were 161 for 2.

We were not to be denied victory, however, and **Prasanna** bowled superbly to shoot the New Zealand side out for 215. He captured 8 wickets for 76 runs—his best performance in Tests. Chandrasekhar got two wickets and Venkataraghavan kept the batsmen in check and never allowed them to take liberties, even though he did not take a wicket. One of the incidents in this Test, which we will all remember, is the time Chandrasekhar bowled Wadsworth to terminate New Zealand's second innings. He was appealing to the umpire, who turned round and said, "He is bowled". I was beside Chandrasekhar at the time, trying to calm him down. The exasperated Chandrasekhar posed the classic question, "I know he is bowled, but is he out?" That goes to show what we thought about the umpiring.

We lost two wickets in scoring the 68 runs needed for victory and champagne was waiting for us in the dressing room. We were one-up, and it's always good to go one-up in the first Test of a series. My debut as captain had been successful. I was back among the runs too with 116 and 35 not out.

Dunedin, where we played Otago, is very *near* the South Pole, but the weather made us feel as if we were *on* the South Pole. It was blisteringly cold and, with the rain coming down occasionally, the climate was certainly not suitable for a cricket match. However, the interruptions allowed me to participate in a match with a rubber ball with the little boys who had come to watch the game. And this made me very popular with the enthusiastic youngsters. However, I did nothing of note in the drawn match against Otago, which preceded the 2nd Test, except to drop Glenn Turner off my own bowling. This prompted Glenn to wonder whether caught and bowled had gone out of fashion. His bowlers had let down a few in the first Test and that must have been fresh in his mind. Anyway, Glenn went on to score an unbeaten 121 runs. Dilip Vengsarkar cornered all the glory by top-scoring with 130 runs, and Brijesh made 73, both in the first innings.

As far as I am concerned, the wicket at Christchurch for the second Test was not a Test wicket. How can one accept a wicket on which the grass is as thick as in the outfield. There were patches of grass on the wicket, which were like big tufts. Besides, the weather was, as usual, bitterly cold and raw. To make things more difficult for us, it rained and seven and a half hours' play was lost. Bedi, leading India for the first time, won the toss. And, when we decided to bat on that track, I thought it was an unnecessary risk. It was like playing into the hands of New Zealand, who had three seamers backed up by Congdon.

I started off by lofting Collinge high over the vacant mid-on position, and followed up with a four over slips' heads for a boundary. It certainly wasn't risky batting as I was only going for the cut when I knew that an edge would go over slips' heads. I had made 22 before an intended drive went to Burgess, off Collinge, at third slip, and I was out. Vishwanath played such a marvellous innings that Mohinder Amarnath's confidence increased during their partnership. Just as they looked set to pull us out of the woods, Mohinder (45) was given out leg-before to Congdon. Mohinder is tall and he had stretched his leg down the wicket and we were all surprised at the decision. Vishwanath was caught in the slips for 83 and Bishen swung his bat merrily to make 30 and boost our score.

New Zealand's batting followed the pattern of the first Test in that we became hoarse by appealing, which were generally turned down by the umpires. Glenn Turner, in particular, survived mainly on his ability to get the ball on the pads. He scored a century (117), but I honestly can't think of a single stroke worth remembering. Even his 100th run was given to him by courtesy of the umpire. When he was on 98, he turned Madan Lal to Mohinder at deep fine-leg and took one run. He was hardly out of his ground to complete the second run when wicket-keeper Kirmani had the bails off from a lovely throw-in by Mohinder. But seeing Turner turn back for his second run, hundreds of boys and girls had taken off to greet him in the middle, and the umpire did not have the heart to disappoint them! Turner got his century and everyone around was happy.

Vishwanath's innings, particularly the way he let the rising ball alone, was fresh in my mind as I embarked on my second innings. My 71 was one of my better efforts and that too because I had Vishwanath's 83 in mind. The wicket, which was not mown and was freshened by rain, made the ball kick about, but our partnership lasted quite a bit and we had soon wiped out the deficit. At the end of the game everybody said we were lucky to draw the game. I don't think so, for we needed only 100 runs more and we would have skittled out New Zealand in the second innings, if the umpires' fingers didn't get stuck in their pockets.

The outstanding performance in the Test was by Syed Kirmani, our wicket-keeper, who equalled the world record of dismissals in an innings—six caught and one stumped—and kept superbly throughout. His catch to dismiss Glenn Turner was astonishing. Turner had turned an in-swinger off the middle of his bat and Kirmani, anticipating it, had already moved, and yet had to fling himself to his left to come up with the catch.

Madan Lal and Mohinder also were our heroes, along with Vishwanath. Madan Lal and Mohinder had bowled their hearts out on this track, with Madan Lal looking particularly dangerous. We saved the match on the last morning because of a knock of 71 by me and another 79 runs scored by Vishwanath.

Two days before the third and final Test at Wellington, the capital of New Zealand, the weather was as warm as in Bombay during December/January. From the second day of the Test, however, the weather deteriorated so much that I can safely say that it must have been the coldest day in Test cricket that I have ever encountered. The match was played on the Basin Reserve pitch, which, with a lot of grass and helped by rain, gave the New Zealand bowlers the type of wicket they had been hoping for.

On the first day we were out for 220, after winning the toss, with Brijesh making a strokeful 81 and Kirmani an enterprising 49. When New Zealand batted, Bedi got Glenn Turner down the wicket and the umpire had no option but to give him out. Bevan Congdon got 52. He had got a 50 against us in all five innings he had played, and he is certainly a stubborn person to get out and we were always happy to see his back. He seemed to have plenty of time to play our spinners and plenty of patience too.

On the third day Bishen didn't come out to field after lunch and I led the side. Within an hour I was also off the field with a broken cheek bone. Lance Cairns, who is a big hitter, swept a ball from Prasanna, which struck me on the cheek as I was fielding at bat and pad, breaking and dislocating the bone. An operation had to be performed to get the bone back in place and, after a day in the hospital, I was back in the hotel with the boys. The only trouble, apart from certain food restrictions, was that it pained when I laughed. Our team was full of funny characters and to spend a day without laughing was impossible, which will give an idea of the tortures I had to undergo. Well, I settled for the pain and laughs!

Prasanna, who was my room-mate, was very upset after my injury, but seeing me back again after 24 hours, cheered up. He told me later that after my injury he wandered about aimlessly in the field without even a sweater in that bitter cold. He had to captain the side after I was off, and it certainly wasn't the best of circumstances to lead one's country for the first time, even if it was a temporary assignment.

When we were to bat we noticed that the grass had not been mown. When asked, the groundsman said that he had, which means he must have used a grass-mower without blades. Bishen remarked at the end of the Test that when the New Zealand team comes to India next, it will find the wickets devoid of grass, because our groundsmen use lawn-mowers with blades in them! With the help of the unmown grass and a spot just short of a length, Richard Hadlee mowed us down dismissing us for 81—the lowest total by either country in Tests against each other.

The series was thus levelled. The New Zealanders were out to win the series, and they very nearly did. However, when they found that they couldn't win they were determined to level the series. And to achieve this purpose any means was good enough. At Wellington the wicket was changed only at the last moment, to get a grassy patch just short of length. In the process, the stumps were pitched at the end of the square and the wicket was at the edge of the plot.

The decisive factor was the umpiring, which was so partial that we thought we must have really played well to win the first Test. In fact, but for the umpiring decisions we would have won the first Test by an innings. Also, we were denied victory in the second Test because of the bias shown by the umpires for the home team. During the series I found that bat and pad appeals were absolutely futile, unless the batsman himself felt some shame and 'walked'.

It made us very unhappy to find the New Zealand Press extremely biased. We never got any headlines, which were reserved for the New Zealand players. If our batsmen got runs the headline would invariably say that the New Zealand bowlers bowled badly and, if the Indian bowlers were on top, the newspapers would blame their home batsmen for throwing their wickets away. The unabashed partiality of the New Zealand Press was underlined by a headline in an important newspaper at the end of the series. It said: "Indian heads Turner and Congdon in batting averages." The newspapers, I must say, did a great job for the Kiwis, doing their best to boost their morale by their lop-sided comments. After some time, we ceased to bother about what they wrote, and opened the newspaper only to see the TV programmes for the day.

The weather also made us feel miserable. If what we saw was the New Zealand summer, I shudder to think what the winter would be like. The only good thing about the country was the people. They were extremely kind and friendly. They tried to make us as comfortable as possible. If only the weather was as kind and the umpires as friendly, we would not only have won the series, but would have really enjoyed the visit.

19

Trinidad, I Love You

The doctor had advised me three weeks' rest after the New Zealand tour and I was allowed by the manager, Polly Umrigar, to spend some time in New York and, if possible, have my injury examined by a specialist. I was still suffering from the after-effects of the fractured jaw, which had, however, begun to heal. Balu Alaganan, the treasurer of the team, was with me and we spent a pleasant week in New York with Dr. S. Ravindranath, Balu's family friend. He turned out to be a keen cricket fan and we talked about cricket all the time.

Meanwhile, the team had gone on to the West Indies after a 30-hour flight from Auckland. The tour opened with matches against Windward Islands at St. Vincent and against Leeward Islands at Monsterrat, both of which ended in draws. Balu and I were to join the team in Barbados on the eve of the Barbados-India match. On the way to Barbados, we spent a day at Orlando, on the west coast of the United States, near Los Angeles, to see the wonders of "Disney Land". However, one day was too short to see everything, but we had to remind ourselves that we were on a cricket tour.

When we arrived at Bridgetown, Barbados, a customs officer wanted to know if I was going to score as many runs as I had done on the 1971 tour. Of course, it was difficult to answer the question, so I could only smile and leave it there.

There were others who warned me about the West Indies fast bowlers, Andy Roberts and Holding. "That maan Roberts, he fit maan". Another person said, "Gaavaska, you gonna hook Roberts maan or not?" There was nothing I could say, except to assure them that I would do my best.

Bishen wanted to rest before the first Test at Bridgetown, Barbados, and I had to lead the side, in spite of being out of cricket for about three weeks. I began the tour on a promising note, getting 62 runs before lunch in the match against Barbados and fell to Padmore when I missed a drive. Wicket-keeper David Murray also missed the ball but recovered quickly to whip the bails to stump me.

I was worried before the match whether I would be psychologically affected by my last injury. But my fears and doubts were dispelled after my innings against Barbados and I felt very confident.

When Barbados play any visiting team, the local supporters are keen to see a Barbados victory. In fact, as I have said earlier, a West Indies victory is not celebrated with as much gusto as a Barbados victory. Barbados is generally regarded as the 'home' of West Indian cricket, and the Island has always provided the bulk of the West Indies team. Of late, however, players from other parts of the Caribbean have dominated the West Indies cricket, particularly those from Guyana and Trinidad..

The first Test at Bridgetown (Barbados) began on March 10. Bishen elected to bat on a beautiful track, after winning the toss. Parthasarathy Sharma, who had shown good form in the Island games, was my partner, replacing Dilip Vengsarkar who had got into a bad trot. Solkar was still on the injured list and had to stand down in the match against Windward Islands. Solkar was hit while fielding at bat-pad and the ball had rebounded off his head to be caught by the bowler Venkataraghavan! When told to go for an x-ray to see if there was any damage, particularly to the brain, some of the players quipped, "What brain?" But, Bedi's comment really raised a laugh. "The blow has done him good. He is talking more sense now," said the skipper. Over the years, Solkar has taken a lot of painful blows while fielding at that position. The strain is now showing and he is no longer at his best in that position as before, when he was rated as world class.

I knew that the Kensington Oval wicket at Bridgetown was a real beauty. The ball came off quickly and it helped stroke-making. I was 37 in no time, before Andy Roberts brought one back and trapped me leg-before, with a ball that kept low. I was most disappointed to get out because I was seeing the ball well and, what is more important, middling it all the time. We were knocked out in the first innings for 177. The West Indies, with centuries from Vivian Richards and Clive Lloyd, and 93 by Alvin Kallicharran, piled up a big score (488 for 9 declared). The Richards we saw was completely different from the one in India. Then he seemed to be bent upon hitting every ball out of sight. The new Richards showed tremendous patience, without cutting away any shots. Only after he got his century did he loft the ball. And he played Chandrasekhar with confidence and ease. On the Indian tour, Chandrasekhar had given Richards plenty of trouble and many anxious moments. But in 1976 Richards was calm and unhurried while facing him, and his records didn't come as a surprise.

In our second innings, I was out to a short ball from Roberts, which never came up and found me skying the ball only to be caught by Jumadeen at forward short-leg. It was an atrocious shot and that too in the first over. What the team needed most was someone to stick around and I certainly let the side down. I was very annoyed with myself and made up my mind not to go for the hook shot at all. Vishwanath, in making 62, completed 2,000 runs in Test cricket, and among others, only Madan Lal and Mohinder resisted. We lost the Test by an innings. It was a very bad defeat for us and a great morale-booster for the West Indies after their shattering 1-5 defeat in Australia barely a month ago. We had dropped a fair number of catches in the close-in positions which proved very costly. We were to learn that dropping Richards (of all people) was certainly not going to pay. But, during the series, Richards benefited most from our poor catching.

Throughout the tour I was finding it difficult to concentrate in matches, other than Tests and, I confess, my attitude to these games was not right. All I did was to go out and slog. I realised this was inexcusable and it wasn't fair to the other members of the side. However, the second innings of our match against Trinidad changed all that. I had batted in the first innings like a man who knows that his time is up and is out to grab all the fun he can. My 52 runs in 72 minutes included 3 sixes and 4 fours. I also attempted to play the back-handed sweep shot. After batting this way, it struck me that I should have played like this in the Prudential World Cup in England. But then, Bartholomew, Julien and Gomes were certainly not up the same street as Snow, Arnold, Old and Lever!

In the second innings, however, I regained my concentration and scored 57 runs in 49 minutes, with scarcely a lofted shot. There was the urge, now and then, to let myself go, but I restrained myself. In terms of stroke-play, it wasn't at all a satisfying innings but, in terms of concentration and determination, I was satisfied with my knock. I had avoided all the flashy, crowd-pleasing shots during this long innings. I was only hoping that I would get more runs in the next Test, because I have always been able to concentrate in Tests. Incidentally, this did not please the spectators, one of whom came and told me, "If you's gonna bat like that for the whole day, then you's gonna put us to sleep. You's better play like the first innings !" I smiled but I had made up my mind not to do anything that would endanger the prospects of the team.

One thing you can be sure of is that there is no dearth of advisers in the West Indies. A man in the street will stop you and tell you about your game and how you should have played. That's pretty common. Moreover, what they love to see is a fast bowler being hooked. Oh yes ! they love that shot in the West Indies.

In 1971, I had given them plenty of the hook shot, thanks to Uton Dowe, who was bumper-happy. But, over the years, I had learnt to be discreet about this shot and I try to avoid it as much as I can.

The first day's play in the second Test at Port of Spain, Trinidad, was washed out by rain. However, when the match eventually got under way on the second, it was Vivian Richards who cornered all the glory. Coming in to bat after Roy Fredericks was bowled second ball by Madan Lal, he played so well that it looked as if it would be impossible to get him out. However, we had the West Indies on the hop as Mohinder bowled Lawrence Rowe in his first over. Kallicharran was caught at deep square-leg off Bedi; Lloyd was bowled by Chandrasekhar's 'loop ball'. Murray, who always seems to thrive in such situations, helped Richards to add valuable runs as Chandrasekhar was tired. Richards at 83, who went out to drive Venkataraghavan, missed and was resigned to being stumped, got a reprieve when wicket-keeper Kirmani fumbled with the ball, and Richards walked back to the crease casually. Eventually, he was out for 130, and Murray was out in the second over after lunch, caught by Kirmani off Bedi. After batting so well, this was an unexpected end. But Julien played a fine attacking innings before Madan Lal dived to his right to stop the ball off his own bowling and then threw down the wicket with Julien trying to scramble back. This was magnificent cricket. The West Indies innings ended at 241.

Our innings was also off to a stumbling start. Dilip Vengsarkar, trying to hook Roberts' second ball, gloved it to the wicket-keeper and was out. Mohinder Amarnath, who went in one-down, took such a long time to come out that, if Clive Lloyd had appealed he would have been justified. Apparently Mohinder had not even padded up and was having a rub down when Dilip was out. He sure had a lot of confidence in the opening pair! However, he was not his ambling self while batting, but very alert. He played some crisp shots, before an ambitious late-cut off Jumadeen ended in his dismissal. Vishwanath was just settling down when he was caught behind, off Holding. A good ball and a good batsman out! Surinder Amarnath played one rousing square-cut off Holding, the ball crashing into the fence, but lost patience against Jumadeen and gave an easy catch to Rowe at mid-wicket, as he tried a lofted shot. Brijesh Patel was aware that this was his chance to make good, so we decided to concentrate on taking singles to upset the field. And, as we knew, the West Indies fielders trying to stem the flow of runs through singles, tried to throw us out, giving us plenty of extra runs in the process. I was 90 at the end of the day, with Brijesh on 42. I was ten short of my century, which would be the third successive 100 on the same ground.

The last ball before tea that day, when I was on 49, I was nearly bowled by Roberts. The ball pitched pretty wide of the off-stump, but cut back amazingly and missed my off-stump by a whisker. Trinidad is certainly not a fast bowler's dream wicket and for Roberts to bowl such a ball, when more than 40 overs had already been bowled, was truly remarkable.

The next day Brijesh prospered along with me and I struck up a good understanding, picking up many singles. It was with one such single that I reached my century, the third in

successive innings at Port of Spain's Queen's Park Oval— a
record for the ground. Knowing that the team wanted more
runs we carried on and were still together at lunch. Michael
Holding bowled a good spell after lunch, and he got me out to
a ball that left me for a catch to the wicket-keeper, when I
was on 156. Brijesh and I had added 204 runs for the fifth
wicket, which gave us a lead of 89 runs over the West Indies.
I was looking for runs and was taking a few risks at that stage
to make the scoreboard move faster. Brijesh and Madan Lal
continued where I had left off. Brijesh was understandably
slow as he approached his first Test century, and Madan Lal
took some time to settle down. Madan Lal, however, played
one tremendous straight drive off Andy Roberts, which was a
real beauty. When Bedi declared at 402 for 5, Brijesh was 115
not out and Madan Lal 33 not out. The declaration left the
West Indies the last session of play, with a first innings deficit
of 161. In that session, we got the wicket of Fredericks. Rowe
batted well the next day, but was out to an ugly cross-batted
swipe off Venkataraghavan for 47.

On the morning of the last day, the 'Richards incident'
occurred. Richards had been off the field for quite some time
when we batted the previous day because of a strained leg
muscle. When he was batting the next day he slipped and fell,
while flicking a ball to leg from Bedi. This seemed to have aggravated the injury, because he went up to Bedi and sought his
permission to retire. Bishen agreed to give him a runner instead,
but he said that, if Richards wanted to retire, Bedi would
exercise his right to dictate when he could bat again. This
was not acceptable to Richards who didn't want a runner, but
wanted to retire. The umpires were brought into the discussion
and the West Indies captain, Clive Lloyd, also joined in.
Richards eventually retired and, as the next wicket fell, he
came in to bat. Bishen's reasons for allowing him to bat at the
fall of the fourth wicket was to try and get him out, since our
bowlers were on top then.

Luckily for us Richards and Lloyd had a misunderstanding, as a result of which Richards was run out. The decision didn't get well with Richards or may be he was just unhappy at losing his wicket. However, his gestures, as he left the field, incited the crowd and, as we came in at the tea interval, umpire Gosein was booed by a section of the spectators seated in front of the pavilion.

I was a little late in joining the team after the tea interval and I ran on to the field with the batsmen, Lloyd and Murray. As I walked along with them, I (naturally) walked next to Murray since he is not much taller than me. I jocularly asked Clive Lloyd, "When is the declaration coming, skipper?" I wasn't aware that Clive Lloyd was annoyed with Bishen about the Richards incident, and was surprised when Lloyd replied with some heat, "You want me to declare when your captain won't let my batsman retire? If he is such a stickler for the rules, I could have been too! I didn't appeal when Mohinder Amarnath took more than two minutes to appear for batting! And, you want to know when I am going to declare?"

Clive Lloyd had, of course, underestimated us. Within half an hour, the West Indies had lost three more wickets and, when the mandatory overs started, they were just 228 runs ahead. Before this Roberts had played back to Chandrasekhar and survived what must have been the plumbest leg-before decision in cricket. In the third mandatory over Roberts again survived a bat-pad catch appeal which was disallowed by umpire Gosein. After the Richards run-out, when the crowd gave vent to its anger, umpire Gosein wasn't going to give anybody out. Oh no! He wanted to see the next day, he didn't dare to take any risk because the crowd was already after his blood. Yet we tried to get Julien and Roberts out. It was only when six overs remained and the West Indies had run up a lead of 54 runs, that we gave up the attempt. When the match ended, the West Indies were 215 for 8. The statistics

may show a drawn game, but never can statistics be so wrong
as in this case. India had morally won the match!

India would still have won the Test if a catch of Lloyd had
not been spilled, because of a collision between Solkar and
Patel. It is difficult to pin the blame on anybody since both are
excellent fielders. At the same time, I feel that Patel should
have left the catch to Solkar, because he has a bigger pair of
hands than Brijesh. The morale of the team suddenly dropped,
and one could feel the change. And then came those Gosein
decisions ! So, we had missed the bus.

When we landed at Georgetown, in Guyana, it started
raining and it just didn't stop. The Bourda Oval, where we
had to play Guyana, was flooded and the match was called
off.

We had our moments of fun though. On April 1, 'All Fools
Day', we sent our manager, Polly Umrigar, and treasurer,
Balu Alaganan, running to the Indian High Commission.
Bishen arranged a phone call to be made to Polly Umrigar
in the morning, to tell him that the Indian High Commission
in Trinidad had reported to the Indian High Commission in
Guyana that the team's behaviour during the last session of
the second Test and generally off the field was bad and not
liked by the Indian High Commission there and would the
manager come and explain the matter. Polly was in a flutter
and rushed to Bishen's room to tell him of the telephone call.
When Polly entered the room Bishen nearly gave the game
away by laughing, but he controlled himself and kept his face
averted by doing some backbending exercises. Polly said he
didn't even have Guyanese currency for the taxi fare. Bishen,
however, asked him to go and find out and not to worry.
Polly carried with him a letter from the New Zealand Cricket
Council which had praised the Indian team's behaviour in
glowing terms, to show to the High Commissioner.

On his way to the High Commission in the taxi, Balu Alaganan realised that it could be an April Fools' joke. His initial reaction was that only I could play such a joke and they should take me along to the High Commission. Umrigar, however, wanted to go and finish off the matter. So they went and to their great relief discovered it was a joke. Polly and Balu both took it most sportingly and we all had a good laugh about it, unlike Dicky Rutnagar, a London-based Indian journalist covering the tour, who was very much upset by the joke played on him so that his relations with Bedi were spoilt.

Dicky got a call, supposedly from the Guyanese External Affairs Ministry, asking him to explain an article he had written supporting South Africa's policy of racial discrimination. The caller said that the Guyana Government's policy about apartheid in South Africa was well known and so 'Dicky' should come and explain. Dicky tried to explain that he had never written an article on South Africa, nor had he visited that country. But the caller insisted that there was a clipping of the article in the Government file and he must come over to the Ministry prepared to explain his conduct. Dicky realised, after going to the External Affairs Ministry, that it was a hoax and he was furious. For one who liked to pull everybody's leg, his reaction was most unsporting. Dicky tried to take it out on Bishen on several occasions and, by the end of the tour, their relations were very much strained.

The rain at Georgetown didn't look like stopping and during this time a visit was organised to an Army camp in the interior of Guyana. I went in the coach with the team to the airfield, but one look at the aircraft and at the clouds which looked pretty menacing, I flatly refused to fly on the plane. I knew there were others who wanted to stay put, instead of flying in the inclement weather, especially in a small aircraft like the one placed at our disposal, but they all put on a brave front and decided to go along. Every member of the team (there were four others, besides me, who decided to stay back) shook hands with us solemnly before they boarded the aircraft. As the plane took off, wobbling a bit while being airborne, I wondered if we would lose the series because only five players remained in Georgetown.

We were, however, destined to win, and the boys arrived safely back, smiling broadly and giving me looks that suggested, "You worry unnecessarily". I didn't miss the message, but I wasn't going to set foot in a plane like that, especially in foul weather. After all, I had become a father while the team was in New Zealand, and I wasn't going to do anything that was likely to stop me from seeing my first born!

Because of the rain, the venue of the third Test was shifted to Port of Spain, and we were back in Trinidad. If people saw me smiling broadly it wasn't an illusion. I had always done well in Trinidad and my lowest score was 65. I was hoping to keep the record straight.

The Queen's Park Oval at Port of Spain in Trinidad certainly is my favourite ground in the world. When I walk out to bat there I feel quite certain that I am going to score runs. It is just a feeling I have, and it has been proved right. Before the 1976 tour, my scores there were 65 and 67 not out, and 124 and 220. Besides, in the game against Trinidad at Guarcara Park I had scored 125 and 63. The crowd has a lot of people of Indian origin and so the feeling is more like playing at 'home' than on a 'foreign field'.

I knew that a Calypso had been composed about me after our 1971 tour and so, when I went in to bat in the first innings of the match against Trinidad in 1976, I was a little tense. I didn't concentrate enough but I timed my shots well and was happy to see yet another 50 against my name at the Queen's Park Oval. It was a short innings and in the evening a West Indian came and told me, "We wanna see you bat the whole day maan, not just for an hour." This made me feel real good.

But, to get back to the beginning of this fantastic battle at Port of Spain and the spectacular victory we eventually earned to level the series. Clive Lloyd won the toss and elected to bat. Vivian Richards, who had been a thorn in the flesh for us during the earlier Tests, showed his appreciation of the Queen's Park Oval wicket. He blasted 177 runs, which was magnificent batting. Indeed, one could see that his transformation from a slap-bang cricketer to a run-hungry batsman was complete. Clive Lloyd gave him wonderful support, with a hard-hit 68. We were worried when, at the end of the first day, West Indies had scored 320 for 5, with Richards still there with 151.

Bishen Bedi spun out the remaining batsmen, and the West Indians were all out for 359. Richards, after lofting Bedi for a huge six, attempted to repeat the shot and was caught on the boundary. This was the signal for a collapse and the remaining wickets fell in a heap.

When we batted Anshuman Gaekwad was out to a dubious decision off Julien for only 6, but Mohinder Amarnath this time did not delay in the dressing room and, as usual, looked completely at ease against the new ball.

Michael Holding always seemed to relish bowling after lunch, and he produced a sizzling spell and got me out for 26—the only time at Port of Spain I had been out for under 50 runs. A sharp in-cutter found me palpably in front of the wicket, but I was surprised to find the umpire not responding to the united appeal of the West Indians. It was the plumbest leg-before appeal I have survived. I didn't stay long, however, to enjoy my luck. One ball later Holding struck me inside my right pad with a yorker and this time the appeal for leg-before was upheld. I thought this was a doubtful decision since the ball had been delivered from the edge of the wicket and I had hardly moved from my guard. Well, I suppose it is this way that umpiring decisions tend to even out in the long run.

There was added pain, as the pad had shifted and I was hit directly on the shin. I limped off wondering whether this was the end of my big scoring in Trinidad.

Now, in Trinidad, the crowds always gather near the dressing room and the players readily mix with them. I had to listen to complaints of a large number of disgruntled people who told me they had lost bets, which they had laid on my scoring another hundred.

We were eventually out for 228, conceding a lead of 131 runs to the West Indies. We naturally thought that, with so many runs behind them, the West Indies batsmen would go on a run riot but, surprisingly, the openers Fredericks and Rowe played so slowly that, at the end of 15 overs, they had scored only 30 runs. The booing from the crowd didn't have much effect. Madan Lal and Mohinder bowled well. When Chandrasekhar came on he had Fredericks caught by Solkar, and Venkataraghavan got rid of Rowe. Richards struck two fours imperiously and we thought that we were due for another leather-hunt. Fortunately, Venkataraghavan had tied him up and made one turn sharply to go off the edge of the bat to Solkar, who took his 50th Test catch.

In the first innings Kallicharran had watched a ball from Chandrasekhar roll off his defensive bat on to the wicket dislodging the bails, even before he had opened his account. In the second innings a similar thing happened. This time, however, the bails didn't fall off and Kallicharran looked up to the heavens to say his thanks. There was already a demand for his exclusion from the team, because there was a feeling that, since he was of Indian origin, he had deliberately thrown his wicket away. Kallicharran is a professional and, though he is very friendly with our team, he certainly wasn't going to sell his wicket cheaply. Taking advantage of this bit of luck and to prove his critics wrong, Kallicharran hammered his eighth century.

We had still to contend with Clive Lloyd, the danger man, and we needed his wicket badly. Vishwanath did the trick when diving to his left, he brought off a superb catch to dismiss him, off Chandrasekhar. Though Murray tried to push the score along he wasn't very successful. The declaration came on the fourth day after lunch, after Kallicharran had got his century, and Holding had hammered two successive sixes. We were left to score 403 runs in the fourth innings of the match, and on the last day.

I was confident that we could save the game, because the wicket was still good; but the thought of winning never entered my mind.

When we batted a second time, things shaped out better. Anshuman Gaekwad and I put on 69 runs for the first wicket, before Gaekwad fell to a catch by Kallicharran, off Jumadeen. Right from the beginning I was middling the ball, with Mohinder Amarnath playing with equal confidence.

On this twin tour Mohinder Amarnath had developed so well as a batsman that the tour selection committee decided to ask him to bat at no. 3. His complete assurance against the spinners made him look like a class player. The only thing that went against him was that he seemed to lose concentration when he got into the 30s and 40s and, with the bowlers at his mercy, he would get out. In this innings he played with so much maturity and responsibility that I was doubly sure that we could save the Test! I kept playing as it came and had 12 fours in my 86 not out at close of play. I particularly remember a cover-drive off Julien and an on-drive off

Holding. These shots gave me a lot of pleasure as the ball
went sweetly off the meat of the bat. We were 134 for 1 at
close of play.

The Trinidadians had taken a century by me for granted
because, at the end of the day, when I was batting on 86, they
were telling me as we left the ground that they were coming
the next day to watch me score a double-century.

I was unusually bogged down the next day. I wasn't timing
the ball well and was restrained by the bowling. It took me
almost an hour to complete my century. The century came
off a lucky shot. As Padmore bowled on the leg-stump I tried
to play a one-handed sweep and lobbed the ball past a lunging
Fredericks to get the two runs needed for my century. But,
my 'glory' was shortlived, as two runs later I was out in
attempting to drive Jumadeen. I missed the ball completely
and was stumped by Murray. I was declared out caught
behind, but actually I had not snicked the ball, but was
stumped by Murray. Since there was still no thought of
winning, but only of saving the game, I thought I had let the
side down at a crucial stage.

I must, however, mention the manner in which the spectators spurred me on as I batted on that eventful day, which
brought me my fourth century at the Queen's Park Oval.
The Calypso song composed about my performances on the
1971 tour was audible right from the morning and until
the evening. Though the tune is catchy even I was a little
tired of hearing it. I wished they would play something else
on the air.

This time when I got my century—the fourth on the
ground—there were no invasions of the field, and I was grateful for that simply because these interruptions are no good for
your concentration. In the evening there were hundreds of
people to congratulate me, and there was the inevitable wise

guy, who shook my hand with the remark: "Maan the Calypso right, you just like a wall". They don't speak the Queen's English there. It's difficult to understand them in the beginning, but once you do it's great fun.

The people of Trinidad are different. They are not like the Jamaicans or the Barbadians, who are extremely partial and blood-thirsty. The Trinidadians also love good cricket. The Indians are popular in Trinidad, because of the large number of Indians who live there. They identify themselves with the Indian team and are India's staunch supporters.

Vishwanath took my place and, with Mohinder Amarnath, carried on where I had left off. The new ball was due at this stage, but Lloyd didn't take it. Instead he continued with his spinners. When he did take the new ball, Vishwanath was firmly entrenched and there was no way of getting him out, unless he became over-ambitious. When Holding bounced once, he got on his toes and square-cut the ball viciously to the boundary. The new ball only increased the flow of runs and suddenly, at tea, victory became a distinct possibility. Mohinder was batting with a lot of patience and this was surprising, since he loves to thump the ball, but he kept the scoreboard ticking by taking singles to give Vishwanath the strike.

Within minutes after tea Vishwanath had neared his century. A cracking cover-drive and he got his first Test century abroad. Only a misunderstanding with Amarnath found him stranded in the middle, to be run out. That was the only way he looked like getting out. But then he had put victory within our reach and, when the mandatory overs started, we needed only 65 runs for victory. Brijesh's robust batting brought us victory in the 11th over. It was the highest score ever made in the fourth innings victory. Out of the four wickets we had lost two were run-out. Mohinder was run out attempting a single and Lloyd threw down the wicket at the bowler's end. He had batted more than 400 minutes for his 85. He kept one end up ensuring that there was no pressure on the others, who went for their shots.

We had never dreamt of scoring 402 runs for victory, but were confident of saving the game. So the victory came as a tremendous morale booster. We were absolutely overjoyed since not only had we levelled the series, we had created a record for winning on the fourth innings score. The champagne really flowed and it was a memorable evening after a truly memorable day. This was undoubtedly India's greatest Test victory. Cables arrived from the President and the Prime Minister of India and other dignitaries. The change in venue had proved lucky after all. Now we were set for the last encounter for Test honours.

Yes, the Queen's Park Oval at Port of Spain has been a happy hunting ground for me. After my last innings there, a number of letters appeared in the newspapers suggesting that, after my sequence of scores at the Queen's Park Oval, the name of the ground should be changed to 'Gavaskar Oval'. My scores there were 65 and 57 not out (2nd Test, 1971, my debut in Test cricket), 124 and 226 (5th Test, 1971), 156 (2nd Test, 1976), and 26 and 102 (3rd Test, 1976). Oh yes, I'd like to take that 'wicket' with me everywhere, but my kit-bag is not big enough. And, what about that super crowd? Where would I pack them? The crowd which loves its cricket in its typically crazy way. Like the man who had a bet with me when I was playing there in 1971. I was fielding on the third-man boundary then and he was prepared to give me 100 Trinidad dollars in return for one dollar if Maurice Foster scored a century. Foster was batting with 99 then! He won the bet, because Foster was out playing on to Abid Ali for 99! After the interval I went and gave him his dollar. He took my autograph on it. When we met again in 1976, he took another dollar from me, when he bet that India would score the required 402 runs for victory. That's Trinidad for you. Trinidad, I love you!

20

Barbarism at Kingston

After our historic victory in the third Test in Trinidad we
travelled to Kingston, to play against Jamaica. Bishen
Bedi rested for this match and I had to lead the side. The
game was the prelude to the fourth and last Test—also at
Kingston which would decide the fate of the 'rubber'.

The Sabina Park wicket at Kingston is supposed to be the
quickest in the West Indies. It is hard and has a lot of bounce,
which is intended to help the West Indies pace bowlers. The
game against Jamaica, however, ended in a draw. My chin
was giving me trouble and it was extremely sore, so I was off
the field for most of Jamaica's first innings. Batting first, the
home team put on 299. In reply, our batting floundered
a bit. Batting at no. 9, I was able to save the situation with
the help of Madan Lal. To make the game interesting, I
declared after throwing my wicket away in the chase for runs.
I was not only surprised but annoyed when Foster, the
Jamaica captain, refused to respond to the declaration, and
continued batting. I felt cheated because I had declared in
good faith hoping that a response would provide an interesting finish to the game. I surely wouldn't have thrown my
wicket away if I had known Foster's intentions earlier. May
be, he was scared of losing after our fantastic victory in the
last Test in Trinidad.

To show my disapproval I bowled slow full tosses. Still,

Egland Captain, Mike Denness, protects Gavaskar from the frenzied Indian admirers who invaded the field after Sunil's century in the Old Trafford Test (1974).

Sunil Gavaskar with Tony Greig,
towering over him, returning to the
pavilion after batting for the Rest
of the World against Australia
(1971-72). With them are the
Chappell brothers, Ian and Gregg

Playing for the Rest
of the World against
Victoria (1971),
Gavaskar hooking
A.F. Thompson

Gavaskar mobbed by spectators after he completed 1,000 runs in Tests in a single calendar year, Delhi, 1976

Foster didn't respond. He surely had a safe score and there was no way he could have lost. He declared only towards the end, leaving us just two hours' batting in which to get 350 runs. He made a complete mockery of the game. And they say the West Indies love bright cricket! The Jamaica game should have warned us of the frustration and desperation of the West Indies team. They had gone to Australia to battle for the so-called 'World Championship', and had been beaten to a pulp. On their return they found that, leave aside being 'World Champions', they were on the edge of being classed a cellar team. Of the team's potential there was no doubt, there was doubt only about its performance.

The fourth and final Test of the series began at Kingston's Sabina Park on April 21. Surprisingly, Lloyd, after winning the toss, elected to field. This decision was apparently based on the assumption that the first morning's wicket would give his quick bowlers the necessary assistance to demolish the Indian batting. It did help the bowlers and the wicket was really bouncy. Holding, in particular, was making the ball bounce from a shade short of a good length. Anshuman Gaekwad survived a dropped chance in the slips. When I was on 24, I turned Holding off my toes to find Holder dropping a 'hot' chance. At lunch we were 60 for no loss. I was on 33. In the first over after lunch I hit a full toss hard back, which landed at bowler Julien's feet. However, he dropped it, because it would have required outstanding reflexes to pick up a catch going the other way on the bowling follow-through.

When Holding was brought from the Radio Commentators' Box end, I was surprised to hear the umpire say that he was going to bowl round the wicket. His first over made his intention very clear. There were three bouncers to Gaekwad.

When I faced Holding, I received four bouncers in an over and a beamer which Holding pretended had slipped from his fingers. I wasn't bothered at this stage, because I thought that

Holding was wasting his energy. However, the next over from him was the same and when he again said the beamer had slipped, I understood that this was a strategy to intimidate us. Lloyd, fearing that his future as captain was at stake, though he had already been appointed skipper for the team to tour England, had given us first knock, only to find us 98 for no loss. He was not only desperate, but utterly frustrated. Obviously, this was the reason why he didn't do anything to stop Holding from bowling so many bumpers! May be, he himself had asked Holding to bowl four bouncers and a beamer in an over.

When Holding pretended to be wiping his fingers to show that the ball had really slipped, it was difficult to believe. After one over, during which all I could do was to keep my head out of the way of the speeding ball, I walked up to umpire Gosein to ask him the definition of intimidatory bowling. It was during the drinks interval at the end of an over from Holding and, as I approached the umpire, I realised that this was the man who had given those decisions in the second Test under pressure from the crowd, and there was no hope of my getting a satisfactory response from him. So I asked Anshuman Gaekwad to stick around and concentrate even harder.

To call the crowd a 'crowd' in Jamaica is a misnomer. It should be called a 'mob'. The way they shrieked and howled every time Holding bowled was positively horrible. They encouraged him with shouts of "Kill him, Maan!", "Hit him Maan!", "Knock his head off Mike!" All this proved beyond a shadow of doubt that these people still belonged to the jungles and forests, instead of a civilised country.

Their partisan attitude was even more evident when they did not applaud any shots we played. At one stage I even 'demanded' claps for a boundary shot off Daniel. All I got was laughter from the section, which certainly hadn't graduated from the trees, where they belonged. The whole thing was not cricket. The intention certainly wasn't to get a batsman out, but to knock him out.

Next morning while we were having a work-out, Tony Cozier, the most respected cricket writer in the West Indies, passed by and laughingly asked me, "Expecting applause from a Jamaican crowd?" The query speaks for itself, and should give one an idea of the character of the so-called cricket-lovers in the Island.

I was bowled after lunch by a yorker from Holding, which I deflected on to my wicket, for 66. The opening partnership was worth 136 runs—an Indian record for 1st wicket against the West Indies. Mohinder Amarnath, who joined Gaekwad, was unruffled and so was Anshuman. The two youngsters struck it out and no more wickets fell by draw of stumps. We were then 178 for 1. The newspapers next day called it "dull batting". Of course, the journalists ignored the fact that only 67 overs were bowled during the day and, in the last 30 overs, there was no question of the ball being hit by the bat, thanks to the tactics Michael Holding and Wayne Daniel applied.

The new ball which Lloyd took the next day was just the missile Holding needed for his lethal deliveries. He slipped one out to Mohinder, who was caught by Julien, when he deflected a delivery trying to defend his head getting knocked off! The first ball to Vishwanath must have been the most frightening delivery he has ever faced. It almost took his head with it. A similar delivery after some time crushed Vishwanath's finger, as he defended his face, and Julien again took an easy catch.

On the dot of lunch, Anshuman, who had taken many blows on the body and his hands, was hit just behind the left ear. It was yet another short ball and it went like a guided missile, knocking Anshuman's spectacles off. And, can one guess the crowd's reaction? They were stamping their legs, clapping and jumping with joy. The only word I can think of to describe the behaviour of the crowd is 'barbarian'. Here was a man seriously injured, and these 'barbarians' were thristing for more blood, instead of expressing sympathy, as any civilised and sporting crowd would have done.

Anshuman Gaekwad represented the splendid fighting spirit of our team. When he was forced to retire, much against his wish, the will to fight got knocked out of us.

In the pavilion there was nobody to attend to him, though an Indian doctor examined him. There was nobody who wanted to take him to the hospital. The Jamaican Cricket authorities showed absolutely no regard for the seriousness of the injury and their responsibility to provide medical aid. Only when I insisted that Balu Alaganan, the team's treasurer, should go and talk to the Jamaican Cricket authorities, was there some action and Anshu was taken to the hospital for treatment. The whole thing was sickening. Never have I seen such cold-blooded and positively indifferent behaviour of Cricket officials and the spectators, to put it mildly, were positively inhuman.

Manager Umrigar was already in the hospital having taken Vishwanath for treatment, when Balu Alaganan joined him with Anshuman Gaekwad. Soon there was a third casualty when Brijesh Patel took his eyes off a ball from Holder and had his upper lip cut open. So, he too had to go to the hospital and had to shave part of his new-grown moustache to get his lip stitched. When we were 306 for 6, Bishen declared, primarily because he did not want to risk any more injuries, especially to our bowlers.

When the West Indies batted Fredericks found himself plumb in front of the stumps, but was relieved to find that umpire Gosein was still in no mood to lift his finger.

The West Indies openers thus prospered; and Rowe, being the local 'hero', was immune to any appeals from us. It was only when he stepped out to Bishen, missed the ball completely and was out by a few yards, that he was given out, stumped by Kirmani. Even then, if Rowe had showed some displeasure the umpire would have given him 'not out'. But Lawrence is a nice guy and he smilingly walked away.

Richards got two 'lives', Bishen failed to hold a hot caught and bowled chance, which aggravated his finger injury. Off Bedi's next ball Kirmani dropped Richards behind the wicket. A lot of people had begun to call Kirmani, Richards' 'brother', for Kirmani had let him off a few times earlier in the series! The West Indies series was disappointing for Kirmani after his marvellous showing in New Zealand, but there is no doubt about his ability behind the stumps.

A further problem was created for us when Chandrasekhar injured his left thumb, in an attempt to catch Lloyd off his own bowling. Later, it was found to be a fracture. He bowled gallantly, nevertheless, and got rid of the troublesome Richards with a googly.

Deryck Murray found an able partner in Holding and the two added valuable runs. Holding also got his first half century in Tests, which prompted the crowd to storm on to the field and mob him. The West Indies were all out for 391—a lead of 85 runs.

With just three batsmen in the team fit to bat, there was no hope of India making a fight of it and we closed our second innings at 97 for 5. Mohinder Amarnath played a gallant innings to score 59 runs, while Vengsarkar contributed 20. It wasn't a declaration but the termination of the innings since none of the others was fit to hold a bat. This left the West Indies to get 12 runs to win the Test, and clinch the 'rubber'.

Madan Lal was starting to bowl at the West Indian opening batsmen. Madan's bouncers would have caused much more damage to the West Indians, but I wanted him to bowl a beamer and then pretend as if the ball had slipped from his fingers. This was just to show Holding and Co. that we were not suckers to fall for that ruse. Balls, particularly beamers, don't slip from the fingers of Test bowlers and, surely, not in every over. All our 17 players had been on the field some time or the other during the match, when Surinder Amarnath, the 12th man, had to be rushed to hospital for an emergency appendicitis operation on the last day.

There has been a lot of comment from every quarter about the Press conference that was called by our manager, Polly Umrigar, to protest against the intimidatory tactics of the West Indies bowlers. Clive Lloyd retorted by asking if we expected half-volleys to be hit for fours. May be, Clive's lenses got fogged but we had hit deliveries, other than half-volleys, for fours! Clive also said that, in Australia, they got similar treatment from Lillee and Thomson, but they didn't complain. True, but all through our tour we heard West Indian players moaning about the Australian umpires letting Thomson bowl from 18 yards, and never 'calling' him even once for overstepping.

Clyde Walcott made a statement that we must learn to play fast bowling, and our complaint about intimidatory bowling was not justified. Imagine Clyde Walcott telling us what is right and wrong. As the wicket-keeper of the West Indies team in India during the 1948-49 season, he walked to the boundary, not once but time and again, to retrieve the ball thereby wasting time, in order to deprive India of victory in a Test. Well, if Walcott could stoop to that level in 1948, no wonder the West Indians under Clive Lloyd touched a new low in a desperate effort to win by having all our eleven players hospitalised! So, for God's sake let's not have any more moralising, and stop trying to teach others how to play.

The West Indies tour ended on a very sour note not because we lost the four-match series by two matches to one; but because of the patently unsporting manner in which the series was won. I am sure, if umpire Gosein is honest, he will admit that a 2-all draw would have been a fair result!

The find of the twin-tour, if you can call a player who made his Test debut in 1969 as such, was Mohinder Amarnath. He is, without doubt, the most technically accomplished batsman in the side today. He needs to develop his temperament to play a long innings and when he does, he will be a force to reckon with in international cricket. This applies equally to Dilip Vengsarkar. He also needs a lot of hard work to earn a permanent place in our Test teams, because he is richly endowed with talent.

Mohinder and Dilip are still very young and, in the years to come, they will be the mainstay of India's batting. Our spinners are not getting any younger and this is one department where we may find a big gap after the present crop of world-class spinners retire. The wicket-keeping is in the safe hands of Kirmani who is a fair batsman as well. He must have learnt quite a lot from the West Indies series and with his willingness to train hard he should improve. These are the players of the future, though there are a few others who are established and will also be in the team.

Never before have I looked forward to returning home as keenly as this time. I was literally counting the days when I would get to see my son who was already two months old. As soon as I learnt when I was in New Zealand that I had a son, I decided to name him 'Rohan' after Rohan Kanhai, the West Indies cricketer, whom I admire so much and who helped me and gave me sound advice during the 'Rest of the World' team's tour of Australia. I am also a great admirer of M.L. Jaisimha, who was my idol when I was a schoolboy. One of the shrewdest cricketing brains in the country, Jaisimha nursed me on my first tour with the Indian team to the West Indies in 1971.

Vishwanath and I first met during the Moin-ud-Dowla Gold Cup Tournament in Hyderabad. Our friendship has developed over the years so much that he is like an elder brother and a member of our family.

So, little wonder then that I should name my son 'Rohan Jaivishwa'. He will certainly have a lot to live up to when he grows up!

I don't know what the future holds out for me. After this long twin-tour, I am not sure whether I would like to be out of the country for such a long time again. It will involve deep thinking, but right now I am concentrating on leading Bombay to victory in the Ranji Trophy. I am also looking forward to do battle with the Kiwis and the Pommies, who will be paying us a visit in the winter of 1976.

Over the years, Indian cricket-lovers have showered so much affection on me that I owe them a run-treat. So come on, ye Kiwis and Pommies!

21

Pleasures and Pains of Touring

One of the most frequent questions I am asked is about the treatment meted out to Indian cricketers abroad and life in the countries I have toured. The general impression seems to be that going on tour is a lot of fun. This is only partly true because, apart from the pleasure one undoubtedly gets, there is the negative aspect also.

The immediate problems when you go to another country is the language and the food. Not everybody in the Indian team can speak English fluently and, by the time one gets used to the foreign accent, half the tour is almost over. For example, in the West Indies, the average man speaks terrible English. The grammar is all wrong and its a very difficult job trying to understand what they are saying.

Food is another problem. The food abroad is so insipid and tasteless that all our boys find it tough to get something to fill their tummies. The south Indians in the team long for rice and the north Indians for spicy food. Luckily in England one finds plenty of Indian restaurants to eat and also some families who invite the boys for meals.

On the recent trip to New Zealand most of the boys were entertained by resident Indian families so often that the boys longed to have some typical New Zealand food. This was bit of a problem in New Zealand, where restaurants close down early and it is not always possible to go and eat that early.

The south Indians patronise Chinese restaurants for the rice and the north Indians empty the chillie sauce bottles in their food.

Weather is another element which takes a long time for one to get used to. However, the players from the north adjust far more easily to the cold weather, than those from the west and south where there is no real winter as such. Playing with four pullovers is certainly not the most convenient way of playing cricket, and keeping your hands in your pockets till the last possible second before the ball is bowled doesn't ensure good catching. Hard hits often are very cleverly avoided and so also sharp close-in catches, especially in extremely cold weather. It's also difficult to get a proper grip on the ball in such weather. I know a few players who catch 'cold' in the plane, just thinking of the cold weather ahead.

Travelling can often be tedious. In England, particularly, it can be really weary. The boys have to check out of the hotel on the last morning of a match and the coach is ready in the evening outside the ground from where the team leaves for the place where they have to play the next match. Because the stay in the County is restricted to two days and departure is on the third morning, few boys bother to unpack their suit-cases. Sometimes the team reaches the next County well after midnight and, by the time one is allotted a room, it is pretty nearly dawn.

On the 1971 tour of the West Indies, we flew in from St. Kitts to Trinidad in the morning and then we had to drive 40 miles to play. Everybody was barely awake, but fortunately Ajit Wadekar won the toss and elected to bat. As Ashok Mankad and I went out to open the innings, there were instructions to bat as long as we could so that the others could sleep. Salim Durrani, who was to bat at no. 3, told us, "Bat as long as you can but please play shots, otherwise I will go to sleep with my pads on."

Travelling by coach, though tiring, is often entertaining. The boys often conduct mock interviews. Farokh used to interview most of the players and the one with Eknath Solkar used to be the most humorous. Bawdy songs are sung and the card addicts sit down to fleece the newcomers in the team.

Touring with the Bombay team is the easiest. Time really flies, with funsters like Solkar, Mankad and Abdul Ismail around. The longest journey is hardly felt as time just flies by. The camaraderie of the Bombay team is unbelievable. The shy newcomer feels at home immediately and his nervousness is soon dispelled. The Bombay team has a 'Sunday Club', where everybody gathering around in the evening has to spend a riotous hour or two. There is a chairman for the meeting and he appoints two assistants who have to look after the refreshments for the rest of the team. The advantage of the 'Sunday Club' is that it not only gets the team together, but also shows the youngsters and newcomers that the senior members are, after all, just like them and, what is more important, enables them to get to know his team-mates better.

The tensions of the game are forgotten at this 'meeting' as well as the success and failures. The player who has been dismissed for a 'duck' has no time to brood over his failure. Fines are imposed for not adhering to the dress specified by the chairman. These 'fines' are normally evenly imposed on everybody, so that the evening's expenses and also future expenses are, to a large extent, taken care of. The Rest of the World team in Australia also had a 'Sunday Club'. One club meeting required the players to attend wearing just a tie and an underwear. And, no one was allowed to come to the meeting in a dressing gown. Everyone had to come all the way from their rooms to the meeting room in the specified uniform. There were a couple of boys who were not on the same floor as the room where the meeting was held, and it was a problem for them to get there without attracting attention. Thus, they had to use the staircase instead of the lift.

When the meeting began the chairman observed that Tony Greig and Hylton Ackerman were not wearing ties and would have to be fined. Greig, however, got up and said he was in fact wearing a tie. To prove this, he lowered his underpants to show that he was wearing the tie around his waist ! His argument was that the chairman had not specified how and where exactly the tie was to be worn! Zaheer Abbas, who was the chairman, was hilarious. He wanted Rohan Kanhai to down his drink in a gulp, so he ordered, "Mr. Kanhai, I want you do bottoms up !" Rohan, taking him literally, put *his* 'bottom' up.

Yes, touring can be fun. There are some incidents which are incredibly funny. One of our boys, after a late night, was caught by the manager as he was returning to his room in the early hours of the morning. The manager had just opened the door of his room for the morning paper when the lift door opened and in walked our hero after a merry night. Though taken aback, he calmly wished the manager 'good morning' ! The manager asked him, "Where have you been so early in the morning?" Prompt came the reply, "For an early morning walk." Surprisingly, the manager believed it, without trying to find out how a person could go for an early morning walk wearing a suit and the hair and tie dishevelled!

Then, there was another manager who clamped on a strict curfew, and would wait opposite the entrance of the hotel, usually behind a tree or a pillar, to catch the late-comers. One evening a few of us decided to surprise him. This time he was trying to stand inconspicuously at a bus-stop which was just opposite the hotel entrance. We were in time for our deadline and so decided to deliberately stroll there. When we reached the bus-stop westopped and exclaimed, "Good evening, Sir. Going out for a late night?" He stammered a reply saying that he was just out for some fresh air after a heavy dinner. Fresh air at a bus-stop!

On yet another occasion three of us decided to go out sightseeing. All of us were not playing in the next day's game so we weren't worried about having a late night. As we walked we talked of what we would do if the manager bumped into us around the corner. We had hardly said this when, rounding the corner, we actually ran into our manager. He immediately looked at his watch and asked where we were going. One of us replied, "You know Sunny (as I am called), how he likes ties. He was taking us to show some ties that have caught his eye." This manager was shrewd so he said he also wanted to buy ties for friends and he would walk with us to see the ties that I was supposed to have liked. With that went our hopes of seeing the lights of the place.

Fortunately, this schoolboyish treatment of the Indian cricketers is over and the managers now realise that a late night, now and then, helps, rather than having the boys in bed by 10 every night. After all, during the Tests nobody really wants to have a late night. Everybody is aware of his responsibilities and will never try to bring about his own downfall.

On a long tour one tends to get homesick. There are days when there is no news from home either by letter or telephone. I know of one cricketer who had booked a call to his girl friend every night of the twin-tour and got it only once, and that too the day before we left for home. Apparently the international telephone operators had never heard of this place in India, and their Indian counterparts always reported that the line was out of order.

Seeing the same faces day and night also can be quite boring and monotonous. Some members of a team are a little short-tempered, and they don't make good room-mates.

The best part of a tour is the friends one makes in the countries one visits. More often than not one becomes more friendly with one from the opposite team. There are also the girls who add colour to the flannelled background.

The West Indies tour is a high-risk tour for bachelors. In 1953, Subhash Gupte got married to a girl from Trinidad. On the 1962 tour, Dicky Rutnagur, who was covering the tour for a newspaper, got married to a Trinidadian; and in 1971 Govindraj met a Guyanese girl and married her on his return to India. In 1976, too, one player had got 'hooked', though whether wedding bells will ring, it is difficult to say.

During our 1976 tour in Guyana I got a very rare and interesting offer. Early one morning I got a telephone call from a girl who said she was in the foyer and wanted to see me. I asked her to wait and added it would take me a long time to come down.

She said she was prepared to wait. When I eventually went down around lunch time, I had quite forgotten about her and was astonished to find her still waiting. She came and explained that she wanted to be a film actress in India and asked me to help her to get to India. I said that I didn't see any problem about going to India, because all one needed was a passport and an air-ticket. She told me that her father had run away and so there was nobody who could sign her application for a passport. In that case, I asked, how was I going to help.

She hedged about a bit and then said there was one way I could help her and that was to marry her and take her as my wife! She assured me that once she reached India, she would go her own way. I told her I was already married, and there were a few bachelors in the team, so why pick on me? "Well", she said, "You're the most famous, that's why." But, that was not the end of the story. After she was convinced that there was no way I could have gone down the wicket and got stumped by her, she asked me to forgive her for the bother and think of her as   sister!

This is one of the hazards of touring. May be, after reading this the Cricket Control Board will include another clause in the contract that the players have to sign before a tour, prohibiting a player from entering into a matrimonial alliance while on tour!

22

Bombay, My Bombay

It used to be said once that Indian cricket was 'Bombay cricket'. Those were the days when Bombay players accounted for half the Indian teams. In fact, on one occasion, nine of the eleven Test players were from Bombay. And not just playing in the side, but making a distinct contribution to the team's performance. Today, there are not more than four or five Bombay players in the Indian reckoning.

There is a misconception that the Bombay cricketer is proud and arrogant. This is not true, even though a Bombay cricketer will not suffer fools gladly. He is more often the one who is the friendliest. On the 1974 tour to England a member of the team from outside Bombay admitted to me that he was terribly mistaken about the boys from Bombay. He said, "Where I come from, I was told that I must watch out for the Bombay boys. But, I find that they are the ones who are the friendliest and who do not form groups."

Yes, Bombay's contribution to Indian cricket has been tremendous; except in the matter of creating dissensions. That has been reduced to a fine art by a few officials outside Bombay. It is really unfortunate that the average cricketer is in awe of a Bombay cricketer. This often results in an inferiority complex, which, in turn, results in jealousy and envy. I know for a fact that Bombay cricketers go out of their way to make friends in the opposite camp. On the field they may be snarling, but off the field they are a mild lot.

The Bombay cricketer knows that he is what he is entirely due to hard work and his own efforts, unlike a few others who have come into Tests with backing from their States. This is the reason one finds most of the 'one-Test' men from other States, while the number of 'one-Test' cricketers from Bombay are negligible.

Cricket in Bombay, at all levels, is tough and no quarter is given and none asked for. Even a friendly fixture is played grimly and with seriousness. Right from his school days the Bombay cricketer is aware that he has to be twice as good as the others, to be considered for higher honours. Besides, Bombay's cricket is organised so efficiently that there is nothing to complain about. The schoolboy cricketer, who rubs shoulders with Test heroes while playing in the 'Kanga League' and other tournaments, is seldom bothered about reputations. Having played with Test stars, he is aware of the hard work they've put in and strive to emulate them. Competition is very keen and there are plenty of cricketers who have played in just one Ranji Trophy game, failed and never again got a look-in. There are always others waiting to occupy the places of those who cannot make good. This keeps the established players on their toes and they can never afford to be complacent and take their place in the team for granted.

Of all the tournaments in Bombay there are two which occupy pride of place: the 'H.D. Kanga League' and the 'Times of India Shield'. The Kanga League is the only tournament that is conducted by the Bombay Cricket Association. It is open only to clubs affiliated to the B.C.A. and has seven divisions, each with 14 teams. The matches are played during the monsoon and, as a result, many of the games played in July are washed out. The wickets are uncovered and are often exposed to rain. Batting on these wickets helps to develop the instinct for survival, and the capacity to take punishment. This is strictly a tournament for bowlers and they invariably reap a rich harvest. Batting ability is tested to the full and often technique is thrown over-board in favour of clean cross-batted heaves.

The outfield, which is not mown, makes the lofted shot a *must* in every batsman's repertoire of shots, because a full-blooded drive will often result only in a single due to the **very slow** outfield. Since the matches are spread over all **available pitches**, one often finds the square-leg position of **one match** and the cover-point position of another facing each other. Sometimes a mid-on of one match becomes the third-slip of another game being played alongside. I myself have contributed to the dismissal of a batsman in another game at the third-slip position. Actually, I was at deep mid-on in our match. This put me next to the second-slip of the game being played on the adjoining plot. An edge from the batsman hit me on the thigh and was gleefully caught by the second-slip on the rebound. The batsman went away cursing his luck, and I was profusely thanked by the fielding side for helping to get rid of a troublesome batsman.

Cricket matches are spread all over the city and, there are occasions, when a game in one area is completely washed out because of rain; while in the other area bright sunshine makes a full day's game possible.

Form can never be forecast and the weaker side often springs surprises on the stronger side. Towards the end of the Kanga League, when the rainy season ends, batsmen come into their own, and there are fewer outright victories. This is the most tense stage when seemingly easy winners are left behind by unexpected opposition. The club of which I **am captain,** Dadar Union Sporting, has been winning the

'A' Division pennant for the last four years. The pair of opening bowlers we have, V.S. Patil and Urani Mody, are unplayable. And, even when we have been dismissed for 60 runs, we have won the match comfortably, thanks to these two seamers. Dadar Union also boasts of the best all-round fielding side in the League, and some of the catches that the boys take are truly unbelievable.

The Club house is unpretentious, but the Dadar Union's contribution to Bombay cricket is enormous. Cricketers like Madhav Mantri, R. B. Kenny, N. S. Tamhane, the Amladi brothers, P.K. Kamath, V.S. Patil and V.J. Paranjape, among others, have played for Bombay and some for India. The present Dadar Union side contains almost all first-class players.

Right from the time of Madhav Mantri, discipline has been the Dadar Union's keynote and this has earned a great deal of respect, not only for the club, but the players as well.

The other important tournament in Bombay is the Times of India Shield. It is an Inter-Office tournament, in which more than 260 office teams take part. All the matches, except those in the 'A' Division, are knock-out matches, played over the week-end. The 'A' Division is divided into two groups and matches are played on a League basis. The winners of the two groups play the final for the coveted 'Times of India Shield'. The competition has led to a lot of commercial organisations employing cricketers specially for playing in the tournament. An average cricketer is, thereby, assured of a job and it is up to him whether he makes use of his opportunity. The last date for joining an organisation to qualify for playing in the tournament is September 1, and in July and August hectic efforts are made to persuade a player to leave one organisation and join another. The matches are played over three days, and are always keenly fought.

There are some impressive performances and many cricketers get a chance to play in the Ranji Trophy on the strength of their performances in the 'Times Shield'.

The only sore point is the poor standard of umpiring, particularly in the 'A' Division. Many interesting matches are ruined by umpiring errors. Admittedly the top umpires, being themselves employed, cannot 'stand' for these matches as they are often played on week-days. I feel that only those on the Ranji Trophy panel should be asked to umpire the 'A' Division matches, thereby eliminating palpable mistakes.

This is the tournament where young boys can watch talent from practically all over the country. Almost every side in the 'A' Division has about five Ranji Trophy players and even some Test stalwarts. When I was in school I used to watch these games and stand next to the sight-screen and try and learn from the Test players in action. I was once caught trying to cross the local railway track, since I was in a hurry to get to the match and this was the quickest way to the ground. I was let off after a great deal of harassment by a Railway sentry, and had to pay a fine for my offence. My regret is not that I had to pay a fine, but that I missed the batting of Ajit Wadekar and Hanumant Singh, because their team had declared the innings closed even while I was pleading with tears in my eyes with the Railway policeman to let me go.

These, and a host of other competitions, prepare the Bombay lad to face all kinds of situations. In the process he becomes a hard-boiled cricketer and a tough nut to crack. This is the stuff of which champions are made and is, perhaps, the reason why Bombay have been Ranji Trophy champions for so long.

A band of smiling officials who are always prepared to

listen to the players, try to understand their point of view, and show utmost consideration to the players, also keeps the Bombay team happy. In all these years I don't think there has ever been a conflict between Bombay cricket officials and the players. This complete harmony makes Bombay what it is— the Champions of Indian Cricket. In fact, I can say without reservation that whatever I am in the game today is due, in a very large measure, to the fact that I have been nursed in the cradle of cricket, that is Bombay.

23

Men and Memories

"Hello, is that Mr. Dilip Sardesai speaking? I am an admirer of his and I want to speak to him."

"I am sorry, Dilip Sardesai is not in please."

"Do you have any idea what time he will be back? I want to present him with a tape-recorder. By the way, who am I speaking to?"

"This is Salim Durrani, his room-mate."

"Oh, Mr Durrani, you are the one who took Gary Sobers' wicket and also Lloyd's, and got rid of these two to make India's victory easy. Oh, I am so happy to speak to you. I have got another tape-recorder for you. Please come and collect it and also the one for Sardesai. I am waiting in the foyer please."

Salim Durrani was in his shorts when the telephone call came through, but he changed into respectable clothes and put on the India tie and came down to the foyer. Looking around he couldn't find anybody waiting with two tape-recorders. He made enquiries at the Reception counter and went back to his room and changed back into his shorts again. Just then the telephone rang, and the caller said, "Mr. Durrani, I am waiting for you, aren't you coming down?" Salim replied:

"I had gone down, but I couldn't find you anywhere."

"Oh, I had gone to the swimming pool to see a friend, but do please come down, I'll be waiting opposite the Reception counter."

So, Salim got back into his clothes once again, knotted his tie, smoothed back his hair and walked down the two floors to the Reception counter.

Well, there was nobody waiting for him. He again asked the Receptionist, went to the swimming pool and back again to the Reception counter. Suddenly, a voice behind him said, "So you want a tape-recorder, huh?" and, from behind a pillar, stepped out Dilip Sardesai who himself had made those calls to Salim. It was so funny that Salim himself started laughing, forgetting the trouble he had taken to dress up and come down to the Reception counter twice in quest of a tape-recorder which just wasn't there.

The joke was on Salim this time, but he himself is capable of some terrific side-splitters. Ask him to tell you the one about the spin of the coin at Hyderabad. If that doesn't make your stomach ache with laughing, nothing will.

Salim, 'Uncle' to all of us, and 'Prince Salim' to his contemporaries of the sixties, is a unique character. I can't think of any left-hander who had as much grace on the cricket field as Salim. The crowds simply love him. During the 1972-73 series against England he was known for his ability to give the crowd a 'six' on demand. The crowd only had to ask and he obliged by banging the ball into the stands. He has a ready-made title for his book, "Ask for a Six". I don't know if he will ever write it, but I do hope he does.

Salim has been a much misunderstood man. He has been called "moody" and this stigma has stuck to him. But, this is not a correct estimate of the man. He treats a Test match as he would treat a club game. The crowd comes first to him and he is a crowd-puller, first and last. He is often accused of not taking Test cricket seriously. This is equally untrue. I recall, during the 1971 West Indies tour when Salim was failing with the bat after a dazzling beginning, how upset he was about his form. He very badly wanted to make the England trip later on, especially because he had missed the 1959 and 1967 tours. Eventually he was not selected for the 1971 tour to England, but he came back with a vengeance in 1972, winning the Duleep Trophy single-handed for the Central Zone.

Salim is not much of a believer in workout at the nets, and this has probably earned him the 'moody' tag.

Money is a commodity which Salim will never be able to keep. He is so generous and warm-hearted that he will go out of his way to help anybody. Just before we left for the 1971 tour of the West Indies, Salim and a few others, including myself, were invited to play against the visiting Sri Lanka team. We had travelled by air from Bombay to Madras but, from Guntur to Madras, on our return journey, we had to travel by train which involved an overnight journey. Salim, with his customary charm, had organised a bed-roll for himself. Having travelled by air I had no bedding for the train journey, and the cold wintry night made sleeping a problem. When Salim saw my predicament he promptly gave me his blanket and a sheet to cover myself. He was chatting away with some passengers and so wasn't prepared for sleep yet.

When I woke up the next morning I saw Salim fast asleep, all huddled up, to keep himself warm. I couldn't believe it. An established Test cricketer and a 'hero' had given his only blanket and sheet to a young, unknown Ranji Trophy player. This overwhelmingly generous and totally unselfish side to Salim's personality is not known to many who only point out his faults. From that day Salim became 'uncle' to me. His attitude towards the younger cricketers is so generous that they forget their nervousness and discuss their problems with him without inhibitions. He is always there to advise young players and give them every encouragement.

People call him a 'wayward genius'. I don't know about his being 'wayward', but he is certainly a 'genius'. A genius whom the authorities have never bothered to understand.

Cricket-lovers all over the world know Farokh Engineer as a wicket-keeper of the highest class. When they watch him behind the stumps, they immediately realise that here is a man who obviulsy enjoys his cricket and is willing to give, in turn, enjoyment to the paying public. His acrobatic dramatics behind the wicket or in front of the wicket always keeps the crowd in good humour. Not only the crowd, but he keeps even the fielders on their toes with his chatter. Hardly is a ball bowled without Farokh saying something, either to the batsmen or the fielders. It doesn't have to be cricket, of course. It can be anything. And with the Indian team he has to speak in Gujarati, very seldom in English.

In the slips he would turn round and ask a silly thing like, "Why don't you talk? After reading *Playboy* last night you aren't talking much." "Dr Hill, ask Eknath how much does 37 and 19 make?" All nonsense and nothing to do with the game, but just to keep you awake and not get bored. Once he stumped a batsman out and asked him politely if he was in a hurry to catch a train home. You can be assured that with Farokh an evening can never be dull. Even if it is a team meeting, Farokh puts his points across humorously.

At a team meeting in Madras, on the eve of the fourth Test against the West Indies, the electricity failed for quite a long time. Venkataraghavan had not come for the meeting for some reason, and the meeting went on without him even after the electricity failed. When the meeting was over, it was still dark and, as **Prasanna** was about to take everybody's leave, Farokh quipped: "Be careful, 'Venky' might be hiding outside." The tenseness of the serious matters that the team had discussed just faded away after this remark.

On the 'Rest of the World' team's tour of Australia, he was always teasing Intikhab and Bob Cunis about their bulk. One day both of them challenged him to a 100 metres race. Farokh kept on postponing the event for some reason or the other. Finally, with everybody fit, it was decided to have the race during the Tasmania match. Bill Jacobs, the manager, was the starter and Tony Greig and Norman Gifford the judges. Farokh came last!

When war broke out between India and Pakistan, Farokh was always practising with his bat how to 'bayonet' Intikhab Alam, and ended up by commenting that he would need a really sharp bayonet to pierce through the Pakistani player's bulk.

Farokh's favourite leg-pull is when he goes in his car to the ground for a match in England. He will tell the person with him that he had forgotten how to get to the ground and would stop the car near a passer-by. Naturally, the person with him would request the man on the road for directions to go to the ground. Just as the man would start answering, Farokh would accelerate the car laughing away, since he knew the way to the ground already. It is a sight to watch the sheepish face of the person next to him. Farokh did that to Ajit Wadekar once and Ajit was so startled by the sudden acceleration that he didn't know what was happening. A camera that time could have recorded Ajit's expression for future laughs.

In spite of his ready-wit and humorous ways, Farokh is not liked in international cricket. Cricketers of other countries think that he is tricky. A serious allegation indeed and Farokh's reply is that all is fair in love and war, and Test cricket nowadays is more akin to a war between twenty-two players.

Even among members of the Indian team he is not particularly popular. This is basically because, in order to hide his own failures, he will put the blame on others. If he has dropped a catch his general gestures will be to show to the crowd that it wasn't really a catch, but a deflection off the pad or some such thing. He has got away with it often. During the 1972-73 series against England he missed 12 chances until the Madras Test and only three were reported by the Press. It is well known that Farokh will go to the journalists in the evening and explain that it wasn't a chance at all, just the excitement made the fielders throw up their arms.

The bowler who shows his anguish at a dropped catch is ticked off for his theatrics. One such remark produced one of the ugliest dressing room scenes I have ever seen. This was between Farokh and Abid Ali during the Prudential 'World Cup' match against East Africa at Leeds. On the field, too, one noticed both saying things to each other heatedly. As soon as the team came in for lunch the fireworks started. It was more like a bout between Mohammad Ali and Joe Frazier, the difference being that both threatened each other with bats. Unfortunately for the bat manufacturers, the stronger bat was never found out, because the other members of the team intervened and stopped the quarrel from proceeding further. Yet, it was horrible while it lasted. The Manager, Mr. G. S. Ramchand, completely forgot about this incident in his report. Of course, he was engrossed in reporting other players to the Board!

Yet, one cannot deny that Farokh Engineer is a player whom the crowds come to watch and team-mates rely upon. He has been India's saviour often and for that Indian cricket owes him a lot. He has truly been one of cricket's rare characters, a man whom the crowds call 'King Farokh'.

In recent years no Indian tour has taken place without 'Ekki' Solkar. At his peak in 1971 he was known as 'Mr. Reliable' and 'Mr. Dependable'. Now, on his own admission, he is not so reliable and dependable. But, from 1971 to 1976, Ekki has remained the same. Incredibly funny and truly a great bloke to have around on a tour. A spirited cricketer, he thrives in tense situations which he has found by the dozen from 1969 to 1974, not only in the Tests but also for Bombay, though much less than in the Tests. If a popularity poll was taken among Indian cricketers Ekki would certainly top the list along with Vishwanath. His spontaneous and infectious smile, even during failures, has made even the most hardened players sympathise with him. And, his attitude during the good times has been that of a man who would like to share it with the others.

He has been the target of many leg-pulls and many a joke has been attributed to Ekki, though he may not even be aware of it. Not very proficient in English, he still manages to get his message across in his own way, leaving the others in the team doubled up with laughter.

He loves a fight out in the middle. A tense situation brings out the best in him. In other situations he tends to relax and pays for his lack of concentration. Dilip Sardesai and he rallied India so often in the 1971 series against the West Indies that some West Indian spectators called theirs the 'Laurel and Hardy act.' In the Barbados Test Ekki had stayed at the wicket by sheer determination. He played and missed often but stuck to his task. While their partnership was on, the ball lost shape and had to be changed. Ekki asked to have a look at the changed ball, at which Gary Sobers remarked, "It won't make any difference since you are going to play and miss anyway!" Ekki's retort was: "You play your way, let me play my way."

Also in 1971, after we were introduced to the Queen at tea

on the first day of the first Test, Ekki said a 'hello' to Geoff
Boycott. Boycott, still smarting from his cheap dismissal in
the morning, mistook the smile for a derisive smile and said
"The next......innings I will be batting with a hundred at this
time and then you won't.......smile." Now, Ekki never likes
to lose in a battle of words and he was replying even before
Boycott had finished, "You bloody wait, next bloody innings
I will take you out bloody." He didn't, but in 1974 he did get
Boycott out four times and the last time was the last Test
innings of Geoff Boycott till today. The result was that Boycott did not give him his benefit tie, which he had earlier said
he would give Ekki.

Ekki is a marvellous mimic. One has to see and hear him mime
to believe that if he hadn't been a cricketer he would certainly
have made a great mimic. When he mimed Durrani, Engineer (whom he calls 'Dikra' Farokh), Pataudi, Jaisimha and
Wadekar, among the Indians, and Sobers, Fredericks and
Kallicharran one can get a stomach ache laughing. He also
mimics Indian film stars very well. I do suspect that Ekki's
secret ambition is to act in a film and, I am sure, the Indian
cricket team can vouch for his acting ability.

Ekki has come up from very humble beginnings. His performances as a cricketer are, therefore, of greater merit when one
considers the odds he has had to overcome. Today Ekki is
such a devoted family man that he doesn't even want to stay
in the dressing room once the game is over, always in a rush
to get back home.

Shopping on a tour abroad with Ekki is great fun. He can
never make up his mind about anything and is always hesitant
before he finally buys something. Very fond of beer, his reason
being that it will help him to put on weight. He is an extremely
poor eater, but still manages to do some wonderful, strenuous
exercises.

In New Zealand he found he was getting persistent head-aches and had difficulty in breathing. The doctor who examined him advised him to forget his beer for some time. Ekki, however, was found sneaking a Peg of whisky to his room. The next day, when confronted with this, he explained that he had not touched the whisky, only kept it under his bed in case he found it difficult to get sleep! A unique sleeping dose, but typically like Ekki, for he himself is a unique character.

People who are used to watching Vishwanath and Farokh Engineer standing next to each other behind the wicket will only see Farokh joking with his customary gestures. Vishwanath is always the silent observer. But, enter the privacy of the dressing room and suddenly Vishwanath will be dispelling tensions with a funny remark made with a straight face. He is quick at cutting jokes and, looking at him, no one would suspect what a tremendous fund of humour he has. If you hear laughter and a mini-riot inside, you can be sure the cause is Vishwanath and the target, in all probability, Eknath Solkar.

I think Vishwanath's ability at wisecracking can be matched only by Richard Hutton. Vishwanath's Hindi will horrify the purist from the north, but his accent and delivery are extremely humorous. When he finds himself stuck for a word, his hands speak a lot more than his tongue. He observes people keenly and notes everything about them, storing away some important characteristic in his mind for future use. Often, he surprises you by recounting something you may have said at your first meeting with him.

Totally unassuming, in spite of his excellent international record, he is averse to giving advice to other team members unless he is specifically asked. Nevertheless he remains a popular man in the team. For sheer popularity in India I don't think there is anyone to touch him. All over India the crowds go wild over him and he has very seldom disappointed them. In Bangalore he is 'King' but then the Bombay and Calcutta crowds love him no less. The applause when he walks in to bat is to be heard to be believed. He is aware of this tremendous affection that people have for him and he is always striving to give the crowd a lot of pleasure by his batting. Even a brief innings from Vishwanath is enough, though such an innings are disastrous, as far as the Indian team is concerned. His batting is an 'education' for young players aspiring to do well. In fact, Vishwanath's entire demeanour on the cricket field is exemplary. He is always in control of his emotions, except once, when I remember he showed a trace of annoyance. This was in the second Test at Christchurch against New Zealand (1976). Glenn Turner had survived yet another appeal for leg-before and Vishwanath turned to me in the slips and said, "If we get the same 'consideration' we will score double centuries in every game."

I am reminded of a funny incident associated with Vishwanath when he and a few others were invited by 'Tiger' Pataudi to play a match in Bhopal. On the rest day they decided to go on a 'shikar'. They had hardly entered the jungle when suddenly they were surrounded by 'dacoits' who fired a few shots from their rifles in the air, warning them not to try anything funny. Vishwanath, Prasanna and the other members of the party were asked to get down from the jeeps and hand over their belongings. When one of the men accompanying them tried to run, he was 'shot' down by the 'dacoit' leader. Vishwanath and Prasanna were told that they were being held to ransom. The petrified Vishwanath, who was tied to a tree, started weeping and explaining that he was an India Test cricketer and the country needed his services. The 'dacoits' had never heard of cricket and weren't in the least bit impressed. They were eventually released, when the ransom was supposedly paid to the 'dacoits' and Vishwanath breathed a sigh of relief.

Only later did they come to know that the 'dacoits' were, in fact, 'Tiger' Pataudi's servants and the whole incident was staged as a big hoax! Prasanna knew this, because 'Tiger' had told him earlier, but poor Vishwanath to this day doesn't believe that it was a make-believe hold-up, and cannot help shivering in fright when reminded of it. Even the man who was supposedly 'shot' down by the dacoits was not enough to convince Vishwanath that he was the victim of a practical joke. The experience was too much for him.

Typically he took it in his stride, as he takes every dig at him phlegmatically. He may pull people's legs, but it is his ability to laugh at himself that makes him so well-liked, unlike Farokh Engineer, who only wants to make fun of others and can't take a joke at his expense in the right spirit.

Another 'character' in the Indian cricket scene is Ashok Mankad. Called 'Kaka', because it also happens to be the nickname of the film star, Rajesh Khanna, of whom Ashok is a great admirer, Ashok is a great story-teller. His recounting of various 'incidents', with just the right mixture of spice and exaggeration, enlivens the evening on a tour. This ability of his to make people laugh makes him a great asset on a tour when one is likely to feel dull. He loves to play cards and comes out with an incredible variation of 'runs'. On all the tours I have been with him, I have never seen him lose, except on rare occasions. Long train journeys are never tedious when 'Kaka' is around. His winnings at cards at others' expense are adequate remuneration for the constant entertainment he provides.

The 1971 tour of England was not a memorable one for Ashok. He just couldn't get going in the Tests, though he scored heavily in the County games. Yet, he never lost his sense of humour. At the end of the series, when he had got into double figures in the last innings, he was telling the English players that they should count themselves lucky that the series was confined to only three Tests. He told them he was just getting into form and would certainly have got 25 runs in the fifth Test!

'Kaka' is an avid cinema-goer and whenever there is a good scene in a film he is watching, he would invariably stand up and applaud. This can be pretty embarrassing for the others who are with him, but 'Kaka' just doesn't bother and he will not change his habit. After seeing the movie "Cromwell", the way he talked to the cab-driver must've made the poor cabby wonder 'where' he had picked up his passengers! The poor cabby, who couldn't understand English beyond a few words, was bombarded with such phrases as, "In the name of the Lord, I beseech you to take us to the CCI", and "I beseech you to drive more slowly." But, how can one blame the cabby for trying to drive fast so that he could be rid of his 'mad fare' as quickly as possible!

Richard Hutton, son of the fabulours (Sir) Len Hutton of England, is the wittiest cricketer I have come across. My first impression of him was of a cocky Englishman whose only good point was that he had a famous 'last name'. Certainly, he didn't look impressive in the first Test at Lord's in 1971. I didn't very much like his remarks, as I took runs off his bowling. Every time I played a shot off my legs he would remark, as I turned for the second run, "Why don't you play where my field is." The next time he said it, I told him to bowl to his field so, may be, I could play where his field was. This chattering went on non-stop, particularly when a batsman took runs off him. He would be waiting for you at the end of his follow-through, with his hands on his hips and the usual question on his lips. We didn't find him amusing at all. After I returned from Australia, I told the others that he was an extremely peculiar person, but I wasn't believed.

Despite Hutton's peculiarity, the Australian tour by the Rest of the World team was thoroughly enjoyable, thanks to Richard

Hutton. I realised on this tour that talking to the batsmen is a habit with Richard. Perhaps he feels his bowling ability is inadequate to get a batsman out and so he likes to have a verbal weapon in his armoury. In the Brisbane 'Test', Hutton was hit all over the place by Stackpole when he bowled his first over. In the second over, Richard found his length and beat Stackpole thrice on the forward stroke. Walking down the pitch he asked Stackpole in all seriousness, "Why are you pulling the fielder's legs, why don't you edge one for a change?" Every time he was whacked by an Australian batsman, he would throw out a challenge, "Just you come down to Sheffield or Leeds, on a green wicket, and I'll see you." Of course, nobody took him seriously. The day before the 'Test' at Perth, we had gone to see the wicket. Richard threw a ball on the wicket and when it bounced back, he quipped, "Eh, it came back. At Leeds it would have got stuck."

Rohan Kanhai was, yet again, hit on the chest during the 'Perth' Test. When he came back after an x-ray, he was greeted by Richard with the remark, "Don't come near me, with all the x-rays you've had taken so far, you must be radioactive." To Clive Lloyd, who was having black coffee, Richard remarked, "Don't be 'racial', Hubert, have some milk too." But, by far, his best quip on the Australian tour was when he was asked at a cocktail party, "How are the Australian girls treating you?" Richard who, till then, hadn't exactly had a roaring time, replied, "Well, it looks like the Australian 'birds' are a good deal colder than the weather."

Richard Hutton loved to go sun-bathing in Australia and was ever looking for an opportunity to slip down to the beach. By January he had a terrific tan and he was telling us how he was going to show his tan off to the Londoners in the cold month of February. Richard was a terrific chairman of the 'Sunday Club'. The standard he set at the first meeting could never be touched by subsequent meetings, and by popular demand he was again voted chairman of the last 'Sunday Club'

Gavaskar playing an elegant cover-drive.

Hooking Derek Underwood to the fence in the Test against England, Old Trafford, 1974. Looking on is Alan Knott.

Gavaskar holding up the Irani
Cup after leading Bombay to
victory against the Rest
of India, Delhi, 1976.

A drive in cover.

A typical sweep shot by
Gavaskar.

before our dispersal and his farewell gifts to the players brought out delighted howls from the members. Our manager on that tour, Bill Jacobs, called him the funniest man he'd ever met. He was not only that, but a good bowler too, only when he bowled to his field, of course!

SUNIL GAVASKAR IN FIRST-CLASS CRICKET

Compiled by Anandji Dossa

TESTS

	Year	M	I	N.O.	H.S.	Runs	Avge	100's	BOWLING Runs	W	FIELDING Avge	Ct.
vs. West Indies	1970-71	4	8	3	220	774	154.80	4	9	0	—	1
vs. England	1971	3	6	0	57	144	24.00	—	42	0	—	5
vs. England	1972-73	5	10	1	69	224	23.88	—	7	0	—	2
vs. England	1974	3	6	0	101	217	36.16	1	5	0	—	1
vs. West Indies	1974-75	2	4	0	86	108	27.00	—			—	1
vs. New Zealand	1975-76	3	5	1	116	266	66.50	1			—	5
vs. West Indies	1975-76	4	7	0	156	390	57.14	2			—	2
Total		24	46	5	220	2123	51.77	8	63	0		17

UNOFFICIAL TESTS

	Year	M	I	N.O.	H.S.	Runs	Avge	100's	BOWLING Runs	W	FIELDING Avge	Ct.
vs. Australia	1971-72	5	10	1	68*	257	28.55	—			—	5
vs. Sri Lanka	1973-74	2	4	0	85	106	26.50	—	1	0	—	4
vs. Sri Lanka	1975-76	1	2	0	203	238	119.00	1	8	0	—	1
Total		8	16	1	203	601	40.06	1	9	0		10

*Indicates 'not out'

IRANI CUP

For Bombay

	M	I	NO	HS	Runs	Avg					Ct
1967-68	1	2	0	5	5	2.50	—	—	—	—	0
1970-71	1	2	1	46*	58	58.00	—	—	—	—	2
1971-72	1	2	0	48	71	35.50	—	5	0	—	0
1972-73	1	2	0	6	6	3.00	—	—	—	—	3
1973-74	1	2	0	108	132	66.00	1	5	0	—	0
For Rest of India											
1974-75	1	1	1	156*	156	156.00	1	12	0	—	0
For Bombay											
1975-76	1	1	0	47	47	47.00	—	—	—	—	0
Total	7	12	2	156*	475	47.50	2	22	0	—	5

AGAINST VISITING SIDES

		M	I	NO	HS	Runs	Avg			Ct
86 & 0	1972-73 for Board President's XI vs. M.C.C.	.	.	.	.	.	.	.	.	2
81	1974-75 for West Zone vs. West Indies	.	.	.	.	.	.	.	.	3
29	1975-76 for West Zone vs. Sri Lanka	.	.	.	.	.	.	.	.	1
Total		3	4	0	86	196	49.00		—	6

*Indicates 'not out'

RANJI TROPHY

1969-70	2	3	1	114	141	70.51	1	21	0	—	6
1970-71	2	3	0	176	307	102.33	2	19	1	19.00	0
1971-72	3	5	0	282	494	98.80	2	0	0	—	8
1972-73	7	12	2	160	579	57.90	3	6	1	6.00	16
1973-74	6	9	1	84	248	31.00	—	—	—	—	11
1974-75	5	6	2	96*	203	50.75	—	4	0	—	4
1975-76	4	5	1	190	510	127.50	3	—	0	—	5
Total	29	43	7	282	2483	68.97	11	50	2	25.00	50

DULEEP TROPHY

1971-72	2	3	0	101	138	46.00	1	17	0	—	2
1972-73	2	3	1	55	65	32.50	—	—	—	—	2
1973-74	1	2	1	53*	65	65.00	—	—	—	—	0
1974-75	2	4	0	41	76	19.00	—	—	—	—	3
1975-76	1	2	0	84	124	62.00	—	37	0	—	0
Total	8	14	2	101	468	39.00	1	54	0	—	7

*Indicates 'not out'

TOURS

West Indies	1970-71	8	16	4	220	1169	97.41	5	62	0	—	2
England	1971	15	27	1	194	1141	43.88	3	190	4	47.50	10
Australia	1971-72	11	20	2	95	559	31.05	—	4	0	—	9
Sri Lanka	1973-74	4	8	1	104	316	45.14	1	1	0	—	7
England	1974	14	26	2	136	993	41.37	3	60	2	30.00	6
New Zealand	1975-76	6	11	1	116	313	31.30	1	40	0	—	7
West Indies	1975-76	7	12	0	156	608	50.66	2	53	1	53.00	5

OTHER FIRST-CLASS MATCHES

Scores						Runs	Wkts	Avg	Ct
39 & 38*	1971-72	Indian XI vs. Rest of India	—			20	0	—	0
34 & 6	1972-73	Board's President's XI vs. Ranji XI				43	3	14.33	0
12	1973-74	Indian XI vs. Rest of India (Karmarkar Benefit)	—					—	0
Total	3	5	1	39	129	32.25	—	63	3	31.00	0

*Indicates 'not out'

SUMMARY

(Up to the end of the 1975-76 season)

RANJI TROPHY	29	43	7	282	2483	68.97	11	50	2	25.00	50
TESTS	24	46	5	220	2123	51.77	8	63	0	—	17
DULEEP TROPHY	8	14	2	101	468	39.00	1	54	0	—	7
IRANI CUP	7	12	2	156*	475	47.00	2	22	0	—	5
UNOFFICIAL TESTS	8	16	1	203	601	40.06	1	9	0	—	10
VISITING SIDES	3	4	0	86	196	49.00	1	—	—	—	6
TOURS	65	120	11	220	5099	46.77	15	410	7	58.57	46
OTHER FIRST-CLASS MATCHES	3	5	1	39	129	32.25	—	63	3	21.00	0

*Indicates 'not out'

CENTURIES (30)

282	vs. Bihar, at Bombay, 1971-72
220	vs. West Indies, at Port of Spain, 1970-71 (2nd innings)
203	vs. Sri Lanka, at Hyderabad, 1975-76
194	vs. Worcestershire, at Worcester, 1971
190	vs. Maharashtra, at Bombay, 1975-76
176	vs. Maharashtra, at Poona, 1970-71
171	vs. Saurashtra, at Bombay, 1975-76
165	vs. Leicestershire, at Leicester, 1971
160	vs. Gujarat, at Bombay, 1972-73
157	vs. Bengal, at Bombay, 1971-72
156*	vs. Karnataka, at Ahmedabad, 1974-75 (Irani Cup)
156	vs. West Indies, at Port of Spain (II Test), 1975-76
136	vs. Surrey, at The Oval, 1974
135	vs. Madhya Pradesh, at Indore, 1972-73
134	vs. Hyderabad, at Bombay, 1972-73
128	vs. T.N. Pearse's XI, at Scarborough, 1971
125	vs. Trinidad, at Port of Spain, 1970-71
124	vs. West Indies, at Port of Spain (1st innings), 1970-71
117*	vs. West Indies, at Bridgetown, 1970-71
116	vs. West Indies, at Georgetown, 1970-71
116	vs. New Zealand, at Auckland, 1975-76
114	vs. Rajasthan, at Bombay, 1969-70
112	vs. Gujarat, at Bulsar, 1975-76
108	vs. Rest of India, at Bangalore, 1973-74 (Irani Cup)
104*	vs. Lancashire, at Manchester, 1974
104	vs. Gujarat, at Bombay, 1970-71
104	vs. Sri Lanka Board's President's XI, at Colombo, 1973-74
102	vs. West Indies, at Port of Spain, 1975-76 (III Test)
101	vs. England, at Old Trafford, 1974
101	vs. East Zone, at Calcutta, 1971-72

*Indicates 'not out'

CAREER HIGHLIGHTS

1. Playing in his first Test series against West Indies in the West Indies, scored 774 runs, averaging 154.80 in 4 Tests. It is the highest aggregate for a player making his debut. This included 4 centuries, with two separate hundreds, 124 & 220, in the last Test at Port of Spain. He is the second Indian to score two separate hundreds in a Test, and the only one to score a century and double century in the same Test.

2. He 'carried his bat' through an innings for Bombay against Karnataka, in the Irani Cup match, 1974-75, for 156 runs.

3. His best bowling figures in an innings are 3 for 43 in the Ranji Centenary match, 1972-73, and 2 for 8 vs. Hampshire, in England, 1971.

4. His aggregate of 1,169 runs on the 1970-71 tour of the West Indies and 1,141 runs on the 1971 tour of England are the highest by an Indian on the West Indies tour and a short tour of England.

5. Was a member of the 'Rest of the World' team which toured Australia in 1971-72. Participated in 'Double Wicket Tournament' at Barbados, 1971; and was also invited to participate in the Garfield Sobers' Benefit Fund match at Barbados in 1972.

6. Was appointed Captain of India vs. West Indies in the Second Test at Delhi, 1974-75, but could not play owing to injury. Led India in the first Test against New Zealand, at Auckland, 1975-76, and scored 116. India won the match by six wickets.

7. Has captained Bombay in the Ranji Trophy, and West Zone in the Duleep Trophy and Irani Cup matches.

8. During 1965-66 Harris Shield matches in the Senior Inter-Schools Tournament, Bombay, Gavaskar hit four hundreds and, in the All-India Schools Tournament for the Cooch-Behar Trophy, scored 760, averaging 152.00 with scores of — 33 & 7 not out vs. Gujarat, 158 vs. Baroda, 246 not out vs. Central Zone, 222 vs. East Zone and 85 & 9 in the final against North Zone. Created record for the All-India Schools Tournament for the first-wicket partnership when he (246 not out) and Anwar Quereshi (203) added 421 runs.

9. Gavaskar (209) and Ramesh Nagdev (349), for St. Xavier's College, Bombay, put on 472 for a record first-wicket partnership, against the Institute of Science, in the Inter-Collegiate Tournament, Bombay.

10. Holds the highest individual record in the Inter-University Tournament, with a score of 327 for Bombay against Gujarat, 1970-71; and also for the Vizzy Trophy Tournament for Inter-University Zonal matches, with a score of 247 not out against South Zone Universities, 1968-69.

11. Making his debut in the Inter-University Tournament for the Rohinton-Baria Trophy in 1966-67, he scored 106 for Bombay against Jabalpur; and 139 not out in the next match against Baroda.

12. Was the recipient of the 'Chhatrapati Shivaji Award' in 1971-72 as the outstanding Sportsman of the Year. Has won the top prize given by the P.J. Hindu Gymkhana, Bombay, to the outstanding cricketer in the country; one of the two cricketers to win the L.R. Tairsee Gold Medal' twice—in 1970-71 and 1975-76—and was awarded the 'S.V. Rajadhyaksha Prize' as the best fielder in the country in 1972-73, when he took 16 catches in the Ranji Trophy matches during the season. In 1970-71, the Bombay Cricket Association awarded him the 'Justice Tendulkar Trophy' as the Best Senior Cricketer of the Year.

INDEX

OTHER  PAPERBACKS

ADVENTURE

KENNETH ANDERSON

Jungles Long Ago	Rs. 15.00
More Tales from the Jungles	FC
Man Eaters and Jungle Killers	12.00
Nine Man Eaters and One Rogue	12.00
The Black Panther of Sivanipalli	12.00
The Call of the Man-Eater	12.00
This is the Jungle	12.00
Tales from Indian Jungles	15.00
Tiger Roars	15.00
: Modern adventurers	15.00
: World adventurers	15.00

ANTHROPOLOGY

MILES BURKITT   : The Old Stone Age   12.00

BUSINESS & MANAGEMENT

PROF DUNCAN   : How to Conduct
Meetings : Company,
Club, Political and
Social   8.00

J.B. DURYEA   : How to Solicit :
A Must for all
Insurance selling agents
and salesmen   10.00

P.K. GHOSH   : Government &
Industry   12.00

CIVIL ENGINEERING

E.H. WILLIAMSON   : Data Book for Pipe
Fitters and Pipe Welders 12.00

DRAMA

OSCAR WILDE : Complete Plays 12.00

COOKING

PREMILA LAL : Indian Recipes 12.00
SIPRA DAS GUPTA : The Home Book of
Indian Cookery 8.00

CRITICISM

TARAKNATH SEN : Three Essays on
Shakespeare 12.00

EDUCATION

H.J.C. GRIERSON : Shakespeare's
Macbeth 12.00
CHARLES & MARY
LAMB : Tales from
Shakespeare 10.00
IVAN ILLICH : Energy & Equity 6.00
The Right to useful
Unemployment 12.00
IVAN ILLICH &
OTHERS : Education Without
Schools 10.00
HUGH JARRETT : How to Write English 9.00
PROF. DUNCAN : How to Spell Correctly 8.00

FICTION (Classics)

ALEXANDER
DUMAS : Three Musketeers FC
CHARLES DICKENS : A Tale of Two Cities FC
: David Copperfield 18.00
: Great Expectations 10.00
: Hard Times FC
: Oliver Twist FC
: Pickwick Papers FC
CHARLOTTE
BRONTE : Jane Eyre 12.00

EMILY BRONTE	: Wuthering Heights	9.00
GEORGE ELIOT	: Adam Bede	FC
	: Silas Marner	8.00
	: The Mill on the Floss	12.00
HENRY FIELDING	: Tom Jones	18.00
JANE AUSTEN	: Emma	9.00
	: Pride and Prejudice	9.00
	: Sense and Sensibility	FC
JEROME K JEROME	: Three Men in a Boat	FC
JOHN BUNYAN	: The Pilgrims Progress	FC
JONATHAN SWIFT	: Gulliver's Travel	9.00
MAUPASSANT	: A Woman's Life	12.00
RIDER HAGGARD	: She	FC
ROBERT L STEVENSON	: Treasure Island	FC
W.M. THACKERAY	: Vanity Fair	16 00
THOMAS HARDY	: Tess of the Durbervilles	FC

FICTION (Nobel Prize Winners)

| IVO ANDRIC | : The Vizier's Elephant : 3 novels in one volume | 6.00 |
| JOHN GALSWORTHY | : Jocelyn | 9.00 |

FICTION (other Novels)

| BIMAL JYOTI DAS | : The Rose and The Lily | 7.00 |
| JOHN COWPER POWYS | : All or Nothing | 3.00 |

FICTION (Crime. Detection and Mystery)

AGATHA CHRISTIE	: Elephants can Remember	8.00
	: Nemesis	8.00
	: Sleeping Murder	9.00
ALISTAIR MACLEAN	: Circus	10.00
	: The Golden Gate	RP
	: The Guns of Navarone	8.00

	: Seawitch	9.00
	: Where Eagles Dare	8.00
	: Goodbye California	9.50
	: The Way to Dusty Death	8.00
BERKELEY MATHER	: The Mem Sahib	12.00
DESMOND BAGLEY	: The Snow Tiger	9.00
	: The Freedom Trap	9.00
	: The Tightrope Men	9.00
	: The Enemy	10.00
	: Flyaway	10.00
ELIA KAZAN	: The Arrangement	RP
	: The Understudy	12.00
HELEN MACINNES	: Agent in Place	10.00
JAMES JONES	: Whistle	18.00
MORRIS WEST	: The Navigator	12.00
	: Harlequin	RP
ROSS MACDONALD	: Blue Hammer	9.00

HISTORY

A. L. BASHAM	: The Wonder That Was India	RP
DR. B.N. PANDEY	: A Book of India	15.00
DURGA DAS	: India-From Curzon to Nehru & After	12.00

HOBBY

LAURENCE MALLORY	: Rightway to Use a Camera	9.00

LITERATURE

BERTRAND RUSSELL	: Mortals and Other American Essays 1931-35, Volume-I	8.00

MEDICAL

JOHN W. ARMSTRONG	: The Water of Life	10.00
MARGERY G. BLACKIE	: The Patient, Not the Cure-The Challenge of Homoeopathy	16.00
PETER DIGGORY and JOHN McEWAN	: Planning or Prevention : The New face of 'Family Planning'	10.00

PHILOSOPHY & RELIGION

L.S.S. O' MALLEY	: Indian Caste Customs	8.00
W.J. WILKINS	: Hindu Mythology	25.00
	: Modern Hinduism	16.00

POETRY

HELEN GARDNER ed	: Metaphysical Poets	10.00
EDWARD FITZGERALD	: Rubaiyat of Omar Khayyam	15.00
PALGRAVE	: Palgrave's Golden Treasury	FC

REFERENCE

ALAN AND VERONICA PALMER	: Quotations in History	16.00
	: Everybody's Family Dictionary	15.00
	: Collins English Gem Dictionary	12.00
	: Collins English Learner's Dictionary	30.00

ERIC NEAL	: A Sentence Dictionary	16.00
WILFRED D BEST	: The Student	
	Companion	10.00

SCIENCE

| ALBERT EINSTEIN | : Ideas and Opinions | 18.00 |

SHORT STORIES

AMRITA PRITAM	: The Aerial & Other	
	Stories	8.00
OSCAR WILDE	: Stories of Oscar Wilde	12.00
ROGER COLET	: Maupassant :	
	Selected Short Stories	15.00
GOPINATH		
MOHANTY	: Ants	8·00

SOCIOLOGY

LUCY MAIR	: Marriage	12.00
JEFFREY MEYERS	: Married to Genius	16.00
ASHOK MITRA	: Calcutta Diary	18.00
	: Terms of Trade and	
	Class Relations	18.00

YOGA

| ARTHUR BALASKAS | : Body Life | 25.00 |

SPORTS & PASTIME

ARLOT & TRUEMAN	: On Cricket	15.00
	: The MCC Cricket	
	Coaching Book	15.00
CHESTER BARNES	: Table Tennis	15 00
DENNIS LILLEE	: The Art of Fast	
	Bowling	20.00
DENIS COMPTON	: Cricket and All That	15.00
AND BILL EDRICH		
DR. NAROTTAM	: Portrait of Indian	
PURI	Captains	12.00
E.A.S. PRASANNA	: One More Over	10.00

FRANK TYSON	: Complete Cricket Coaching	25.00
FRANK WORRELL	: Cricket Punch	10.00
IAN CHAPPELL	: Chappelli	15.00
MIHIR BOSE	: Keith Miller	15.00
SIR DONALD BRADMAN	: Farewell to Cricket	12.00
SUNIL GAVASKAR	: Sunny Days	15.00
TONY COZIER	: The West Indies : Fifty Years of Test Cricket	15.00
VINOO MANKAD	: How to Play Cricket	7.00